DON'T CALL ME MOANA

Don't Call Me MOANA

A Daughter Reckons with Her Hawaiian Heritage

NINA MACHEEL

Nina Macheel
with best wishes

LUMINARE PRESS
WWW.LUMINAREPRESS.COM

Don't Call Me Moana
A Daughter Reckons with Her Hawaiian Heritage
Copyright © 2022 by Nina Macheel

All rights reserved. This book or any portion thereof may not be reproduced or used in any manner whatsoever without the express written permission of the publisher, except for the use of brief quotations in a book review.

The cover photo is of the author's mother, who changed her Hawaiian name from Lillina to Norma, dancing *hula* in Wisconsin in the early 1950s.

Printed in the United States of America

Luminare Press
442 Charnelton St.
Eugene, OR 97401
www.luminarepress.com

LCCN: 2022915059
ISBN: 979-8-88679-024-5

For my children
Keone, Malia, and Aja

TABLE OF CONTENTS

Author's Note ix

How Do I Look? 1

Her Home Away from Home 9

Remembering What We Never Knew 35

You'll Hear It Call You 47

Having a Wonderful Time 59

Stirring the Pot 67

See You, See You 83

Lots of Jobs, Women, Beautiful Beaches 113

Adrift in the Āina 125

Teapot to Melting Pot 137

Anything Else? 143

Don't Ask, Don't Tell 149

Hiding in Plain Sight 165

Aloha in a Bowl 177

Why'd He Have to Go? 189

What's in a Name? 199

Years of Respite 221

Nowhere to Run 231

War Bride 251
Ambition and Ambiguity 269
Home Together, Forever 285

Acknowledgements 297
About the Author 299
Notes & References 301

AUTHOR'S NOTE

The takeover of their land, the overthrow of their sovereignty, and the dilution of their culture forced my Hawaiian ancestors to the margins of the places where they'd always belonged. These pages trace their struggle to regain their foothold amongst the islands of their birth, and of their birthright. The imprint of their grit and grief lives on in my grown children, the fifth generation from where this story begins, and girds my own journey for identity and belonging.

This narrative is composed of collected oral memories, research, and imagined truth that are correlated to key milestones of Hawaiian history. In the absence of verifiable references, I have used conscientious visioning as an approach to verisimilitude. The gift of this methodology has been a felt sense of my ancestors. In honor of the Hawaiian tradition of oral history, I have called these sections "Talk Story."

He aha ka hala i kapuhia ai ka leo, i ho'okuli mai ai?
(What was the wrong that forbade the voice?)
A traditional Hawaiian saying

Chapter 1

How Do I Look?

She looked different. Anyone could see that, even me. But I didn't see that it mattered, or why it should. She was my mother, and I was used to her. She tried her best to be like everyone else – like all the doughy German and Scandinavian women married to hearty farmers who lived in that Midwest backwater where my father took us to live in the early 1950s. It was up to her to get those people to accept us, and she worked hard at it, though there wasn't a manual for how to do it. I was not yet five years old when we got there, but I picked up on their suspicion, which they chased away with curiosity, after deciding that we were not dangerous. Someone might clear the way for us with a whisper that she was with my father, a hometown boy who'd won medals in high school track before going to war. Then they'd move over and make room for us, or at least seem to. This lightning-fast calculus, triggered by my mother's facial features, was the social dynamic of my childhood.

She, of course, knew that her differences went far beyond how she looked. But she was realistic. She was so far from the Pacific islands where she'd grown up that she had no choice but to feign enthusiasm for where she'd landed. People were always asking how she liked it there in Wisconsin. These questions were not unfriendly and seemed less nosy than they were a bridge to friendship. My mother seemed more at ease with their curiosity than the people poking about for tidbits from her, about her. She put folks at ease while making sure that they remembered that she wasn't really one of them.

Straddling the line between belonging and remaining an outsider, my mother created a field of racial and cultural ambiguity that made it harder for me to understand that if she was different, then I must be too. Though everyone knew I was her daughter, I didn't look very much like her. I was grateful for that, relieved in some private way that shamed me. I felt lucky to be spared her narrow eyes and wide, flat nose, the features that signaled that she wasn't from those Midwest parts. Waiting beside her in the grocery aisle, the vestibule of the church, a line in the post office, I'd notice the glances passing over us and wish that I had a mother who looked like the other kids' mothers. Something about having *this* mother put pressure on me to divest myself of her, to blend in with the people who found ways, even if friendly and well-meaning, to let us know that we were different.

Amidst the banality of mid-century social norms, one lived in perpetual discomfort. There were strictures against deliberately, consciously making another uncomfortable. Today we have a term, *implicit bias,* for the subtle attitudes and projections that cracked the surface of what is known as "Midwest nice." To a child who is racially different but has not yet recognized it or its implications, among the first observable behaviors is friendliness to everyone who is white and antipathy toward those who aren't. A child who is not considered white – in other words, almost all the world's children except for those of northern Europeans – distrusts the surface niceties that keep interactions civil. She lives with the angst that something nameless is coming inexorably toward her and that sooner or later she will take a direct hit. What she'll suffer is the assault of racism of which she may know nothing, but suddenly comprehends everything. The existential dread of racial confrontation traps the child in a primitive but elevated state of "fight or flight" that is so swiftly activated that it is beyond intellect. That child intuitively avoids situations in which she is "other," knowing an incident could actualize anywhere, out of nowhere, but will usually come when she wants inclusion. A child who has witnessed one separated because of something she cannot help, or has felt the threat of it in the air, feels helplessly exposed and vulnerable. She knows with certainty that it could – and probably would – happen to her, because racism lies just a paper-thin layer beneath the surface of decency.

When my mother was not with me it was not apparent that I was multi-racial. Being anywhere with her sparked unwelcome recognition that I, too, was different. Today I would say that I was multi-racial, but in those days people on the brown to black spectrum were called "colored" or, in the more overtly racist areas, the "n" word. With our monolid eyes, and had folks not known we were Hawaiian, we'd have been called "Oriental," a label that conjures many stereotypes: a place in the Far East where rugs were made, a seedy inner-city ghetto called Chinatown, a place that sent stealth bombers to attack Pearl Harbor. They were all, indistinguishably, Oriental, in the same way that Americans lumped the culturally and geographically unique tribes of our First Nations as Indian.

In the Wisconsin region where I grew up – as in virtually every region in the United States – there'd once been a racial group with whom I might have related, had I had more than the most cursory exposure to them. We called them

Indians, and we knew that the land we lived on had once been theirs. They literally left shards and vestiges of themselves in our soil. As children, we poked around in the dirt for Indian arrowheads and lived in towns with names from the cultures that had once inhabited our acreage – Waukesha, Milwaukie, Waunakee, Oconomowoc, Menomonie, Winnebago. Despite these ubiquitous references, we were not encouraged to wonder where the Indians had gone or why they'd left. They were mentioned in our school history books only in relationship to whites: they'd resisted white settlers on their land, they'd helped the French fur trappers, they'd scouted for the Lewis and Clark expedition. Had they been visible in our community they might have triggered in me the desire to discover and "wear" my own racial origins.

Lacking a tribe with the same physical characteristics as I had led me to wish I could shed the things that made me different. Without my nose and eyes and mother, and the vague backstory attached to us, I could fully enter the world that mattered. And that world, as every child of any color perceives early on, is white. The racial description Caucasian, formerly prevalent, is fading out as racism is increasingly reduced to the colors of skin, of which any that is not white is implicitly inferior.

My mother understood bias and bigotry, but she never discussed it nor coached us on how to maneuver within it. She'd learned from direct experience, growing up in Hawai'i's so-called "melting pot," where interracial marriage was common at a time when many states still had laws making it illegal. She'd gone to the Midwest after World War II as my father's "war bride" to live amongst people who had little exposure to people who looked like her or who knew to how to live within a culture of racial diversity.

Wisconsin, circa 1950. Christmas in the first house my parents bought in my father's hometown: George and I are on the floor, age three and four; Anne, age two, is on the hammock.

But she knew what mattered and made sure that I and my siblings always aspired to fit in as *haole,* which in her native language meant someone who wasn't a Hawaiian Islander. In other words, someone who is white. To Hawaiians of her generation, to be white meant to be privileged, dominant, and genetically superior.

Though most people in our Wisconsin town couldn't distinguish between a "Jap" and a "Chink," they could grasp that my mother was Hawaiian. This opened doors to acceptance, since being Hawaiian qualified her as American, though at the time Hawai'i was a U.S. territory and would not achieve statehood until 1959. That she was a war bride and had survived the attack on Pearl Harbor entitled her to a modicum of respect. She'd arrived in my father's hometown with three babies, a 20-inch waist, a wide, flat nose, and those eyes derogatorily called "slant" or, more poetically, "almond eyes." Many townsfolk weren't aware that Hawai'i had electricity and frame buildings. My mother entered a world where folks tried to imagine her bare-breasted, living in grass shacks. Surely, many thought, a civilized place like rural Wisconsin in the 1950s was a step up for her.

My mother's choice to leave her island home, and the factors leading to that decision, were more complicated than most could understand, then and now. She knew it was important to ensure racial acceptance of her children. She drew us under the mantle of Hawaiian because identity as a native from the fabled tropics deflected attention from our other race, which was Chinese. Ignorant as the stereotype of a Hawaiian may have been, it was better than the prevailing impression of the Chinese as unsanitary, ghetto-dwelling opium addicts. Evil, shadowy icons like Dr. Fu Manchu and the Dragon Lady were the face of China in American pop culture of the time, and even today Chinese men are typecast in film and TV as obsequious and devious.[1]

Setting the record straight that Hawaiians were not primitive, my mother declared herself a worldly "cosmopolitan." Few in her adopted community would've known the meaning of such a lofty descriptor, but I'm sure she intended it to be intimidating. She wanted respect from those people who'd never ventured far from their fields and farmhouses, nor had ever endured the violence of war. She would manage to conform to this new world while remaining distinctive, to belong while remaining separate, to make sure that they knew that though she was among them, she was not of them. She'd come to Wisconsin to create a home, but it would never be her real home.

Chapter 2

Her Home Away from Home

Picturing my Hawaiian mother trying to fit into my father's hometown in rural Wisconsin, I see a lithe, slender whisp of a woman with wiry black hair that she struggled to bend into the tidy buns favored by the local women. I picture her sitting behind them at Mass on Sundays, studying their felt hats with a frill of tulle or contrast of grosgrain ribbon, trying to picture a flower tucked behind their ears. Most of what she observed about Midwestern style and comportment she'd learned at church, a place where she felt comfortable. She'd grown up Catholic, and the ponderous red-brick Catholic church on the banks of Wisconsin's mud-colored Rock River anchored her in that place that she called "just like Siberia." Any friends she'd make, or stature she'd achieve, would come from that church. It was where she'd show that she could adhere to the local norms while signaling that she was still true to her origins. She'd learn to pin back her hair in the prim style of her new neighbors, except that she'd tuck carved celadon jade hair combs into her *chignon*. Dressing like them would take longer. Why should she suit up in gray gabardine the color of storm clouds when, before leaving Honolulu, she'd gone to the Chinese tailor to order clothes in the palette of the tropics: a suit the color of the torch ginger flower, with a flattering peplum skirting her narrow hips, and a felt hat to match. She would not force her feet into sensible, lace-up oxfords when she'd brought navy blue leather heels with cut-out toes. Her three new sisters-in-law, for whom my father would always be a baby brother, were thin, shrill women with penciled-on brows and pinched, tight lips. They advised against her green and lavender jade pendants hanging from a black silk thong. Better to wear a strand of pearls, even if they are fake, they suggested.

"I grew up in the Crossroads of the Pacific," she would tell them, "and lived through the war, wearing this jade. It is good luck, this jade."

Eventually, bit by bit, she acculturated to the Midwest. Or surrendered, as I think of it. She pushed to the back of the closet the garments that went with the fragrant flower lei my father had once lifted to kiss her neck. She accumulated clothes the colors of rodents and mongrels. I was old enough to notice this transition and the loss of a certain insouciance. I remember it as the time that she began staying in the dark, unable to rise from the couch in the shade-drawn family room that cradled her misery. But she'd pull herself together to get dressed for Mass, "putting on airs," as she called it. She would march down the aisle to the front pew, with me and my brother and sister in tow, relishing the humorless stares fixed upon her. She knew they were working out if she was yet one of them or still an alien from some savage place they couldn't imagine ever visiting. Sinking into a genuflection and sliding onto the padded kneeler, making the sign of the cross, she'd pray to be forgiven for believing my homesick father's promise of a faraway heartland of warm-hearted kinsmen who would love her just as he did.

Making the best of it, she'd say that these Wisconsin people appeared to be nice. But they all seemed the same to her, and she couldn't figure them out. They all looked alike, just the reverse, she realized, of how all Orientals looked alike to them. The Midwest uniformity was more disorienting than where she'd come from, where everyone looked uniquely different. She'd grown up tracking and itemizing racial blends with curiosity and precision, because to understand each other's ancestry and culture was to understand how to be comfortable with one another. Although she'd grown up with the Japanese field laborers who picked pineapples and maintained the most immaculate neighborhoods in Honolulu, in the Midwest she lived among people who could not distinguish a Hawaiian from a "Jap." How could she explain the nuance that lay beneath her discernment: how Hawaiians had learned to sort through conflicting loyalties, like figuring out how to continue trusting longtime Japanese neighbors after the Pearl Harbor attack? How could these Wisconsin people know it was not about race, she would explain, talking to herself, because there was no one else who would listen. It was about culture.

Within our household, racial labeling seemed normal as a tool to help Hawaiians get to know and understand each other. I never questioned this approach to relationships nor understood the need for it until I was about ten years old and discovered a trove of glossy, yellowing photos showing my parents and the way we'd lived when I was an infant, too young to remember. The photos opened a window onto a young girl who seemed to be my mother, smiling from a place my father had once inhabited. He alone, among the family and community he'd brought her to, among anyone in the world outside of Honolulu, was party to the experience those photos portrayed. To that point in my life, any place outside the one we had was unknowable. People in those days did not travel, especially when so many were attached to a farm with animals that could not be left. The black and white photo images of people, plants, buildings – a whole world apart from ours – were my first glimpse into that nebulous "home" she'd talk about, which wasn't the one we were living in.

Housebound by weather and the short, sunless days of winter, I came upon the disheveled mess of photos tossed into the drawer of a side table in our living room. I seized upon them, less interested in their content than in having a project to fill the hours. I would organize them into the empty albums that lay nearby with a crackling cellophane sleeve of glue-on corners, half of them spilled into the far reaches of the drawer. Sorting by subject and dates, arranging them by what would fit on a page, I fell in love with the rail-thin young man and the slender young woman with fat babies, finding it hard to realize that they were us, our young family in another time, another place.

I quickly used up all the corners, tethering the photos' brittle, deckled edges to the thick, cottony black album pages. Needing more, I pocketed a quarter from my babysitting earnings and a few nickels my grandmother Elizabeth had pressed into my hand the last time she came to see us. I bundled up for a late afternoon dash to our town's Main Street. The light was dimming from soft to steel gray as I crossed the bridge over the Rock River. I passed the John Deere farm equipment factory on its banks, its windows tipped open and emitting the drone of manufacturing, wondering where in that teeming assembly line my father was at that very moment. I trudged on toward Schneider's Shoe Store on the corner, glancing at new leather oxfords displayed in the windows, crossed the street toward Ulmer's Furniture, and arrived at the musty Hallmark store.

I loved the Hallmark store. It smelled of old wood and scented lotions and the sugary fruit of the penny candy. Pushing the door open, I tripped a cheery overhead brass bell. The pink-cheeked old shopkeeper with the white halo of frothy hair rose from his creaky oak swivel chair. He was always there, every time I'd been in there, sitting behind the high counter working over blue-lined ledger books. He called me "young lady" and took the empty cellophane sleeve I handed him. He knew just what I needed. He nodded and shuffled off. Before disappearing behind the shelves of squat candy jars and their array of penny candies, he pulled a small paper sack of horehound drops and handed them to me. "Compliments of the house," he wheezed. I popped one in my mouth as he moved, humming to himself, toward the wall of brass-rimmed drawers. He opened one after another, tsking and humming, finally looking up with a smile. "The last one we've got, young lady," he said in a quavering rasp. "That will be a nickel." I extracted one from my coin purse and slid it across the worn leather desk pad. He handed me the new stash of 200 corners and waved as I opened the squealing door with its jangling bell.

The walk home was dark and cold. I watched the vapors from my breath appear and evaporate in the bitter air. I stopped on the bridge over the Rock River to stare at the water with its fathomless black swirls and hovering mist, partially iced over, then continued up the hill past stalwart houses storm-windowed against the cold. I poked the toe of my thin rubber boot into bubbles of air frozen beneath glazes of ice where the pavement met the grass. The icy concrete was strewn with charcoal and clay-colored coal furnace ashes to prevent slipping. I tried to find clear patches to slide a few feet across, all the while thinking about how I'd arrange the remaining photos on the pages left to fill.

My mother had written dates and details on the back of most of the photos, in the tidy hand she'd learned from the nuns at her Catholic school in Honolulu, a place and name I only knew from the pictures and her notations. I noticed that everyone in the photos looked warm, posing near banks of blossoming bushes, wearing clothing alive with bold patterns in fabrics that fell softly, loosely, leaving arms and calves bare. People smiled and clowned while we children squirmed in their arms and grimaced against the sun. The people in that place my mother called "home" did not seem like anyone I knew in the place that I called home.

My favorite photo was the one showing my brother George and me in a galvanized aluminum tub, splashing water over a patch of grass, labeled "Honolulu Naval Housing, 1948." My mother had scribbled "George and Moana" on most of the photos, which seemed unnecessary, because my brother and I were always together, and who could forget that those fat babies playing with the hose on the lawn in Hawai'i, those same toddlers that later photos show padded in layers of drab coating, dwarfed by the towering, leafless trees in wintry Wisconsin, were George and me? I noticed that after the other babies arrived, the picture-taking stopped. I knew the ones we had were precious, and I took care not to leave fingerprints on their shiny surfaces.

The photo project was my first attempt to infuse order into my mother's disorganization, and to understand my origins. Compartmentalizing our lives had begun early: there was the time before we left Hawai'i, and the time after, when we lived in the Midwest. The times when my mother wore drapey dresses and a hibiscus behind her ear, when she seemed soft and tender, before the Wisconsin years when she bundled herself to keep warm in coats fastened from her chin to her knees with black buttons the size of half dollars. The times relaxing like any young family anywhere, away from the need to project an image and drag the rest of us into it.

Wisconsin, circa 1951: Our family on a picnic with the rare treat of soda pop for us kids

I saw early photos of myself, among the few taken of us as children in those days of Brownie box camera snapshots, that verified that I was as fat as my mother always said I'd been. I saw myself standing under the elm tree squinting into the sun, my hair kinked up beneath the starchy veil flowing over the itchy white dress in a photo labeled "Moana

First Communion," and I hated the way I looked that day, my face too round, my self-concept already at odds with the pudginess of my pre-pubescence.

Those photos show everything that was going on in those days, if you look beyond the surface to what is hiding in the shadows. You can find the evil, gap-toothed Russian Premier Nikita Khrushchev with the wart by his nose, holding a cob of corn in the air like he might hit someone over the head with it, or banging his shoe on the desk at the United Nations. You can see the stealth visage of polio, the scourge of the 1950s, in a photo of a church procession of Catholic children, in which I am paired with a girl named Carolyn whose leg is shriveled by polio. You can almost hear the clucks of sympathy and dismay as she and I came down the aisle, but you can't know how I'd resented the way she deflected from the attention I'd wanted for my dress. It was made of embossed pink satin in that empire-waisted style with a little fabric bow tacked at the bust line – simple and elegant like Jackie Kennedy would wear. Of course, I pretended to be more kind-hearted than I felt, as though I'd offered rather than been assigned to walk with her by the nuns at my school.

You could do that with those photos, take them for what they were, or make of them what you wanted to see. I loved the one of my delicate mother splashing water over me under the Hawaiian sun, which I look at now with an ear cocked to each figure's backstory, in the way that I cocked an ear to all the whispering in my childhood, because in the 1950s folks did not say things out loud. I never understood those hushed voices, or who might overhear what one said: were there lurkers with ill intent? I'd looked around and hadn't seen any – maybe the lurker was me? Or maybe being overheard wasn't the fear – maybe it was fear of losing something we had. Khrushchev and polio were the only evils I ever heard spoken of that seemed able to take shape and come out, storm into, or slink through, our streets and hurt people. I wondered what evil would want from our dismal landscape of dirty snow, crusty fields of corn stalk stubble, and featureless streets of nice, bland people? Why bother to attack someone like Carolyn in the middle of the night, leaving her legs twisted and gangly and weak? The folks who were supposed keep us safe – parents and teachers and shopkeepers – seemed just as baffled. Everyone hid under private clouds of worry. But though I wondered, I never worried. Khrushchev was a faraway old man who needed to be made to shut up. We were assured there were people who would do that. I was confident that one of our stern nuns could have fixed him.

Polio was sneakier. It could be anywhere, even on our street, in the swimming pool in the park, in crowds of strangers at the county fair. My mother took polio seriously. All around us were examples of paralysis, and there were rumors of fatality. Perhaps, to my mother, polio harkened to Hawai'i's history of decimation by infectious disease brought by Captain Cook's crew in 1778 when they introduced sexually transmitted diseases. Later foreign arrivals brought smallpox and measles. These were deadly to an isolated island population. By the 1820s an estimated one third of Hawaiian islanders had succumbed to the newly introduced microbial bacteria and viruses.

But my mother's fear of polio went beyond Hawaiian history. She knew from direct personal experience that invisible, unpredictable maladies can alter lives. After all, we had all wound up in the Midwest because my father could not live among Hawai'i's tropical allergens. We'd been driven to the farm country of his youth, because it was the only place he knew to go. When we arrived there, bedraggled and exhausted and strange-looking, we were welcomed because everyone had known my father since he was a little boy. They knew that his father had abandoned their family when my father was a small child, in the middle of the Great Depression of the 1930s. They were charitable and helped him get his footing after he'd done his part in World War II. They were kind even if he'd returned with a bride who looked Japanese, like the enemy, who'd grown up in a place they knew about from Arthur Godfrey. He was a 1950s television star who played the ukulele, wore a Hawaiian shirt, and deliberately mangled Hawai'i's name, chuckling to himself as he rolled out "Hawhya, Hawhya, Hawhya" until it became a stereotype that remained in American culture long past its prime. Townsfolk who'd known my father as a child were curious to talk to this Hawaiian he'd brought back with him, to ask her about the images of Hawai'i they'd seen of dancers swooning under swaying palms while gentle waves lapped at the shore.

The Hawaiian music that I knew came from those scratchy, long-playing 78 rpm records that my mother brought home from her occasional trips to Hawai'i, when she briefly infused Hawaiian culture into our house after it'd been re-awakened during her visits. I had no counter-images of what Hawai'i was like, but wondered how my mother could endure having to continuously explain that Hawai'i was somewhat like, and yet not at all like, those songs suggested. She suffered no fools, but she knew where to put attention. We would focus on keeping polio from crossing our threshold so we could assimilate into my father's hometown.

THE PRESS OF POLIO UPON MY MOTHER, ON TOP OF coping with racial bias and cold shoulder from my father's family, made her hypervigilant. She condensed all the speculation about where polio lurked and how to beat it away into a simple solution that she could manage: to keep her children cool and rested. She'd heard that this was an effective preventative practice, and it seemed to make sense to her. Every summer afternoon, when I'm sure she'd have loved for us to remain outside, she called us inside for a nap. We hated this. For one thing, we were too old to have to nap like babies. Besides, we couldn't see the point of it. We couldn't see or feel polio, and the people who got it were not yet visible to us, so it seemed like something that adults made up to get us to do their bidding. For another, the naps took place during the hours we'd ordinarily be going to the city swimming pool at the park. I wasn't fond of the pool, which was always overcrowded and not very sanitary, but it was our town's only summer recreation, along with the bike ride to get there, and sometimes lolling in the small park behind the bathhouse. That small window into friendship and fun closed when we were called to lay quietly in the room from which we were ordinarily banned.

"George! Moana! Get your sister and get in here." My mother never cajoled or enticed; her voice was always the harsh bark I would later hear among the elders bartering in urban Chinatown open air stalls.

Reporting to the living room with dread, as if we'd done something wrong, we'd find her holding crumpled white bed sheets in arms extended toward George and me. We knew our part: take a sheet and spread it flat and smooth across the living room floor. We made a short game of holding the corners and flapping the fabric up and down, creating a waft of warm breeze. She'd bark at us to "quit playing around" and we did as we were told, letting the sheet settle over the wall-to-wall, mauve-gray carpet. She forbade us from walking across that carpet – afraid we'd wear paths in its pile – at any time except the nap. The carpet was a splurge that my parents had made, using my dad's Christmas bonus, to cover the worn chocolate brown, orange-flecked linoleum that had been there since before the War. The privilege of lying across that carpet underscored the gravity of this necessary nap. Everything else about the hour of our nap became ritualized: George and I would crawl onto the double bed sheet we'd just laid on the floor, and our younger sister got the crib sheet spread on the sofa. She'd fall asleep quickly and soundly as our mother pulled down the shades, shutting out the afternoon sun, dimming the room, and dulling the carpet to a dusty gray.

"Now you hush until it's time to get up," she'd say, flashing us an "or else..." look. Then she'd set in motion the other purpose for these naps, which was to free up time to talk on the phone. Poking her finger into the rotary finger holes of the kitchen wall phone, she'd set the dial coursing through its clicking rotations. Then she'd greedily pull the coiled receiver wire to reach the nearest comfortable chair – the one with arms my father sat in at the head of the dining table in the next room. She'd set upon those calls like a dinner she'd been putting off and finally had a chance to devour.

"Now you be quiet," she'd repeat, aiming her voice in our direction, "or I'll come in there and lick you."

But she never did, because soon after she left us, she entered and immersed into the world of her grievances.

Her best friend Pat, who lived on the other end of town, seemed to have unlimited time to hear all the ways the "in-laws" were insulting, rude, ignorant. Didn't thank her for the Christmas gifts she'd sacrificed her own children's needs to buy. Didn't invite us to family parties. Passed right through our town without stopping to say hello. Before calling her sisters, who were married to career military men and scattered across the country – one in Denver, the other in Waltham, near Boston, and a cousin in Binghamton, near Niagara Falls – she took long distance rates and time zones into account. With them I heard more "uh huh, uh huhs" as she gave their stories of alienation and loneliness equal time as her spoken complaints.

    Confined to the white sheets in the next room, I couldn't avoid listening. Her voice rose and fell with variations of the same old complaints. I felt frozen by the harsh recounting of incidents where I'd been present yet hadn't felt them bite as she had. I hadn't seen what she'd seen: was there something wrong with her, or with me? She struck out at the "damn Germans" irrationally, punishing us children because she couldn't land a strike on the perpetrators of her perceived slights. The loss of my given name, Nina, was the irrational result of one of her frustrations. She was irritated that the name was consistently mispronounced, with the hard "I" rather than the Latin way, "like the Nina, the Pinta, the Santa Maria," or Nina Simone, so she took my name away and gave me another that was more unusual, more prone to mispronunciation and misspelling, a name that tied me more closely to the Hawaiian Islands when she was grooming me to fit in as Caucasian. It was an illogical solution, reactive in a way that came to characterize the way she mothered me.

But there were also times when she was light and sweet, her voice alive with reports of small victories, proud of what she had gotten out of and gotten on top of. At those moments my brother took advantage of her good humor to wiggle quietly to the side tables beside armchairs to examine the tchotchkes we were not allowed to touch. She'd laid them out in a way that was easy to dust and could be noticed by the few people that ever visited us. There was a crystal ashtray that the insurance man used on his annual visit, and a spoon set in a wooden box with a glass cover from our trip to Niagara Falls. We'd helped pick it out that year that we'd all piled in the car and drove out there, four of us in the back, bouncing around without seat belts or air conditioning, breathing second-hand smoke from my father's unfiltered Camels. The end table drawers were jammed with decks of playing cards with glossy reprints of classic paintings – Pierre-Auguste Renoir's *Two Sisters on the Terrace* with the red hat and Jean-Francois Millet's *The Angelus*, with the peasants pausing to pray in the field at sundown – awaiting the bridge club ladies who came on the third Wednesday of the month, and for whom my mother always baked a pie. On afternoons when she was too absorbed in her calls to check in on us, I dared take the cards out of their sturdy cases and organize them by numbers and colors and shapes, and I tried to shuffle them with the same snap that my father achieved when dealing a poker hand. Sometimes George pulled a *National Geographic Magazine* from the shelf and we'd furtively study the pictures of dark-colored women with drooping breasts and lips stretched by big disks before turning the page to a feature on lizards and rabbits that turned colors. On the coffee table rested a giant conch shell with "Waikiki Beach" hand-lettered in crisp black ink across its cool, flesh-colored curl. George showed me how to press it against my ear to hear a semblance of the sound of waves inside. Then he'd have to explain what a wave was, maybe flipping through other magazines to find a picture of one. He was always good about helping me string things together I could not have otherwise known.

"How'd the wave get in there?" I whispered.

"It's not a real wave. It's like a ghost," he said, "telling you not to forget the ocean."

"What if we do?"

"Bad luck," he'd say. "Anyway, it's just for Ma, since she's been there."

My mother liked figurines of pale children that looked angelic. Her favorites were the porcelain ones that came from Spain, from a company called Lladro, of slender girls with milky white aprons and blond hair falling across their backs like veils. I wondered how she'd come to appreciate them, since no one we knew looked like those virginal creatures. She also liked the Hummel figures of chubby children in shabby clothes, seemingly depicting old world agrarian villages of simpler times. Her favorite was the little boy and girl under an umbrella that reminded her of my brother and me when we were little. Her face got soft and tender when she looked at it. I never saw the connection, because my brother and I were wiry, brown and "Oriental" while those kids looked pale and plump. I later learned that the Hummels were made by the ones my mother called "those damned Germans" but she seemed to overlook that when she conflated my brother and me with those innocent statuary children with their rosy smiles.

The Germans she despised were my father's family and our neighbors, many of them just one generation removed from a country that had catapulted the entire world into

World War II. Those first- and second-generation Germans and Prussians, who'd only a few generations earlier carved tidy farms out of the Wisconsin woods, asked my mother how she'd learned such good English. These questions galled her. No doubt they were meant to be friendly, conversational. But they were hard to take coming from people she saw as Germans rather than as Americans, people who didn't seem sorry enough for the tragedy they'd hoisted on the world, the defining trauma of my parents' generation. "They have no idea!" she'd spew, banging things around the kitchen after enduring some thoughtless or patronizing comment on the street, in the church vestibule, or while visiting my father's sisters. She'd seen the devastation of war first-hand while those Germans had stayed behind plowing the fields. She spit out her loathing for the population of my father's hometown with two terms of derision, one racial and the other nationalist: "damn haole" and "damn Germans."

My mother's most bitter epithets were more personal, directed at my grandmother Queen Elizabeth, as she called her. But she only made them when Elizabeth wasn't there, which was virtually always. She came about once a year, an arrival that put our household into high gear. My mother would bake a fruit pie, wanting to show how well she'd adopted the German arts, and because it is a Hawaiian tradition to offer food to guests. Elizabeth, as we called her, never ventured past the living room, where she sat in the gold cut-velvet chair reserved for company, like the priest on his yearly visit or a Hawaiian cousin passing through. From that chair my grandmother Elizabeth would call us grandchildren to her, one by one, so she could get a close look at us. I would prepare for this inspection by making a perfect part in my hair, donning my blue plaid dress with the square white pique collar, and scrubbing my hands to get them whiter, because she once told me that if I washed hard enough, I could get the brown out. I wasn't sure what to make of that, but I understood that lighter skin would be better skin. She also told me to never pick my nose because it was already bigger than everyone else's and picking it would make it worse. I never told my mother that Elizabeth had instructed me in these ways. I knew it would set her off, and she raged about Elizabeth enough as it was. The rest of us hated to have to hear it.

"They don't know nothing. Don't know Jap from *pākē*." Fuming, she'd slide into her childhood words, ignoring that few within earshot knew that pākē was what the Hawaiians called Chinese persons. Such words, and worse, fell along the continuum of her bitterness, sometimes at the rise, sometimes in the full swell or after the crash, as the surge receded. Against the storm of her rages, listening in but wishing we didn't have to, my brother and I huddled like the Hummel kids, holding onto each other as the wind of her fury ravaged our flimsy umbrella. We knew that when she had worn herself down on the in-laws, she would begin comparing this God-forsaken Wisconsin outpost to "home."

SHE HAD ANOTHER HOME. THIS WAS A FACT THAT WE TOOK for granted. There were things attached to that other home, like certain words and foods, but these blended seamlessly into our home life, which is where they stayed for us only. I understood that outside our home these things would be meaningless or ridiculed. Her other home was in a place far, far away called the Hawaiian Islands or just the Islands, for short. That they were very far away is the one indisputable thing everyone knew about the Hawaiian Islands. Letters written by military personnel who'd been stationed in Hawai'i during World War II described Hawai'i's unimaginable beauty: flowers and beaches and warm winds and gentle surf and swaying palm trees. They wrote of so much exposed skin, brown skin, while conceding that in Hawai'i it made sense to wear less clothing.

The thing about my mother's "home" was that it was hers, not ours, and she didn't invite us there. Partially this was because it was too costly and arduous to go there, partially because she seemed to want to limit our exposure to it. She went happily every few years, after my parents had saved enough money, disappearing into that mystical, faraway place that seemed just for her. While she was gone my father took care of the four of us kids. His mother and sisters did not help, but that didn't seem unusual; we didn't know about the ways normal families pitched in to help in such situations. My father asked aged, bent-over Mrs. Braemer, who lived across the street and was usually out in her garden, to keep an eye on us while he went to work. Sometimes I went over to pick her hollyhocks and make dollies out of them, or to help her pick up rotten crabapples and toss them into a dented, galvanized bucket. When my father came home from work, walking the few blocks from the John Deere factory in the days before every family had a car and commuted, he fed us Depression-era food like soda crackers soaked in warm milk with a sliver of butter melting across the pale white surface. Sometimes he opened a Mason jar of string beans that my mother had put up and stored on shelves in the cool, dark basement.

After a few weeks, just about the time we were getting used to my father running things, he got us all cleaned up, borrowed his brother-in-law's car, and drove us to pick her up at the Milwaukee airport. She came back looking new and shiny, with fat suitcases stuffed with exotic gifts that spilled across the house. She brought my father cellophane bags of dried miniature shrimp from China that he rationed in a nightly treat of five or six to eat with a beer. She brought a few avocados for herself, unheard of in the years before refrigerated trucks opened the Midwest to faraway perishables. She hoarded them for herself – not that anyone else wanted them. She sprinkled them with sugar and scooped out the buttery innards with a spoon. For us kids she brought a small log that looked like a thick Tootsie Roll, kept moist in a sealed bag. It was a *ti* plant (which I confused with *tea*), which Hawaiians traditionally plant along the borders of their yards to ward off unfriendly spirits. We put ours in a dish of water and coaxed out a few green shoots, which seemed an achievement because we didn't know they grew to be several feet tall. Within a few weeks we'd have to toss it out, its soggy bark coated with a film of gray mold. She always brought back a vinyl long-playing record of Hawaiian music that she played and sang to for a few weeks, until it went back into its thin paper sleeve and lodged on a shelf with other albums from other trips. It was the only music we had in our house. For many years I believed that recorded music on a black platter was unique to Hawai'i.

My mother was always brighter after visiting the islands. Our house would be fragrant with foods she'd brought back, and she'd revive her use of words from the near-extinct Hawaiian language. She'd tell my father news about her relatives, none of whom we kids had ever met. The part of her that was different from everyone around us seemed more pronounced, and she seemed to relish herself as unique. Eventually she'd enfold those parts of herself under wraps in their usual place of shadows. Within a few weeks we'd all be back to the usual confusing dilemma of masking the differences between us and everyone else, while avoiding being like everyone else. My mother gave us no direct guidance on how to achieve this tricky balance. She wanted us to pass as haole, provided we didn't wind up behaving like them. She wanted us to blend in with them without becoming like them.

My father's family, which my mother called "the relatives," personified all the attributes we were to avoid absorbing. She was vigilant to any of their traits taking hold and yanked them out before they set in for good. My father, who was quiet and subdued with us, was never free to talk about his mother or what things were like for him as a child, though it was always known that they were very poor. Lacking much time with his side of the family, who lived fifty miles away in the Milwaukee area, we never got their stories or memories of our father as a young person. The few times we visited, they seemed nice enough, contrary to all we'd heard from my mother. My father's sisters were vivacious, noisy, and animated, compared to his self-effacing quiet. He never mentioned his mother, knowing it would trigger a tirade from my mother, who never forgot an insult and never passed up a chance to rail about whatever had happened the first time she came to Wisconsin. Her wounds were easily torn open and she lacked the skills to heal them. Her rage was fearsome: stomping through the house with enough force to rattle dishes in the cupboards, throwing pots of food at my father, accusing him of letting his mother stuff us in the dusty attic after we'd arrived from Hawai'i. This story was so often retold that I could almost imagine that I remembered it: my parents arriving at his family's door in 1949 with three babies born in three years, forced to leave the beautiful islands because of my father's allergies. Though she weighed just 90 pounds and was still recovering from a difficult pregnancy, none of them – Elizabeth or my father's three sisters – helped them settle in. There were no meals sent over from neighbors, nor offers of childcare. My uncle with a dairy business hired my father to deliver milk, then refused him credit for his purchases, though most customers ran a tab and paid monthly. My mother chafed at this insult, which she seemed to think had something to do with her and was being delivered through my father. "Damn Germans," she'd spit out. "Think I'm a Jap."

Across the threshold, laying on our backs during those periods of forced rest and listening to the rants, I'd stare at the ceiling as if our mother's complaints were projected there like a movie.

"What's a Jap?" I whispered to my brother.

"Don't know," he said.

I didn't believe him. He was a year older than me, nine, and seemed to know everything. But he didn't know about this important thing.

"Well, Kurt Schutz called me a Jap," I whispered, revealing an incident I'd been keeping a secret. Kurt had cornered me behind a shed, his white-blond butch-cut hair glistening over his sunburned scalp, his blue eyes menacing. I'd run away, and he'd yelled "Jap Jap" until I ducked into an alley. I could not have explained what a Jap was or why I feared this word hanging off me. But I avoided being near Kurt at school or on the way, as if the word Jap was something I could catch, like polio.

"Don't tell Ma," George said. "And stay away from Kurt."

"What's a pākē?" I asked him. I was already aware that our mother had a language we only used in our house. This was one of those words that she used that my father seemed to know about, but I sensed no one else would.

"Chinese," he said. "Our grandpa is pākē."

I didn't know what Chinese was either, or that we had a grandpa, or what all of it had to do with polio. But they seemed related, because when our mother ran out of steam on the relatives, she started in on polio. She lowered her voice, as though polio was out on the street, hiding in a tree or squatting behind trashcans in our alley, plotting how it would come in the night and take away our legs. She whispered about taking those kids that polio got to an iron lung, whatever that was. I wondered whether my father and mother would let polio take me away and not come get me back. I wanted to think that polio was kinder, friendlier than my mother's hushed tales. Maybe just an ogre up the beanstalk that was scary but did no real harm.

"Everybody sick in this cole, cole, cold climate," she'd say, only adding the "d" – a letter that does not exist in the Hawaiian alphabet – on the last word in the series, as if it would be a waste to use it unnecessarily. "I would not have come to this place if I knew everybody's sick all the time. Damn haole."

Whoever was on the other end of the line took all of this in, and no doubt had their own fears and resentments. My mother's sisters were scattered around the country, but they'd all grown up in Hawai'i and they knew the history of white folks bringing diseases that ravaged the islands.

After a third of them were killed off by microbes, the haole stole their land and threw out their queen and made them Americans. And now that we were on the United States mainland, where we had a right to be, they treated us like we were dirty, with our darker skin, like my grandmother Elizabeth had implied. I knew all this was festering because out of the blue, at random-seeming times, my mother would mutter, "The nerve!" Like while getting us into our baths, to keep us clean of the haole diseases, she'd splash us with tepid water, telling us as though we were old enough to understand, that "Hawaiians died like flies, seven out of ten," her voice lowered to convey the gravity of these numbers.

It had happened before her time, in the early 1800s, so she hadn't seen the putrid bodies carted off in the heat. But she seemed to have a vivid image of it and to have felt it in her bones. We all knew about the leprosy that crumbled noses and ears and fingers until they fell right off. We had learned about this in Catholic school because there were so many saints who were lepers. Hawaiian leprosy came from the Chinese, and unlucky Hawaiian lepers were rounded up by bounty hunters, shipped off to the turbulent bay outside Kalaupapa on the island of Moloka'i, and thrown into the water with their satchels of belongings. The ones who couldn't swim were not rescued; the ones who could get to shore would stay there until they died, exiled forever. Same as the polio kids, also carted off in the night, the neighborhood whispering for days afterward and shrinking back from contact with the afflicted families.

From the adjacent room, I could see my mother sitting on her bare feet, her knees pushed up near her chin, like a crouching animal ready to spring. Outrage pushed wind into her voice as she lit upon her plan. She worked it out right in our earshot. "These kids, they get along with these damned Germans. They pass for haole here. I need to make them haole," she said. In other words, she would protect us from the haole by making us into haole, a plan springing from the part of her childhood in Hawaiʻi and her ancestry in China that was tenaciously survivalist. Having laid down her intention, she began her descent onto the plateau of the everyday Midwest, signaled by a glance at the clock and the realization that she had to get off the phone because my father would soon be home.

I looked at George, scared. I wasn't exactly sure what it meant to be Hawaiian, but at least we knew we were Hawaiian, not haole. Being Hawaiian made us different from the folks in that Midwestern plain where we'd landed. But in this case being different was better than being haole, because we always heard our mother cursing about the haole, usually in the same breath as her rails against the Germans.

"She wants us to be haole?" I whispered to George.

He frowned and scrambled to his feet.

"Wait," I said, pulling on his leg, "Let's hear the rest."

But George broke away and went to the window.

"You'll get in trouble," I warned.

He pulled the crocheted circle that dangled from the middle of the shade, releasing its spring. The shade clattered open, winding itself around the wooden roller in a tight, decisive snap. The dim room flooded with sunlight, making of my brother a stark silhouette against the lower half of the window.

"George," I hissed in a loud whisper. "Come back here. Listen to her."

"I don't want to listen," he said.

"Well, she's gonna lick you," I said.

He reached up to lower the shade, but the pull-ring dangled out of his reach. He gave up, not even trying to find a way. He came back to the sheet and pulled the corners, straightening it out, removing signs of our restlessness. Then he lay down again, knowing our mother would soon hang up and check in on us. I propped up on my elbow and looked at him, expecting him to tell me what he was thinking. But he didn't say anything. I laid back down and listened to her plotting our future as haole.

Chapter 3

Remembering What We Never Knew

I never saw it as a problem that my mother came from a faraway land that she called home. The problem was that she did so little to enfold us, her children, into a sense that anything about her other home might extend to us. She kept all but the most general personal memories and experiences about Hawaiʻi to herself. As a curious child, I mentally gathered and stashed the little bits and glimpses of Hawaiʻi that randomly crossed my awareness, though I didn't go out of my way to find them. The photo album project is an example of trying to piece snatched images of Hawaiʻi into a whole I could attach to. My mother did not look over my shoulder as I sorted out all those black and white snapshots of us as babies in Hawaiʻi, as I would have done were my kids taking on such a project, seizing the moment to share stories of us all in that sunny, verdant place. Thus, the images never took on a life beyond my absorption in them as a task for a wintry afternoon. I never crossed the gap between seeing images of myself as a baby bathing under palm trees and identifying with them as integral to my heritage. The albums have disappeared, like so much about our ties with Hawaiʻi.

After a few years in the Midwest, my mother began teaching my sister and me, and another childhood friend from our Catholic school, to dance the Hawaiian hula. Our repertoire was limited to a few well-known island favorites: the "Little Grass Shack" and "Lovely Hula Hands." She'd returned from one Hawaiian visit with a suitcase full of skirts made of strands of fluid red cellophane, a simulation of the fabled grass skirts, and she'd fashioned tube tops of red satin and elastic. She volunteered for us to dance as the opening act to her solo performance at church bazaars and school fundraisers. I never had the pelvic flexibility to dance the hula with grace, and I was too self-conscious to pull out the radiant smile my mother kept yelling at me to produce. Lessons with my impatient mother were stressful, and I hated getting on that riser in small-town venues to proffer our culture. It was an awkward time for me – the mid-1950s when I was too old to be cute and too young to be alluring. But the dancing was something concretely Hawaiian that she shared with our community, and people appreciated that we did it. Pulling out her oriental hat, my mother also helped the Ladies Altar Society raise money by hosting a Chinese sit-down dinner in our dining room. The twelve lucky diners were chosen by lottery tickets and paid a rather hefty sum to be led into new culinary realms, far beyond the limp canned chop suey boiled in a pot that passed as Chinese food at that time. She used fresh ginger and the stir-fry technique that was novel to casserole cooks who threw in a can of salty creamed soup to pull their efforts together.

The success of using her culture to enrich her community was a breakthrough for my mother. She basked in the praise heaped on her as a woman of worth and charm. Recognition of her value, by extension, reflected admirably on my father, who'd taken a risk in returning to his hometown with a war bride from another land. He'd found himself mired in unforeseen complexity with few tools for guidance. My parents probably didn't see the practical, much less psychological, value of keeping our island heritage and identity alive, though my father loved and understood Hawai'i. It was up to my mother, and she was deeply conflicted and afraid. But when she finally opened her Hawaiian heart to the community, I'm sure my father was as proud a beneficiary as the rest of us.

My mid-life drive to identify and reclaim my racial and cultural roots would have surprised my parents. It surprised me. It was insistent, yanking me by the collar and pulling me back to Hawai'i for purposes beyond a beach vacation. It was a need to reconcile beliefs I'd carried with facts I'd learned throughout my fifty years. It was the necessity of assimilating layers of experience, education, reading, and relationships. The pull seemed natural, and I'd have been remiss to ignore it. As one disparity settled, another arose, and each triggered more curiosity, vexation, and even cynicism. I realized, long after I was already in it, that I was in the natural process of cumulative, iterative root-finding. Each revelation was a thorn in my side, a stone in my shoe, a niggling irritation like a dull headache or low-grade fever that doesn't go away. Eventually, the force that had grabbed me and not let go took the shape of a visage, and then presented herself with a name. She was Waipuilani E. Paki, and she was my great-grandmother.

Waipuilani came to me at a gathering of relatives I'd invited to come together at an oceanside house I'd rented on O'ahu. We'd had a day of backyard barbecuing, kayaking, and sharing news. After dishes and the remains of our evening meal had been cleared away, as the sky darkened from twilight to the velvety blackness that is unique to seaside, my cousin brought out the diagram of the family tree and spread it across the table. I was surprised to see our family history so carefully documented and felt sad that it'd never been shared with family members who lived on the mainland. It seemed to be in the care and keeping of one cousin, the second eldest among us, and I resolved to ask her if we could get together so I could learn more about its entries. Running my glance up and down the trunk, and out and across the limbs, I came to a full stop at the name Waipuilani E. Paki.

I was immediately in her thrall. My cousins said she was called Tutu Wahine. They offered a few sparse details about her: she had black skin, only spoke the Hawaiian language, and had grown up in the wild, primitive uplands of Western Maui. Their description was too cursory, too offhanded, for the reverence I was already feeling for her and her place in our ancestral lineup. I'd already mentally elevated her to the top of my list of things that I'd missed out on but wanted to give myself. The most important of those was the steady, grounding presence of grandmothers, which I believed would be impossible to manifest since they were all deceased. Nevertheless, I felt her compel me, from across the veil, to wake up and do my work.

In the Midwest world of my childhood, everyone I knew had a grandmother. These women were a family fixture, a source of comfort, rather like central heating in a cold climate. They were solid and substantial, providing continuity of skills and traditions. The grandmothers I knew of, and envied my friends for having, tended to live on nearby farms. They had cows to milk and haylofts to play in and berries to pick for pie. They looked like dumplings, powdery and soft, and seemed to come with plates of warm cookies and feather beds in their dormers. Everyone went to their tables for Thanksgiving, like the song we sang in grade school every November: "Over the river and through the woods, to Grandmother's house we go."[2]

My family didn't have that typical Midwestern grandmother. Elizabeth was nearby but she was physically and emotionally inaccessible. Our Hawaiian grandmother was physically far away, but she fortified my mother across the vast distance in time and miles. Seeing the ways my mother needed her mother, I wished that Grandma Rosa were nearby. She could've helped my mother, and she could've imparted grandmotherly wisdom to me. I'd needed the steadying ballast of a *kupuna,* an esteemed Hawaiian elder attuned to the earth and the ethereal.

Encountering Waipuilani, seeing her arise like a hologram from her box on a genealogy chart, I felt compelled to meet her. She had knowledge to proffer, even posthumously. She could help fill the voids where I'd been struggling to ground. She catapulted me into a liminal reality that was both jolting and calming. She would help open doors that had been shutting me out and, equally important, help close some that needed to be closed. I'd read, but I had not experienced, that "As Native Hawaiians, each of us has the ability to tap into a preconscious reservoir of past experiences and to access all that exists in a storehouse of knowledge called ancestral memories."[3] I had come to windward Oʻahu for the purpose of remembering, she seemed to say, not merely enjoying a long vacation. My *kuleana* (life purpose and responsibility) was to engage with her. That was why she had

turned up at my party. "People don't *believe* in spirits here.
. .They *live* with them," I'd read.⁴ I would live with her. This
meant starting at the beginning, defining who Waipuilani
was, her roles, and her place in time. I, as a mother of daughters, had to know these roles and consequences.

I began by sitting in appreciation for what each woman
in my lineage was to the other. Waipuilani was my mother's
grandmother, she was my grandmother's mother, she was
my great grandmother. It was important to list and contemplate each relationship, because each shaped the woman
who came after, just as each was shaped by the ones who'd
come before. This recitation of her place seems elemental,
but it is also seminal, because Waipuilani did not come to
me until I had cleared a path for her. She'd arrived during
a period when I was vegetating in empty-nest blues and
professional limbo. Needing a getaway to plot out my
next steps, I'd rented my friend's house at Punaluʻu, a tiny
windward Oʻahu town along the two-lane Kamehameha
Highway that rims the island. I hadn't planned to dive into
family history, which I'd been trained to sidestep. But I'd
landed in the right time and environment for Waipuilani
to show up, to shake me out of my ennui, and to give shape
to my aimless Hawaiian hiatus.

After my ethereal encounter with Waipuilani, I remembered having hiked twenty years earlier in Western Maui's
remote Honokowai area. Though I now believe that Honokowai was Waipuilani's place of origin, I had no awareness
of her on the day I'd bushwhacked through the area's thickets and overgrown trails. I'd been on a business trip, visiting
the Wailea Beach resort my Honolulu-based company was
developing. Seeking an adventure, I'd found Honokowai
about an hour's drive west and north, and headed there

one day after my meetings. Honokowai had once been a district of traditional Hawaiian *ahupuaʻa,* which was a wedge-shaped area of land that followed natural watershed boundaries and was self-sustaining with the flora, fauna, and organizational practices its community needed. Remembering that hike, I could envision the geographical isolation of her childhood. The ahupuaʻa system of barter, trade, and sharing gave inhabitants little reason to look outside their boundaries. People of those times, and of that culture, were not driven by the "grass is greener" wanderlust that drives young people today. She may have had limited exposure to the world beyond the boundaries of their rugged enclave, may have known little about the whaling, plantations, and boatloads of people coming from other lands. Descending to the coast and taking the shoreline trek to the whaling port of Lahaina would have been arduous. The decision to leave their traditional, indigenous way of life must have been forced upon them by circumstances they were powerless to derail. Thinking back to that hike, I knew that understanding why she came off the mountain was the key to understanding our family destiny, right up to how we all wound up in Wisconsin.

E. Waipuilani Paki, or Waipuilani E. Paki – I've seen official documents where her name is shown both ways – was born November 19, 1871, in Maui, Kingdom of Hawaii. Internet research readily coughs up data of this sort, but sheds no light on what shapes a life unless someone has a memory, an anecdote or fact, and takes the initiative to go online and embellish the record. Even then, one questions how accurately the information had been passed down, given that memory is selective. For example, I learned through online records that the E. in Waipuilani's name stands for Elizabeth. This waylaid me as I contemplated the irony that I already had an Elizabeth in my lineage of grandmothers, the unloved Elizabeth who was my father's mother. That she had this improbable English name tells me that she was named in compliance with the 1860 Act to Regulate Names, imposed by King Kamehameha IV, requiring children to be christened with English first names. This tells me that Waipuilani's family was near enough to regulatory agencies to know and abide by their strictures.

I began researching what was going on in Western Maui in the 1870s, hoping to thread events and circumstances into the trajectory of her life. I had cursory understanding of the cascading effects of loss of land and culture through ethnocide, and the ways that forced disruption leave us with residuals called epigenetic inheritance.[5] I felt the Hawaiian pain of loss encoded in my DNA, compelling me to learn what forces broke our ancestral bond to the land. Knowing this would inform me of ways that they affected not only Waipuilani, but also her daughter Rosalie, and Rosalie's daughter Lillina, and then me, and ultimately my own daughters.

One thing we know for sure: after leaving the mountain, Waipuilani went to Lahaina, where she met and married Sun Akana Wong, a man born in China who was twenty-six years older than her. He'd come to Hawaii in his youth and had become a Hawaiian citizen in 1866, six years before Waipuilani was born.* He'd fathered nine island-born chil-

---

*I've written Sun Akana Wong's story based on records available to me at the time I was researching our family genealogy. Since that time online ancestry site entries have been expanded to record a man with that name who lived on Maui and was born in 1861. I leave this account as written since it reflects information available at the time that I queried him. With website ancestry records on open sites in continual states of update

dren, the last five with Waipuilani. He was significant to me for reasons beyond heading up our limb on the family tree, where his position is nondescript, another name on another branch. But his genetic and cultural footprint is outsized: he brought the Chinese into our bloodline for all generations to follow. His children with Waipuilani, and presumably with the other island women with whom he procreated, were *hapa* (the Hawaiian word for half), the burgeoning multi-racial sector that would define the Hawaiian population forever after.

I have tried to imagine how Waipuilani came to be with a man so much older than her, and how they functioned together. It is said that she did not speak English, though Sun Akana Wong may have, given how long he'd been in Hawai'i. No doubt their children spoke English or *pidgin*, the organically evolved mash-up of languages that island people of mixed origins used to communicate with each other. My mother had no direct experience with her grandfather, since he died in 1923, and she never spoke of him. The discovery that she grew up without a grandfather, just as I'd never had one, struck me anew with the perpetuation of dysfunction across generations and the loss of knowledge about our forebears. Being in this place where my parents met, and where I'd been conceived and born, compounded the obvious: I could not know myself without understanding the Hawaiian part of my mother, which came down from Waipuilani. Thus, I had to understand Waipuilani to understand my mother, and my Grandma Rosa as the link between them. Mothers of the 1950s were more private about the details of their lives, while women of my generation embraced the therapy that required probes into

---

and revision by anyone who chooses to contribute, verification is a challenge.

our mothers' experience. For years I'd been caught in the proverbial Catch-22: without knowing what our mothers withheld, we couldn't know if they were withholding.

I mused on these things without restraint, grateful for the rustic, ocean-viewing decks of my rented house, rocking in chairs to the rhythm of the waves. I reflected on how the fluidity between pairings and abandonments may have hardwired in me tendencies toward singledom. Reining in my thoughts when they moved too quickly, or when I jumped over too much that was yet unknown, I felt anger toward the temporizing males who'd left Waipuilani and Grandma Rosa impoverished, with their children foraging food, while they moved on to form new families in the sprawling, overlapping entanglements that my mother never wanted to explain to us.

Contemplating the waves slapping against the sea wall was both mesmerizing and exasperating. Every metaphor for every mystery was embodied in the unceasing tidal rhythm that is the pulse of Hawai'i. I meditated on the ocean's ephemeral colors, trying to capture them in a daily writing practice, describing the ever-transforming shades of blue, gray, and green as they transformed from what they had been only seconds before, from silvery to leaden, reflecting light and then absorbing it, the spectrum of gray, blue, or green, or bluish green, or grayish blue, or greenish gray, or some variant of all of those, sometimes with a hint of lavender or a splash of gold or surge of ecru, with flashes of lacy white and burnished copper. Were those the colors of the water, or the reflections on the water? That taupe – was it the water, or sand churning in the waves? Did it matter? It was ungraspable yet it was engrossing as metaphors for my self-identity which coalesced as much around what I wasn't as what I was, and for the fluid blending of the people and cultures of those baffling islands.

One day, watching the clouds over the reef gather and reflect the sunset on the other side of the island, I realized that I had to look far beyond myself, even beyond Waipuilani, for clues to what triggered our family migrations across the 19th and 20th centuries. Our story began back in 1778, the year Captain James Cook arrived in those islands where I was spending so many hours cataloguing colors.

Chapter 4

You'll Hear It Call You

For thousands of years, in what cultural anthropologists call the "pre-contact years," the Hawaiian Islands were the most isolated land mass on Earth. Anthropologists believe that the original "discovery" of Hawai'i was in 400 CE by Polynesians thought to have journeyed in sailing canoes from the Marquesas Islands two thousand miles away. Discovering the string of volcanic protrusions that we now call Hawai'i, they went ashore and over many centuries cultivated the barren landscape into a fully self-sustaining society ruled by warrior kings. Captain James Cook arrived in 1778, with his ships HMS Endeavour and HMS Discovery, and their crews of about 170 men. Their coming, and Cook's descriptions of Hawaiians as heathen savages, triggered an influx of Christian missionaries from New England states. Their coming was the beginning of the American colonization of Hawai'i, which has been described as "the slow, insinuating invasion of people, ideas, and institutions. . . that dismembered the *lāhui* (the people) from their traditions, their lands, and ultimately their government."[6]

On the face of it, and with the kings' blessings, the missionaries' extensive cultural transference provided advancements that would enhance Hawai'i's habitability not only for people who already lived there, but also for the Americans and Asians who came in the missionaries' wake. These diligent emissaries of progress brought in Hawai'i's first printing press and created an alphabet for the Hawaiian language. They taught Hawaiians to read, to sew, to cover their bodies, and even to make quilts – which Hawaiians had no practical need of, given the climate. They built frame houses of the sort they'd had back in Massachusetts. They cleared land for polo fields and brought in horses to play. Their offspring, with names still recognizable today – Castle, Cooke, Baldwin, Dole, and Parker – became Hawai'i's first entrepreneurs. They engineered Hawai'i's inexorable transition from centuries-long sustainability on their own land to landlessness and dependence on imported essentials, including food.

Waipuilani was the last in my family's lineage to have lived in the traditional Hawaiian self-sustaining ways of being. Mapping her childhood to the dramatic changes in the islands' business and culture, it's important to know that she grew up during the reign of King Kalākaua, who was called The Merrie Monarch because of his love of world travel, song, playing the ukulele, and traditional hula dance. During his reign from 1874 to 1891, the years when Waipuilani grew from young child to young woman, King Kalākaua's far-ranging policies left a deep imprint on island life. He reinstated the public performance of the hula, which the missionaries had forbidden, triggering a revival of Hawaiian dance arts celebrated to this day in the Merrie Monarch Festival held every spring in Hilo. He irrevocably altered the Hawaiian economy by negotiating agreements with American business and government agents, such as the Reciprocity Treaty of 1875, that allowed the United States to import Hawaiian sugar and other products duty-free. This singular initiative vastly expanded the markets for island products and accelerated Hawai'i's momentum toward plantation agriculture. He also granted the United States permission to use Honolulu's Pearl Harbor, which laid the foundation for Hawai'i's strategic role as America's military base of operations in World War II.

King Kalākaua's sister Lili'uokalani ascended to the throne after he died unexpectedly in 1891 while visiting San Francisco. She became Hawai'i's first female monarch when Waipuilani was twenty years old, entering adulthood and her life as a mother in Lahaina. In my search to understand Waipuilani, I imagine her receiving the news that her queen was imprisoned by a band of Honolulu's haole businessmen just two years after she'd been enthroned. Those men took over the Hawaiian government and forever ended Hawai'i's standing as a sovereign nation. Losing their Queen stripped the *Kānaka Maoli*, the native-born Hawaiians, of any advocates in positions of power who would safeguard their well-being. The wanton illegality of overthrowing a sovereign queen was sanctioned with a gentlemen's "wink and a nod" between island entrepreneurs and politicians in Washington D.C. who wanted to use Hawai'i as an American barrier defense. Queen Lili'uokalani languished under house arrest in her own Iolani Palace, until she abdicated in 1895, while the self-appointed governors conducted illegitimate government affairs in adjacent rooms. In 1898, finishing off their collusion with the islands' white patriarchy, the United States government annexed Hawai'i and dissolved the Hawaiian Kingdom.

These disruptive threads of cultural disintegration and upheaval were the backdrop of Waipuilani's youth. While the entrepreneurs of Lahaina flourished, island-born

Hawaiians like Waipuilani were increasingly marginalized and without recourse. One needs only to look at the United States' theft of Native Americans' lands to understand the behaviors at work in the taking of Hawai'i from its sovereigns and people. Once United States agents were ensconced in Hawaiian affairs, they subjected the Hawaiian people to classic methods of cultural genocide: they barred Hawaiians from speaking their own language and from giving their children Hawaiian names, and they propagandized Hawaiians to accept that these edicts were in their best interest. Accustomed to a monarchy, Hawaiians were habituated to taking direction from persons of legitimate authority. Powerless, and trusting the indoctrination, they acquiesced.

As a woman who came into adulthood in the early days of feminism, and in reverence to the islands' matriarchal order of the time, I wince at the image of the Hawaiian queen so brutally "handled" by the plantation gentlemen in their white linen suits.

MY MOTHER, CHRISTENED MILDRED LILLINA, WAS BORN in 1925, the third of Grandma Rosa's daughters. She spent her childhood summers on the outskirts of Lahaina with Waipuilani, her grandmother called Tutu Wahine, who lived in a frame shack without water or electrical power. This gave my mother firsthand experience living in many of the "old Hawaiian" ways. She spoke of these without any sort of cleaving sentimentality. Her perspective was how one coped with and adapted to stark poverty. She may have grown up overhearing the elders grumbling, unhappy with their displacement, their relegation to the lowest rungs of service and manual labor. These dissatisfactions, alongside the increasing haole affluence and U.S. military empowerment, molded her awareness of where things were headed for young people of her circumstances. She began developing a mental checklist of situations to avoid, a list she passed on to me when I began dating a generation later. High on the list was to avoid being anyone's doormat. To one of her circumstances and race, gaining and sustaining agency would require grit, a feisty resilience. This she developed, or perhaps she acquired it in her DNA as an inherited survival trait from Waipuilani and Rosalie.

When I stand back and consider Hawaiʻi's ever-shifting sense of itself – by which I mean its self-concept as opposed to any externally imposed identity – I see myself as the fourth generation of women in my family wrestling over how to be Hawaiian amidst the dominating presence of haole. While archiving my mother's black and white photos so many years ago, I seemed to be savoring her Hawaiian memories for her while she languished in ambivalence about the life those images captured. I was baffled that she seemed okay with letting them fall into a past from which she'd moved on. She never explained to us who the Hawaiians were as a people, nor expressed who she felt herself to be as a Hawaiian – much less the Chinese I came late to acknowledge and integrate with what I knew about our racial make-up. In that vacuum, I saw myself as a haole whenever I could delude myself that I was. This clouded my acceptance that I am a racially mixed bundle, an amalgamation of all the migrations that pressed into Hawaiʻi based on accretions of desperation, abandonment, and hope.

The bottom-line truth that I stalled having to acknowledge is that I belonged "neither here nor there." In that space, I felt both free and deprived. It was easy to turn my back on

Hawaiʻi as a place for tourists, the military, and my mother. It was not a place for me. Never in my mother's hectoring lectures about what to do in my life, rank-ordered, did she suggest that I go to Hawaiʻi, meet our relatives, and experience the "Paradise of the Pacific." In the 1960s, when I was in high school, I imagined enrolling at the newly created University of Hawaiʻi Center for Cultural and Technical Interchange Between East and West (known as The East-West Center). I was drawn to study the crosscurrents between those vast and disparate realms. It was a fanciful idea, but it tugged at me enough to wonder aloud to my mother whether having Hawaiian roots might help me get admitted, and if our Oʻahu relatives could put me up and show me around until I got settled on the Manoa campus. Her response was strident and harsh: I would not like it there, I would not be welcomed, and I should forget about it.

That sprout of nascent interest withered, but it left a root in the wall, an errant tendril that Waipuilani instructed me to tend to and bring alive. Other references about Hawaiʻi turned up randomly, throughout my youth, like a used paperback copy of James A. Michener's sprawling novel *Hawaiʻi*,[7] published in 1959, the year that Hawaiʻi became a state. I checked the book out of the library when I was in high school and was immediately entranced by its opening paragraphs. I could envision the bird that Michener described carrying a seed across the dark, seeming infinity of oceanic distance and dropping it onto the islands' volcanic land mass. I could envision that seed taking root, growing to give vegetative sustenance to the earliest men to step foot onto the abrasive cooled lava we call Hawaiʻi. Michener's novel expanded my concepts of the islands beyond the corny 1950s cliches I'd grown up with. It had weight and substance: a fictional 19th century society of Christian missionaries turned Hawaiian business entrepreneurs; Chinese and Japanese laborers who came to work the land the haole had taken from the Hawaiians and turned into plantations; generations of interracial co-existence creating the diverse population we call the melting pot. This was perfect summer reading for dull, sweltering Wisconsin afternoons. Sprawled across the daybed of our screened-in front porch, I settled down for a long summer read. I'd hoped the book would help open a dialogue with my mother about her islands. One day she noticed what I was reading and furiously ripped the book out of my hands and forbade me to read it. I did not understand then, nor in later years when I got another copy and finished reading it, what about the book had so agitated her.

As an introverted adolescent girl on the social margins, I always had my nose in a book. Reading was how I escaped small town monotony, and the small-town-ness in myself. It was how I tutored myself in the ways of the larger, more sophisticated world that I intended to make myself at home in one day. Most of the books I read were from the library or loaned by teachers who'd taken interest in me. This is how I came to have another historical novel about Roman gladiators which had cover art showing a woman in a ripped tunic. My father found this offensive and snatched the book from my grasp, generating an argument that ended with my getting slapped hard across the face. But my interest was vast and bottomless. Undaunted, I took up tales of the Moghuls in India, the lives of the great composers and saints, Victorian gothic novels and philosophical selections from Aristotle, Socrates, and Sartre. I even tried to teach myself Hebrew.

When I wasn't reading, my escape from my small-seeming life was listening to musicals. Our family didn't have a music system, so I saved my babysitting money and bought a used Motorola high fidelity record player. I checked out recordings of operas and Broadway musicals from the library and played them over and over until I knew every word of every song. I was enthralled with the wartime romance of Rogers and Hammerstein's *South Pacific*[8] which depicted the World War II Hawaiian history that my parents had lived through. I drew no association between them and the musical's characters and situations, nor did my mother or father weigh in to help me understand the plot lines. We missed many instructional moments because my mother lodged herself in the middle ground between censorship and indifference. That left me free to drift into *South Pacific*'s spell of enchantment without understanding the underlying themes. I was free to imagine myself floating on my own special island, "Bali Hai," and to thoroughly miss the lesson of the handsome Lieutenant Cable's song "Carefully Taught," [9] with its bitter lyrics to be "afraid of people whose eyes are oddly made, and people whose skin is a different shade." I failed to connect how that issue might relate to me, or to see that my own father had not heeded the warnings when he'd been in the same situation.

Though musicals helped me escape adolescent boredom, I set them aside in high school to focus on achievements to enable an actual escape. At school I was a nerd and an outlier. I was not so much socially ostracized as socially challenged, because I was so often being punished. For weeks at a time, I was arbitrarily grounded and denied use of the phone, making me unavailable to friends. Eventually they stopped inviting me to their outings. Alone and isolated, I chose activities that I could do from the living room or front porch – reading, practicing piano, knitting. I didn't have boyfriends and felt romance, which I only knew from musicals, was out of my reach. But romance found me, right in my hometown, suddenly and euphorically.

I met him the summer before going to college, on a rare night out that I was allowed to go out with a girlfriend. She picked me up in her mother's pink convertible, the top down, and we drove to a dive bar at the edge of a cornfield a few miles outside of town. It was my first time in a bar. I felt dizzy before the wall of neon lager logos, the throngs of people on the make, the smell of beer and body odors. Within minutes I saw a stranger across a crowded room, just like in the *South Pacific* song, and I was living my "Some Enchanted Evening"[10] fantasy. We had eye lock and he pushed through the crowd to introduce himself to me. He was a gangly, brainy Harvard sophomore from the neighboring town who was home for a summer job. We left the bar and walked to a pier on a nearby pond where mist rose and hovered over the surface. Because I thought of love in terms of song, and because for me the veil between the music and reality was thin and permeable, I began singing to him. He'd been learning French and asked if I knew any, so I sang him the only French I knew, which was the "Dites Moi" children's song from *South Pacific*. I felt vulnerable and otherworldly in a childlike way, but fully ready to step into another existence.

We were smitten, and it took me decades to fall out of love with the idea of him, though our romance only lasted a few years. After he told his mother about me, she made inquiries and learned something that led her to forbid his seeing me. This catapulted our tender new love into a classic young lover's dilemma. Convinced that if his mother met me, she'd love me as much as he did, he took me to his house. She got up and left the room without a word or a glance in my direction, and later gave him an ultimatum: he must choose between me or their funding his Harvard education.

Baffled by his mother's rebuff, I confided in my mother. Something about the situation seemed beyond mere rudeness. Though I rarely sought her counsel, I sensed she'd know what was going on. She instantly called the woman "prejudiced," the word then used before being honed to the word "racist" used today. Like the cynically poignant song from the *South Pacific* musical, my young man had not been "carefully taught." Nor had I. We secretly soldiered on over long distance, after he returned to Cambridge and I stayed in the Midwest, but the lines between us frayed and eventually snapped. Over the time we spent together, mostly on school breaks where I'd go to his campus or he'd come to mine, and for forty years after, I threw myself into perfecting perfectionism. I lived my life as a testament to how wrong he and his mother had been about my worthiness. I was convinced that in some random moment our paths would cross somewhere on the planet, and he would see that passing on me had been a monumental mistake. That first racial wound took so many decades to heal because I'd not seen myself as anything but white and had no skills to cope with anyone who did. In her misguided way, my mother had tried to prepare me for this inevitable situation by forcing me to remain on the periphery, or by striving to blend in so seamlessly as a haole that I felt invisible.

In the thrall of that first love, I put myself on a fast track to graduate college in three years. My goal was to catch up with my love and finish the same year as he, then I would move East to be with him. I'd cooked up this plan without insight into its obeisance to my mother's many lectures to get an education and travel and, specifically, to *not settle down*. Although the romance didn't last, I bee-lined to New York City within days of college graduation, took the subway to the Upper West Side to enroll in Columbia University's School of General Studies, and got a job with a research team in the Graduate School of Business. I went to ballet and opera, the museums and theater. I left after two years to volunteer for the Peace Corps in Turkey, then hitchhiked around Europe, Russia, and North Africa, living out of a backpack and accountable to no one. I was untethered.

Once I left Wisconsin, where I was known as Hawaiian, I was surprised at how often I was asked if I was Chinese. In Europe it wasn't a question, but a statement: people pointed at me and said "*Chin*." Chinese tourists were rare in those years of Mao's Cultural Revolution, so I was a standout. At times it was preferable to being called American, at a time when the U.S. identity was fraught with the CIA and Vietnam. The ones who called me Chin or chink were friendly and seemed to be groping for an explanation, because other than my face I seemed so American. Sometimes I explained that I was Hawaiian, which elicited a delighted response. But usually I let them think I was Chinese, or whatever combination of races and nationalities they came up with. It didn't matter to me what they called me because I couldn't see a negative consequence associated with whatever racial identity they pinned on me, as there had been with my first lover's mother.

Chapter 5

Having a Wonderful Time

By my late twenties, I'd traveled to many faraway and exotic places, but I'd never been to Hawai'i. My chance came when the Honolulu-based company that I worked for in San Francisco sent me to Hawai'i on business. I eased into the islands easily, going to my meetings and touring company projects, barely giving a nod to my mother's years of angst about my going there and meeting ruination. I immediately set an intention to bring up my children to feel at ease with their ancestral home, and went back with them not long after. I wanted them to experience Hawai'i while they were young enough to absorb it without filters and old enough to remember. While on layover in Los Angeles, I called my mother in Florida to tell her how excited the girls were to see where their Granny had grown up. She scolded me for spoiling them and said I should not get my hopes up for an embrace from the relatives or expect to feel at home there. In other words, we should not expect *aloha,* the fabled Hawaiian expression of welcome, love, peace, compassion, and goodwill, said as both greeting and farewell and theoretically expressed, to beloveds and strangers alike, at every chance in between.

Undeterred, I took my family to every beach, historical attraction, and cultural sideshow, from coconut stands along the highway, to lei stringers in the jungley upland neighborhoods, to climbing the steep steps to the Diamond Head lookout. We snorkeled reefs, splashed about in waves, and visited the Pali above Honolulu where in 1795 King Kamehameha 1[11] had driven Oʻahu warriors off the cliff in one of his battles to unify the Hawaiian Islands. We took the solemn tour of the Pearl Harbor National Memorial where 1,177 servicemen are buried at sea in the bombed remains of USS Arizona. We wove baskets using traditional techniques at the Bishop Museum craft workshops while listening to Hawaiian elders chanting in the courtyard. On the island of Kauaʻi we kayaked up the Wailua River and swung from vines over pools along the way, and splurged on a helicopter tour over the wettest place in the world while Neil Diamond crooned into our headphones. The memory of my children meeting the ocean for the first timid, tentative moment, then breaking through to plunge in, is one of those priceless gifts that we parents give to ourselves without ever regretting the effort or expense.

Perhaps because I was so attuned to my children's impression of their ancestral home, I noticed how often we heard Hawaiʻi described as the melting pot. It was in everything we read, every presentation we heard. This simplistic and seemingly benign metaphor enabled them to comprehend how they fit in this place that was so unlike their ski town home in Utah. They could, and did, go deeper than most tourists who did not have a Granny who'd grown up in Hawaiʻi or a Grandpa who'd lived through the bombing of Pearl Harbor. They could feel that Hawaiʻi was a part of them, while understanding that they were not a part of Hawaiʻi. Without judgment or emotional baggage, they understood that everyone of Hawaiian ancestry, even ones like themselves who look haole and were growing up in the Rockies, was forever altered by the Asians and Pacific Islanders who migrated to Hawai'i in the 19th and early 20th centuries to work the plantations. They were able to connect the dots between those historical events and their Granny's experience as a little girl, which is as far back in their imagination as they could go. We did not talk in depth about these things because I wanted them to sponge up their days in Hawai'i as an integral aspect of their own make-up. Young as they were, they already knew, by experience and intuition, much more about being Hawaiian than I ever had.

Striving to give my kids the full, unvarnished picture, I looked for material shedding light on how the Hawaiians felt about being a melting pot. They had wound up in the stew, like it or not. That trip was before the internet and smartphones, so we'd accumulated stacks of descriptive brochures. I poured over them, seeking a narrative about the direct a-to-b-to-c sequence of travesties that had led to the melting pot while resisting the whitewashed veneer of "aloha" and Hawaiian Hospitality being fed to tourists. Whichever element one represented – the ubiquitous tourist or the overrun Hawaiian – the reality is that both sides are codependent, though one element is in the interaction by choice and the other by necessity. Far away from the marketing machines and tour operators, the melting pot seemed to be boiling over. The closer we came to what we thought was authentic Hawai'i – a papaya stand along the highway, a person selling fish out of a cooler on the North Shore, a shrimp shack operating out of a repurposed van – the more passive-aggressive and resentful the transaction seemed.

And why wouldn't there be resentment toward visitors, even to those of us who had a tenuous claim to Hawai'i? The toxic undercurrent probably goes back to the post-

World War II years, the time of my mother's youth, which were the initiatory years of promoting Hawaiian tourism. There is irony in her raising us to be like the mainland haole that so many island residents loathed. No doubt it was her alternative to obscurity in the melting pot. But for us it meant melting into the Midwest pot, the very opposite of the Hawaiian container where folks could retain their racial differences in mutual appreciation and tolerance. The Midwest pot would be where one melted *away,* lost identity, and forfeited what was unique. I sensed that my ancestors' experience was a bit of both, and my mother's aspiration was the latter.

Having never heard our ancestors' names chanted, which is the traditional Hawaiian way of remembering, I wondered whether multi-racial Hawaiian Island families abandoned the tradition when Chinese, Korean, and other names became part of the lineage. My children loved their granny and knew she was Hawaiian, but they did not ask about anyone further back than her. I would not have been able to tell them much, for which I'd have felt defensive. I can envision myself covering my ignorance by explaining that, except for my parents, our family had been shaped and fractured by men who had left their women behind. I'd say that I didn't know what happened to them, but they'd probably found themselves in the pot and melted away

ABANDONMENT IS IN OUR FAMILY GENES. WAIPUILANI is the first ancestor I know to have been abandoned. The pattern of men absenting themselves has been intergenerationally transferred and shows up in many permutations to this day. I cannot say whether it is culturally commonplace in

Hawaiian familial structures or is peculiar to our lot. We are mum on the subject, our silence conveying that our energy has gone into adapting and there is none left for explaining. My parents were practicing Catholics, so adultery and divorce was sinful. Yet they were aware of, and tolerant of, all manner of tenuous liaisons amongst their family and friends. They referred to these occasionally, obliquely and without detail, so I grew up with little specific knowledge, judgement, or curiosity about them. But later I would see examples of one person abandoning another in all the branches and twigs on the family tree. Abandonment went on before the war, and before anything I knew about my Hawaiian family. My father was abandoned as a young boy in the Midwest. His father walked out during the Great Depression and never reached out to his family again, though he lived until he was in his eighties, remarried and living in Idaho. I grew up with shadowy references to the several men who were my serial step-grandfathers, and to an auntie who was said to have five children by four men, and another who is said to have married a World War II soldier though he already had a wife "back home." I married a man who abandoned our children for alcohol and the ski resort town partying that went with it. My children, now young adults, tend toward partners who've been abandoned by their fathers, whether by death or drugs or divorce. My son was abandoned by his natural father and then by his stepfather, who was the man I married. My son's children grew up without him, their mothers acknowledging his parentage but denying him access to them. He has cousins who were separated from and never got to know their fathers.

In Hawaii, the intergenerational pattern of choosing mates who abandon, or who have themselves been abandoned, extends back to the arriving and departing ships of Captain Cook and through to World War II. Each arriving vessel triggered a round of copulation between the seamen and island women, right down to my own Hawaiian family mating with military stationed in Honolulu. The generations that followed have their own list. In few cases is the abandonment acknowledged for the ways it ravages the ones left behind, nor is it described by its name.

I want to make sense of the complex threads knotting and fraying in the tapestry of abandonment in our family. I want to weave them back into a less tortured and consequential pattern. The obvious place to start is Waipuilani's marriage to Sun Akana Wong, an act that crossed so many lines – of age, culture, race, language, spiritual practice – that it's hard to know whether her decision to marry was a simple capitulation or circumstantial, driven by survival. We don't know whether Waipuilani thought about breaking the Hawaiian bloodline. We don't even know whether, in those times, maintaining Hawaiian racial purity was valued. We tend to appreciate and sentimentalize such things after they are lost. Our default is to accept who we are and respect the decisions our ancestors made to get us here. Self-love, ego protection, and even apathy, preclude us from saying "I wish she had never done that, because then things would be different."

For those of us who are hapa, this can lead to an existential ambivalence about our racial make-up, particularly for people born in my post-World War II era. More recent generations tend to be more comfortable naming who they are, be it racial, religion, gender preference, or political leaning. A "hapa pride" movement that gained momentum in the 1990s helped young Hawaiians gain and maintain a positive self-identity as multi-racial beings. I never felt the pride that they heralded, but neither had I ever felt diminished by my race. What I felt was abandonment. I needed, and sought, welcome from Hawaiian Island *ohana,* the Hawaiian word for extended family. In all my trips to Hawai'i seeking it, I never got beyond a sense of being stuck outside on the stoop, knocking on the door. I realized that being hapa haole from the mainland was an entirely different realm than being hapa Hawaiian, hapa Asian, or other racial variants of people living in Hawai'i. I felt the privilege of the haole part of my racial mix when I was outside of Hawai'i, and the sadness of it when I was there.

Chapter 6

Stirring the Pot

For centuries before missionaries arrived in the Kingdom of Hawai'i and taught Hawaiians to read and write, the lore was passed down orally, often through chant. Today we know this practice by its pidgin moniker *talk story*. Before 1795, when King Kamehameha I united the Hawaiian Islands under one rule, lineage was traced back to the tribal leader under whom one was born. Each generation delegated one person to learn and hold the family genealogy until it could be passed on to the next. This was a sacred privilege and duty. These genealogies could go back forty generations, over a thousand years, and take over an hour to recite through chant. Talk story remains a vital form of Hawaiian storytelling, although it is now less focused on accurately preserving records. Implicit in today's more casual, organic form is the understanding that memory is selective, and truth is interpretive.

In this mindset, I appreciated the chart of our family as an amalgam of contributions culled over time from a collection of verifiable truth and squishy impressions. On the night when I first saw the chart, most people at the table could readily pick out any revision or addition made since their previous viewing. Everyone knew the exact place their name appeared as a twig on their branch. Not knowing mine, I went to the head of our limb to start at the beginning, which was where I encountered Waipuilani E. Paki.

The contemplations that followed my "meeting" Waipuilani are what is called magical thinking, in the sense of experiencing a causal link between my inner reality and the external physical world. It was important for me to wiggle my way into the embrace and heart of people I believed to be ohana. I wanted them, my extended family, to validate me as a Hawaiian and set me straight, or redirect me, or whatever else might transpire in the dialogue that I longed to have with them. I had rented a perfect place to get together with them and relax, and I invited everyone to come freely and often. My mother had many times described the "Hawaiian style" way that people dropped over, informally, without being asked or calling ahead. Gatherings in the Midwest were structured, calendared, prepared for in ways that exhausted and vexed my mother. I'd formed an idealized image of the always-open door, one of the few cultural transmissions I absorbed with deep yearning.

The first gathering at my hiatus house was, of course, by invitation. It got off to a late start, which was also "Hawaiian style." My cousins spent Sunday mornings at Mass. Perhaps that would have been a place to bond with them, but I'd not been to Mass in a very long time. I'd hoped they would arrive in time for kayaking and dips in the ocean, enjoying it so much that they'd come back often. They drifted in by mid-afternoon, in a caravan, including my Kāneʻohe cousin's blue van hauling a stainless-steel grill on wheels and a canister of propane. He set this up under a canopy of trees and his wife brought out trays of Korean *kalbi* ribs and the *teriyaki* salmon she had marinated the night before. These went on the grill before most of the others had parked under the coconut palms on the prickly yellow grass, reached into their trunks and pulled out the "sides" picked up from the Food Land market: seaweed and macaroni salads, *poke* and *mochi, taro* chips and smoked *ahi* dip. I arranged everything on the table while folks explored the premises. The young ones, my grand-nephews, took turns kayaking and paddle-boarding, sometimes taking their mothers out to the edge of the reef where the spearfishers lurked all day looking for baby octopuses. They came back, pitched the paddles on the deck, took quick douses in the outdoor shower near the rock wall, grabbed plates, and headed over to the grill. As twilight fell, our 90-year-old Auntie Jan and my daughters strummed ukuleles while the rest of us relaxed on the low seawall and the weathered teak benches scattered across the deck. My cousin never left his place at the grill, and I joined him there to watch the kababs sizzle, their fatty juices dropping onto the coals. When everyone was *pau,* the Hawaiian word for finished, and began carrying their plates to the kitchen, my eldest cousin wiped down the table, adjusted the overhead lights, and summoned everyone to gather.

This was the moment that the genealogy chart came out of its tube and was unfurled in a mood of reverent hush. Its handler was my second eldest cousin, the acknowledged keeper of the genealogy. She anchored its curling corners with flatware from the kitchen, then stood back to make room for everyone to lean in. I got a flashlight from the pantry to help illuminate the tiny, smudgy writing. Many of the names were Hawaiian, which can be twenty or more letters, broken by the okina symbol, which indicates a guttural hard stop when the word is spoken. Straining to see in the dim light, I found the names of my Grandma Rosa, my mother's sisters Winnie and Jan, and several of my first cousins. I saw the names of my mother's two brothers, Val and Larry, neither of whom I'd ever met and wasn't even sure whether they were full or half-brothers, although they had the same childhood surname, Young, as my mother. My impression of my mother having brothers was ill-formed; she had never mentioned that we had Hawaiian uncles. Yet if she had brothers, we had uncles. I grasped the reality of their existence, concretely, for the first time, after seeing them on the chart. I stepped away from the table, into the periphery of the room, near the windows. I was in the bosom of the ohana, yet I felt sad and detached. What did I know about any of them, about any of us on that chart?

I wanted more time to study the names on the limbs and branches and asked if I could get my own copy of the chart. I'd said many times that I'd come to Hawai'i to learn more about our family, which I'd missed out on by growing up so far away, so I stopped short of blathering on about that yet again. The request hung in the air awkwardly. I filled the silence by suggesting that my cousin and I meet at a print reproduction place so the document wouldn't have to leave her hands. Taking the continuing silence as a no, I aimed my flashlight beam to my mother's branch and followed her lineage back three generations to my great grandmother Waipuilani Paki, at the head of a branch about half-way down the chart and off to the side. Not an auspicious position, overall, but the spark of connection I'd felt had rattled me.

"So, tell me. Waipuilani. What was she like?" I asked.

With everyone chiming in with the little bit they knew, I conjured an image of a wiry, dark-skinned woman who was illiterate yet smart, who worked hard and drank a lot. In her later years, after she'd had five kids, she took up with the Hawaiian boy she'd loved in her youth. "See, that's him, Makatu," a cousin said, leaning in and jabbing his finger on the map. Makatu's name was penciled in next to Waipuilani, floating on its own and unattached to anyone, unconstrained by the lines of a box, an acknowledged but tentative part of her backstory, though census records show that they eventually married. As quickly as the sparse details about her were offered, they dribbled off. This was old territory for them, and they didn't have time to dawdle in Waipuilani. They had to get home, work the next day. They gathered their platters and packed up the leftovers, gave me the two kisses, one on both cheeks, customary for an auntie, and trundled across the grass to their cars. I remained where I was, waving from the veranda, listening to the muffled sounds of departure play against the waves pounding the sea wall. I was grateful that I had a whole year on Oʻahu to unravel Waipuilani's mysteries. She would help me understand why my Hawaiian roots felt like such a stranglehold.

 The last car honked as it edged onto the dark, two-lane Kam Highway, heading to the H-3 onramp and the cruise into Honolulu. I walked out to secure the high wooden gates, part of the evening routine, stepping over smashed breadfruit laying across the drive. Learning about my great-grandmother left me feeling agitated, yet I also felt deflated. I'd imagined diving into and swimming excitedly through a large pool of family lore, the floodgates open and tales spilling freely into the channels of my imagination. The reticence to provide me a copy of the chart presaged a year of cold shoulder not only from my family, but from many Hawaiian vendors, business owners, and neighbors I tried to get to know in my small town on windward Oʻahu. I often felt the sting of their assessment of me: an entitled ho, without invitation or welcome, presumed to ₁ne between local and outsider. I didn't get points ₁g Hawaiian blood or for returning to live among ₁ felt their antipathy and perceived that I needed their permission to call myself – even to think of myself – as a Hawaiian. The rebuffs were subtle but ever present: a sneer in the local grocery mart, a haughtiness while buying fish from roadside vendors, a ridicule if asking directions to something like the nearest carwash, for which the answer was a finger pointing to a hose. I often felt inept and shut out, just as my mother had predicted.

THE HAWAIIAN LANGUAGE TRANSLATION FOR MY GREAT-grandmother's name, when separated into its parts, means fresh water (*wai*), forcing (*pui*) and heaven (*lani*). Put together, per the Andrews and Parker Hawaiian Dictionary, Waipuilani means "a waterspout; water drawn up into the clouds or poured down from the clouds." The significance of this name would be mine to plumb, I was certain, because "when a Hawaiian name is bestowed, a connection is made, a story told, history preserved, someone honored, a hope expressed."[12] I would honor the portents the name suggested and call her Waipuilani, though the family called her Tutu Wahine, the traditional Hawaiian name for grandmother. She was described as "pure Hawaiian," an English translation of the Hawaiian Kānaka Maoli, who were the indigenous or aboriginal people of the Hawaiian Islands and their descendants. I like to imagine that Waipuilani could trace her ancestry straight back to the Pacific navigators who landed at South Point on the Big Island of Hawai'i about 400-800 AD. There was strength and majesty in that, and I respected that she came from people who stayed amongst themselves, closed off from the many ethnic groups that poured into Maui in the 19th century. I favored the image of her childhood as isolationist and protected, and pictured her as nurtured on simplicity and the strength of traditions. I wondered whether my strong draw to mountain living originated in my ancestral home on Western Maui's Mauna Kahālāwai (which means "house of water"), an example of how deeply, even fancifully, I was reaching to relate with her.

After she left her home in the Honokowai region she met and married Sun Akana Wong and was eclipsed by marriage, motherhood, and an international enclave of foreigners. After she gave birth to our family's first generation of hapa children, we and our offspring would forever after be part of the mixture that made us different from her. No matter what transpired in her tumultuous world, she would never relinquish her place as Kānaka Maoli.

When my mother was a child her mother Rosalie sent her five kids to spend summers with their Tutu Wahine on the outskirts of Lahaina. The oldest of them might remember their grandfather Sun Akana Wong during those visits, and perhaps they also encountered Waipuilani's longtime love Makatu. He'd returned after Sun Akana Wong had left Waipuilani, or perhaps Sun Akana Wong left because Makatu had returned. I can be certain of none of this, except that he and Waipuilani married after her children were grown. My mother never spoke of her grandfather and stepgrandfather, nor of anything else about her girlhood visits with her Tutu. Had I known about them I'd have plied her to describe how her Tutu Wahine looked, how she behaved, what she believed, what it was like to be with her, and I'd have begged for *anything* about Sun Akana Wong. These details bring, and keep, an origin story alive. They could also shed light on my mother's characteristics and behaviors, which could in turn help me understand my own. In the absence of any endearing memories, I conclude that my mother was not fond of those times or of those people. I was disappointed that my mother couldn't fill the voids I'd felt when I was yearning for grandmothers, imagining them tucking me into feather beds made of down from the geese out in the yard. Tutu Wahine was not that grandmother, I knew, and I liked having the clean slate to formulate a visage of her. But I wanted that image to be realistic.

Luckily, by the time I became aware of Waipuilani there was one person still living who'd spent time with her – my 90-year-old Auntie Jan, who was my mother's youngest sister. I was on borrowed time with her, given her age and myriad health conditions, so rather than waiting for a family party and its random reminiscences, I drew up a list of questions, called to tell her I was coming, and drove across Oʻahu to the Kapolei area where she lived. She settled me on her lanai, enclosed by thick plants entwined in lattice walls. I launched into my list: What was Waipuilani like? What was my mother like when she was with Waipuilani, and what was Waipuilani like with my mother? That my female ancestors were strong, plucky women I was certain. But were they tender, cherished, beloved? Had there been a rift between Tutu Wahine and my mother to explain why she never reminisced about her?

Looking out to the hazy topaz-blue ocean near Barbers Point, as if childhood images were there to be culled and plucked, Auntie Jan sighed as though wondering where to begin. I could see that she remembered patchily, though she enjoyed reminiscing about her childhood. She had probably curated her memories and cultivated the images she wanted to outlive her, as is human nature. She suggested that we move inside and make a glass of tea. Her living room was crowded with knickknacks and tchotchke neatly laid out on tabletops, shelves, and behind glass in dark mahogany cabinets. I picked up a 1950s hula dancer doll with brown skin and told her that Grandma Rosa brought me one just like it when she visited us in Wisconsin. As if the doll had triggered a memory, Auntie Jan began describing Tutu Wahine. She was a sinewy woman with a face like Pele, the ferocious goddess of fire often depicted in Hawaiian art and mythology. Her skin was the color of the dark, smooth inside of a coconut; her dense and wiry black hair cascaded over her shoulders like a spill of lava. She had a broad Polynesian nose and wide-spaced eyes separated by a flat nose bridge. Under the spell of Auntie Jan's poetic description, I mentally melded Tutu Wahine and Pele for a few moments, and I liked that the imagined infusion of one into the other gave Tutu Wahine the righteous power I wanted to believe she had. I asked how she'd lived and spent her time, nudging Auntie Jan's recollections while taking care to allow her to remain deeply entranced in her private memories.

Maui, circa 1935: My great-grandmother Waipuilani. This is the only photo I've been able to locate, which makes it very precious.

"Tutu Wahine had nothing," she said. "Her shack kept out the rain, that's all. She was always busy in her yard, going here and there, like a bird pecking at this and at that." Her mellifluous voice tightened as she recalled that Tutu Wahine was unpredictable and sometimes volatile, probably from drinking the *ōkolehao*, a fermented liquor made from the root of the ubiquitous ti plant. She brewed okolehau in a bathtub in her backyard and drank it with anyone who came over. They all got drunk and swore at the *keiki*, the Hawaiian word for children. "Your mother hated it there," Auntie Jan said. "She hid in the dark until they all fell asleep or went home. She swore she would never drink, and she never did, her whole life."

Indeed, my mother had always set a high bar for respectable behavior. She never drank nor used a swear word stronger than "damned." Perhaps her Tutu Wahine's environment had become so abhorrent to her that she shut her out. Forgive and forget was simply not part of my mother's nature, as I knew from the way she never forgave our grandmother Elizabeth.

Everything Auntie Jan said led me to ask more questions: why had Sun Akana Wong lived apart from Tutu Wahine, and did he take in the keiki when they ran to his house to escape Tutu Wahine? But anything Auntie Jan knew about him was hearsay, so I moved the focus back to Waipuilani. What was her life like as a child, and how could a child born on a mountain without electricity, communications, or paved roads, wind up in the raucous shipping port of Lahaina with the pākē? Her fluid talk story cadence rolled like waves arriving on shore, each delivering a delicate splash before slipping away to regenerate itself into another swell. Auntie Jan explained that, in the late 1870s and 1880s, the time of Waipuilani's childhood, Hawai'i's transition from sustainable farming to the sprawling commercial plantations had long been underway. The impact of that transformation even reached areas like the Kahālāwai where Waipuilani was a child living in the old ways. Not far away, Lahaina was a bustling center of over twelve thousand people. Seamen spilled off ships bringing commerce and migrant labor from faraway ports, places Waipuilani would have had no knowledge of, culturally or geographically. While I had imbued Waipuilani's pairing with Sun Akana Wong with significance and portents, to Auntie Jan it was common and inevitable, an organic response to rhizomatic changes irrevocably spreading across the Hawaiian Islands.

Among the tens of thousands of Asian and Pacific Island laborers recruited to work the plantations came the harness maker and cobbler from South China, Sun Akana Wong. They met, they married, my aunt said. It was rather matter of fact.

SPECULATING, IMAGINING, AND RESEARCHING Waipuilani's youth and life as the wife of a foreign-born Chinese man gave depth and structure to my year on Oʻahu. Though it is the most populous of the Hawaiian Islands and my rented house was easily accessible to Honolulu, there was an undeniable sense of isolation and monotony to island living. Baked into my plan for encamping to the less developed windward shore was the promise that family and friends would visit from the mainland. I extended aloha on the night of their arrival with fish tacos, or seafood purchased from roadside vendors, that I grilled on a hibachi and served with Vietnamese sauces I'd learned to make in cooking school in Hanoi. I joined their hikes and beach basking and relaxed with them afterward in the embrace of appreciative company and the spell of the tropics. As the months wore on, I felt more and more inclined to stay in my enclave with its meaty library of Hawaiian books: volumes of history, geography, art, myths and lore, and memoirs about growing up in Hawaiʻi, along with oversized books of Hawaiian art, interior design, and landscaping, and children's books illustrating charming, simplified versions of the Hawaiian legends, flora, and birds.

By Thanksgiving, half-way through my year on Oʻahu, I was frustrated. My imagination of Waipuilani's life and times was stuck in one-dimensionality, like she was a paper doll. I wanted to flesh her out. Nor was I getting closer to my Hawaiian relatives or feeling any love from my daily ventures to the nearby towns along Oʻahu's coast. I could get to Punaluʻu, a town of about one thousand people, by walking twenty minutes north along the Kam highway. Punaluʻu's three-acre beach was a bit shabby and usually deserted. The sand comes right to the pavement across from Ching's Store, a low-slung, bright red building with hand-printed tag board signs in the windows claiming to have something for everyone, like tropical floats, fishing and diving supplies, and ethnic snacks called *Ono Pupu*. Every now and then I'd walk to Ching's for an odd sundry – a flashlight battery or a tube of sunscreen. Entering the dark, cluttered cave of Ching's was to immerse in a jumble of random artifacts collected for tourists who buzzed by on the highway, the spearfishermen who probed the reefs, the upland gardeners who tilled the ravines and sent their produce to Honolulu's Chinatown stalls. A few beat up trucks were usually parked outside, their engines idling while their drivers dashed inside Ching's for soft drinks, beer, or locally made butter mochi. Or they might be grabbing a bite from the bright yellow mobile Shrimp Shack painted with instructions to "Suck, Peel, Dip, Eat." Ching's had everything one could want, except the ambiance of welcome to a woman wanting to feel like a local auntie. That I was tourist and haole in my core, if not in my facial features, was revealed as soon as I unknowingly used a haole word, like scallion rather than spring onion, when looking for something. I often felt the sting of correction, though I never doubted that it was clear what I wanted.

Pushing past the prickliness, I continued exploring the islands, attuned to the magical *frisson* that both dazzled and humbled me. Several times a week I drove further north to the beaches at Maleakahana and MokuʻAuia, places where local people came together with each other and the ocean. I'd begin with a few miles jogging the pedestrian track that ran alongside the highway. Then I'd cross over to the beach and plunge into the foam of waves washing onshore. I was a bobber, not a swimmer, so I'd get shoulder-deep and tread water and let the people playing in the surf infect me with their joy. Their ease in the swells was something I wanted but, having grown up in the landlocked Midwest, knew I'd never have. But I could absorb their jubilance and I did, shamelessly, carrying it with me to where I'd left a lounge chair in the frail shade of wispy ironwood trees. I'd towel off and settle for a session of people watching. Their laughing buoyancy, their intrepid paddling to meet the next thunderous wave, calling out to each other, mapping their motions to the water's rhythms, showed me the meaning of birthright.

On Christmas Day of that year, I went to a picnic at the ancestral retreat of my longtime Hawaiian friends, a place preserved in land trust on Oʻahu's leeward side. The grounds are pristine, with pathways for wandering, but I was drawn to linger in the *mana,* the energy of power and strength, emanating from the lagoon. Three sacred sea turtles and a rare Hawaiian monk seal had hoisted their bulk out of the water and were resting on the warm, sedating sand. In the contemplative spell of these creatures, my friend Jon asked if I was loving the islands. He is a person who compels truth, so I admitted that I was finding Hawaiʻi a hard place to love. Of course, I hastened to add, the weather, the beauty – how could one not love it? Yet, as I made my way through what should have been one idyllic day after another, I often felt like I had a stone in my shoe. "It is good that you struggle," he said. "It keeps your feeling for the islands alive. People come here and too easily love it, and then they fall asleep."

Chapter 7

See you, See you

As the months on Oʻahu ground forward, I was sinking into deep introversion and considered skipping the family Thanksgiving gathering at my cousins' house in Kāneʻohe. But I was on the hunt for a taproot that burrowed across time and geography, and this gathering might be fertile ground. Perhaps, over the course of talk story and feasting, I'd unearth something new.

My cousin and his family lived three blocks off the central artery running through downtown Kāneʻohe. Their carport was the family party place for Easter, Christmas, birthdays, and other fêtes. It also sheltered the cars and accumulated detritus of three grown sons and the teen daughter who still lived at home. Pushed against a rusted washer and dryer, stacked boxes of uneven sizes sagged and caved in on themselves after years in the island humidity. Against them leaned a collapsible stroller missing a wheel, tubular aluminum lawn chairs with shredded plastic webbing, a pile of cloudy snorkel masks spotted with mold. At the edge, fronting the curb, space was cleared for these chaotic yet predictable holiday gatherings. The ones who came early helped set out folding tables and scattered a dozen white molded plastic chairs in conversational groupings. A path toward the kitchen door was kept clear for the folks bringing something to add to the buffet.

Easing into the neighborhood after driving down from Punaluʻu, I crept along the clogged streets looking for an opening where I could park. Similar gatherings were going on up and down the *cul de sac*, some with big-screen TVs hauled outside to broadcast a football game. It is the Hawaiian way to celebrate holidays, just as it is on the mainland and other places in the world – lots of food, people, rounds of chit chat repeating the same news, and a televised game going on in the background. Aunties sat at the tables bouncing little ones on their laps, fanning straw hats to fend off flies, fingering the lei* they'd been gifted that lay hot and cloying on their necks. Behind me a line of cars inched along in the same futile quest to find parking, and people already gathered in the yards and carports craned to see if the new arrivals were for their party or another one down the street. Everyone seemed to know everyone else and waved, or else everyone waved at everyone whether they knew them or not. I found myself waving back, like a favorite auntie, knowing they were thinking "Who's that?"

My cousin, the host, was broad and big hearted, like a Buddha, with a butch haircut and wide smile. He greeted me by my childhood name. "Eh, Moana, what you want? Beer? Pop?" He plunged his hand into an oversized cooler's sloshing, icy water while calling over his shoulder to whoever was in earshot "Eh, this is Cousin Moana from mainland." I waved, took a can of iced tea, and headed into the kitchen to find my female cousins, intending to pump them for bits of family history. They were fussing over the buffet while the hostess moved inside and out, taking trays of pupu to

---

* In the Hawaiian language, which does not have the letter s, the proper way to say the plural of lei is, simply, "lei." Although the modern spoken usage often Anglicizes the word to leis, the classic Hawaiian form will be used throughout this narrative.

the guests outside. I gave up the conversation thread as everyone broke in to exclaim over a new dish that had just been brought in or a new person who'd just come. The feast materializing minute by minute was an eclectic blend of Hawaiian and haole favorites – salmon that is tenderized by gentle massage that Hawaiians call *lomi lomi*, and steamed *laulau* packets of ti leaves wrapped around rich butterfish – with standard mainland fare: Stove Top brand cornbread stuffing beside a Safeway-roasted turkey resting on its shiny black plastic platter. There were doughy, candy-pink guava rolls wrapped in cellophane from Longs Drug Store, and molded trays of sushi roll nested on bits of green plastic clipped to resemble grass. Getting my two elder cousins, who would best know the family lore, to focus was a challenge, but I pressed on since these gatherings were the only opportunities to converse with them.

"Tell me about Tutu Wahine, Grandma Rosa's mother," I said, hoping to trigger a memory by mentioning Grandma Rosa. I envied that they'd been close to her in their childhood. "I saw her on the chart that time you all came to Punaluʻu," I prodded. "Remember?"

"Tutu Wahine was pure Hawaiian. Black skin. Didn't speak English," my cousin said with the matter-of-fact authority of her position as eldest. She emptied a bag of potato chips into a yellow plastic bowl. "Born in a cave in the ahupuaʻa above Lahaina." She glanced up, silently questioning: did I know what an ahupuaʻa was?

Yes, I could have rattled off, it is a wedge of land where indigenous Hawaiians worked together in harmonious co-dependency, under the authority of local chieftains, back in the days when the kings ruled, and so on. This could have been an entire conversational offshoot, as appreciation for the ahupuaʻa was robust that year, a topic in school classes and TV spots as an ongoing part of the reclamation of respect for traditional Hawaiian culture. But I had to stay with Waipuilani. I piled napkins and sorted the jumble of mismatched chopsticks at the end of the table, wondering how to move the conversation to new material.

"And she drank a lot," my cousin continued. She had a fistful of serving spoons and spatulas, of aluminum and carved Monkey Pod wood and stained whitish plastic with burned black ridges. She drove them into the bowls of stew and macaroni salad and purple Okinawan mashed potatoes. "Tutu Wahine made her own *ōkolehao* in a bathtub behind her shack."

"She was mean when she drank," the second-elder cousin chimed in. She sat at the edge of the buffet table, weighted into her chair by a sleeping grandchild, her first. She wore a short denim skirt, plaid blouse with buttons that strained against her breasts, and opaque dark glasses that she always wore, due to an unexplained eye condition, that made it harder to get to know her. "But she was strict. The keiki were afraid of her," she added. I nodded as each tidbit was added to the store of detail I'd already cached, clucking as if this was a new insight, though I'd heard most of it before. I wanted to think more deeply into her later, to add into the picture what she'd been through that might have driven her to drink, to feel into her struggle and her heart. And, in that moment, I just wanted to keep the conversation flowing.

"But she loved children," she went on, "even if she was strict. But your mother did not like Tutu Wahine."

"My mother spent time with her?" I asked, not giving away that Auntie Jan had already told me about the summers with Tutu Wahine. This cousin was Auntie Jan's daughter, so we were probably drawing from the same well. "She never told us anything about her."

"Every summer," she said. "Grandma Rosa sent all the keiki to Lahaina to stay with Tutu Wahine."

"That's when they lived on Moloka'i? She sent all of them? Winnie, Jan, their brothers, my mother?"

"For the whole summer. All of us," Auntie Jan said, entering the room with a pie plate of coconut *haupia* pudding for the dessert table. I paused to wonder if she was truly ninety years old. She was tall and fashionable, with emerald green toenails and metallic threads running along the border of her sweater, and she carried herself upright like a model. Unlike my mother, who'd let her hair go white, Auntie Jan colored hers the original black of her youth. Her D&G sunglasses were tilted on her slightly off-center nose that looked like it had been broken and never set right. She pushed the frames into her hair and her bright eyes darted about.

"Tutu Wahine only spoke Hawaiian," Auntie Jan continued. This was significant to her. She had re-learned the Hawaiian language of her youth during the 1980s when Hawaiian activists made an all-out effort to pull it back from extinction. The language had re-acculturated Auntie Jan into things Hawaiian and in turn she'd infused her reborn cultural fervor into the generations following her. It was hard to remember that she had left Hawai'i for decades after marrying a military man during World War II. She'd raised four daughters while circulating among military bases from Alaska to Alabama, before marrying her third husband and settling back on O'ahu, where she had a son. "Your mother told her, 'Speak English.' Your mother was stubborn, just like Tutu Wahine," Auntie Jan continued, speaking to me. "Grandma Rosa would tell your mother

'You must not be sassy to your Tutu,' but your mother was independent. Stubborn and independent."

"Those are the exact words my mother used to describe me. Stubborn and independent," I said.

"Well, your mother was those things, too. She made up her mind. She did not like Tutu Wahine. Drinking all night, ōkolehao. All the keiki shooed away. Your mother wanted something else. To curl her hair and tie it in pigtails with ribbons."

I tried to imagine my mother's coarse black hair in pigtails. As a child I'd tried to help bend it around spongy pink curlers, but it would not take shape or curl. "How was Tutu Wahine with my mother?" I asked, sensing a chance to step into new ground in my knowledge of Waipuilani. "She must have been ok, if Grandma Rosa sent her there every summer."

"'Sassy, *nuha* little pākē, little hapa,' Tutu Wahine called your mother," Auntie Jan said in a string of English, pidgin, and Hawaiian words that translated to "sassy, moody little Chinese half-breed."

I bristled on behalf of the little girl who was my mother. I held back my retort, "How could Tutu Wahine make a racial remark about my mother, when she was the one who broke the racial purity?" It was not the time to introduce the loaded subject of racial dilution on my elderly auntie, so I reframed the question. "How could Grandma Rosa send my mother to Tutu Wahine if she was so harsh?" This question embodied a judgment, since I would never have sent my own children to stay with anyone who caused them to feel bad about themselves.

"Grandma Rosa told your mother that her complaints were all nonsense. She said, 'We are all what we are, and we are all beautiful' and that was that." Auntie Jan took a sip from her frosty can of Coke, pulled from the cooler on the way in. "Tutu Wahine was strict. That was the old way. But she loved us children. She loved us."

There. I'd gleaned a new detail about Waipuilani: she loved the children. I held onto that as the first wave of hungry ohana pulled open the kitchen door and shuffled in from the carport, as if a bell had clanged that dinner was ready. Half a dozen young boys led the charge after kicking their misshapen Locals brand flip-flops onto the pile near the door stoop. They bent to Auntie Jan's cheek and kissed her, then turned to me. "Aloha Auntie, Aloha Auntie," they recited without any idea who I was or how I fit in. But they kissed me on both cheeks anyway, in the Hawaiian gesture of respect, before snatching a grilled rib or swiping a chip through one of the pastel-colored dips.

While we'd been chatting in the kitchen the carport had filled up with half- and great- and grand- cousins and nephews and uncles, along with "holiday orphans" from their places of work, school, church. There was the beefy eldest son, one of four, who worked at the naval shipyard. He balanced his baby girl and a plate of food while keeping up a conversation with his brother, a sports commentator on Honolulu TV. My grandniece, a hula champion who would be called upon later to dance, rescued her infant son from her mother's lap and joined the others inching along the table with a running commentary about the food, who'd brought it, and where they'd gotten it. Spatulas dipped into the gallon-sized tub of sour, grayish-mauve *poi*, the Hawaiian staple made from pounded taro root that they could now buy at Costco. There was talk of how the octopus had been pulled out of the reef just that morning, and banter about the game on TV in the next room, or the job just left, or the opportunity just ahead.

I stood apart, watching them disperse with their laden plates. They'd been courteous and had dutifully made small talk with me, an alien auntie from the mainland. I would ask more questions about Waipuilani later, after the last of the decimated cakes from Zippy's and remaining dollops of haupia pudding had been cleared away. Then the family record keeper would coax the tattered family chart out of its cardboard tube, just as she had at my gathering months earlier. She'd point out any changes she'd made in the past months, including her first grandson's name at the bottom. I'd look for Waipuilani E. Paki mid-way up the tree to affirm that she existed. I needed to see her name again, to concretize her after so much research about her yielded nothing. I sometimes wondered, in my solitary musings, if I'd made her up to stand in for all the lost and obscure ancestors that we never knew.

I'd spent the previous few weeks trying to ascertain whether Waipuilani was directly descended from the first Polynesians believed to have landed over 2,000 years ago at Ka Lae, the southernmost point on the Big Island. From Ka Lae there is uninterrupted ocean all the way to Antarctica. I was surprised at how much I wanted our origins to go back to that place of power, which I'd visited on earlier trips, and to have been a part of such a voyage of discovery. I longed to hear our genealogy heralded by the call of a conch shell and chanted out loud, each name pronounced with pride and reverence, going all the way back to our beginnings on the Big Island. I wanted to think that our intrepid genes, which I've seen evolve in my siblings in various forms, are descended from that adventurous impetus. Waipuilani and her ohana had withstood the forces of racial dilution for almost a century after the haole arrived in Maui – a long time, considering that she lived within fifteen miles of Lahaina. The taproot I sought bore deeply into a place in which haole opportunists had no interest until they discovered something there that they needed, and could be easily extracted from the people who'd lived there for hundreds of years.

Suddenly, in that room where the remnants of turkey and leftover salads and sides were being sealed into containers while children clamored for seconds of dessert, I envisioned Waipuilani among us. She was the forerunner to the five generations of descendants together that day, all of us hapa. Each had uniquely shaped eyes in shades ranging from hazel to black, each pair a bit different than those of the cousin or grandchild or sister beside them, as a distant gene asserted, or another receded. Each of us was thinking, in our own way and for our own reasons, about all that had to come together for us to wind up here, the whole of our lineage summarized in an inked name on a metaphorical image. I'd been nosy to the point of haole aggression, but I'd gleaned little new information about Waipuilani or about the generations preceding her. What I'd gained was a new question. Would she have left her ancestral Maui mountain home of her own volition?

The answer to this question was swift and clear. I knew in my bones that she been forced to leave. Her most significant action, then, was not that she took an older Chinese man as her partner. It was that she had gotten up and left her mountain.

DESPITE MY PERSONAL HISTORY OF FLUID LEAVE-TAKING and my ease with relocation, I found it painful to imagine

Waipuilani's departure from her family's ancient place on Mauna Kahālāwai. Did she feel helpless or hopeful, frightened, or adventurous? Did she leave with her childhood love, who we know as Makatu? How and why did they separate? Learning about Makatu was like coming upon a book that had fallen open to a chapter I'd skipped over, a chapter that I wanted to go back and read but had pages ripped out. This could have been a rich talk story, but only the barest bones of it have been passed down.

After the Thanksgiving gathering, I realized there was little more that the ohana could, or was willing to, tell me about Waipuilani. I turned to Google. Clicking from one link to the next, each time wondering how deep I was willing to go, I'd fall into the proverbial rabbit hole, then crawl out and look out over the glittering ocean. Then lather, rinse, repeat. This was my process for weeks, with my extensive house library of Hawaiian books for when my screen-weary eyes wanted to rest on paper. Eventually I concluded that the dissolution of our family's cultural hegemony, and the reasons why Waipuilani left her childhood home on the mountain, began with the dispersal of the royalty-owned lands in the Great Māhele[13] act of 1848. I was so stunned by the unintended consequences of this land division enactment from King Kamehameha III that I blew open my inquiry to far beyond our genealogy. I began freely wending through Hawaiian history, American history, and the history of the Chinese in America. I put myself through a riveting cram course beyond what I ever thought I'd want to know, or would need to understand – the impact of the Civil War on the evolution of the Hawaiian sugar industry, the lure of the California Gold Rush on Hawai'i's Chinese contract laborers, the effect of United States anti-miscegenation laws on Hawaiian statehood. All of these factors played into how and why my family has evolved as it has.

FROM MY YEAR ON WINDWARD OʻAHU I WENT ON TO live a few years on the stormy Washington coast. Five years had flown by since the Recession of 2007 had derailed my career, and the nature of technology had evolved past the enterprise software systems that had been my domain. The world of personal, agile apps that could be downloaded to smartphones and used to run our lives was a sea change. I'd become a dinosaur, and retrofitting myself back into pre-recession life in Portland was unrealistic. Reluctantly, and with little fanfare, I retired from gainful employment. I bought a small granny cottage beside a bucolic lake near the Wisconsin town where I'd grown up. After more than fifty years in the western states, my choice to go back to the Midwest baffled many. Most incredulous were the questions from people who'd long lived there and had long fantasized about moving somewhere else the minute they could. "You want to live *here*? Have you heard about our winters?" was a common reaction. But I yearned for a simple, uncomplicated landing place where I could continue wondering and writing.

One spring day, for a change of scene, I went to spend an afternoon in the huge State Historical Society reading room at the University of Wisconsin. This had been my favorite place to study as an undergrad, and it was still just as I remembered it: the long wooden tables, perfectly aligned emerald-green glass lamps extending row upon row across the expansive room. The space exuded the diligence of more than a century of scholars who'd hunkered down in the ambiance of focus and respectful silence. Every now and then there was the echoey noise of a chair scraping against the floor or a far-off, faceless person coughing. I settled into the room's cushioning quiet to contemplate the possible reasons Waipuilani had left her mountain. I wanted to be specific and had narrowed my focus to necessity. She would not have elected to go for a "change of scene." She wouldn't have had the luxury of capriciousness. She would only have made the move if required in order to survive.

For guidance in survival, indigenous Hawaiians looked to the elements, so I decided to begin there. Fire, perhaps, but there were no active volcanoes on Maui in Waipuilani's time, and the area was too damp for forest fires. Air, signifying extreme temperature changes that destroyed plant cycles and animal habitat? No, their climate was reliably temperate, thanks to the trade winds crossing the Pacific ocean that surrounds Maui for thousands of miles in every direction. Earth? The Hawaiians revered the land and were beholden to it, as embodied in the Hawaiian term *aloha'āina,* which means "love of the land." They revere the interconnection between land and water, individuals, and communities. Hawaiians had always been bound together by the land, rather than driven apart by it. So then, water?

Sitting in that somber room so far from the *kai,* the Hawaiian word for sea water, I was struck with what felt like a tsunami of truth. Of course. It had to be about water. Wai, the Hawaiian word for water, was in the very place names of Waipuilani's youth: Honokowai, Kahālāwai. It was in her very name. Stunned, I sat back. I felt rattled, but also settled, like I'd finally gotten somewhere. I fought down the urge to take a break, to sit somewhere with a cup of tea and let myself imagine how it would be to run out of water if you were an indigenous Hawaiian living off the land. But I stayed where I was and plowed on, researching the sources and flow of water in Western Maui during Waipuilani's time.

To an isolated people who'd lived sustainably for hundreds of years without any exchange with other nations, fresh water was everything. It made possible all life forms, flora, and fauna. It determined where they settled and how long they remained. When it was plentiful and clean, it held people to a place; when it was contaminated or ceased to flow, or overflowed in flood, it forced people to leave. Disruption to the water supply in the Kahalewai region was, even without disturbance to the other elemental factors, enough to drive Waipuilani and her ohana to leave their mountain.

Pressing on, I went to the U.S. Geological Survey website and downloaded their topological maps of Western Maui. Even magnified on my laptop, they were difficult to read. I brightened my screen to increase contrast but still had to squint at the faint lines squiggling across the elevations. After a while, I lifted my eyes for relief, gazing out the tall, leaded windows to the tender spring buds swelling, ready to burst from their nodes. When I looked back at the map I noticed fine, straight horizontal lines superimposed over the wavy topological grade lines. Such straight lines seemed inorganic and out of place with the natural irregularities of the topology. I magnified the view so I could read the fine print beside those lines and made out the word "ditch" in the Honokowai area where Waipuilani had grown up.

Honokowai, which means house of water, was an area where three to four hundred inches of rain fell every year. The rain poured off the slopes of the mountains and ravines, tumbled into gullies and re-gathered in rivulets that morphed into streams and collected into the ponds that irrigated the trees and plants that fed the kamaʻāina. They used what they needed and let the rest flow to the lowlands for others' use in fishponds before moving on to the sea.

Along with the lines signifying ditches were dotted lines representing tunnels. Working together, they mapped the rerouting of water away from the people of the land and toward the Pioneer Mill[14] that had been built in Lahaina in 1860. I found other maps of the Pioneer Mill Company irrigation system and traced the Honokohau and Honokowai streams to where they met at what was called the Honokowai Siphon. There they came together and flowed into ditches that dumped into two reservoirs, the Wahikuli and the Crater, north of Lahaina. The water waited there until there it was needed by the mill, which used what is colorfully named Groundwater Pump M to move tens of thousands of gallons a day into their mill ponds. The water enabled the Pioneer Mill to elevate Maui's sugar production to half the output of all Hawaiian Island plantations combined. Putting this together in that cavernous room on my old Wisconsin campus, so far from the days and the places where the taking of the water had transpired, felt like a kick in my gut.

I flashed back to a book I'd found in the library of the Oʻahu house I'd rented. It was an unassuming, thin volume that was bound with paper that felt like a brown grocery bag and titled Sugar *Water: Hawaiʻi's Plantation Ditches*.[15] I'd flipped through the book's maps and diagrams, more curious why anyone would want to write or read about ditches than I was interested in its content. A Ph.D. dissertation, I'd concluded, putting the book back on the shelf. Later, I saw the book on a friend's shelf in her Honolulu apartment and asked about it. She explained that to understand modern Hawaiian history one had to understand the ditches. Once again, I'd put the book back on the shelf and had forgotten about it. But there, so many thousands of miles away, staring at the topo maps on my computer screen, I remembered that unassuming book. Could the trajectory of our ancestral destiny have been catalyzed by a ditch dug during the years of Waipuilani's childhood?

The first Pioneer Mill well was dug in 1883, when Waipuilani was about ten years old. That first spade hitting the land of the Western Maui made the Kānaka Maoli living there what we would now call "collateral damage," a brutally callous term for people hurt as an incidental result of another destructive activity. The ditch and well digging signaled that the colonialist needs of the plantations superseded those of Hawaiian people whose survival depended on that water. The ditches facilitated the capitalist takeover of Hawai'i's useable land and enabled the islands' evolution to a plantation culture, which necessitated the influx of migrant laborers. Their presence diluted the cultural homogeneity of the Kingdom of Hawai'i and turned it into the so-called melting pot.

HAVING THREADED THAT NEEDLE, I IMPLODED INTO what felt like revealed truth. My compulsion to learn Waipuilani's story had led to the most mundane determinant of Waipuilani's fate. It all came down to ditches. This led me to reframe my image of Waipuilani's mountain home from a place of security and sustainability to one of instability. Untold numbers of Hawaiians were forced to relocate because their water had been rerouted away from them.

They became refugees in their own land. Waipuilani would have entered Lahaina as a kānaka, the derogatory racial tag (as distinguished from the respectful name Kānaka Maoli that is now commonly used for native Hawaiians) used by plantation bosses to distinguish island-born laborers from contract laborers from different countries. That kānaka were considered lazy may have spared Waipuilani a harsh life in the cane fields. But neither was she a good candidate for domestic service in haole homes. This work would have been cleaner and less taxing than field work, but she was unworldly and spoke little English. Her ohana was also struggling at the margins and could offer no support or helpful connections. She'd trudged from the mountain into Lahaina at the outer bounds of hope.

Having stitched these momentous discoveries together, I pulled back from the tedium of research and let my imagination roam. I wanted to envision Waipuilani in the stages before, during, and after her transition to the multi-national, commercial world of Lahaina. For this I would need a change of scene and a cup of tea. I gathered my notebooks and shut my laptop, hearing the clap of its lid meeting its base push through the dense quiet of the massive room. I left the Historical Society and headed across the street to the cavernous, vaulted Rathskeller at the lakeside Memorial Student Union. Sitting at one of its scuffed wooden tables, surrounded by students on break from their own pursuits, many a third of my age, I let myself visualize Waipuilani and what the world was like for her.

TALK STORY: *Waipuilani in the mid-1870s*

> They were sun-browned and barefoot, working side by side on their family land. Waipuilani had always

looked to Makatu, who was a year older, to show her where to go, what to see, how to do what she had to do. They were like brother and sister, or cousins – all the lines blurred and unimportant in the ways that ohana took everyone in its fold. He was strong like a spine that kept her upright and moving, and he was pliable like the ligature that kept her agile. Their life was simple and pleasing. They helped keep their patch of mountain tidy so food would grow. They played when they could, when there was a break in planting and harvesting, digging, and tending. They dove off the high rock over the pond or dove under water and held their breath as long as possible to see who came up first. In the background the elders talked about the water. Every year less flowed down the slopes to their taro and fishponds. But Waipuilani and Makatu never paid attention to these things.

When Makatu was twelve he was sent to work higher up the mountain. Soon after he was strong and tough enough to be paid for his labor, so he signed on to the digging crews working on the tunnels and ditches that would funnel mountain streams into Lahaina's reservoirs. He never connected this work to the slowing flow of water to his ohana's taro patches, where Waipuilani still toiled under the torrid sun.

After work Makatu met Waipuilani in one of the secret places they'd played in since childhood. On the hottest days they met in the gulch, where the sun stayed outside the high banks of packed dirt. They crouched in the ferns clustered near the trickle of an old stream, digging runnels in the mud with their toes. When Makatu worked late, Waipuilani scampered up the stony path to meet him with food from the evening meal: a bit of fish and a dab of poi wrapped in a ti leaf, with a scoop of mashed yam. They sat on their haunches on a ledge and watched the sun drop toward the horizon. As the ocean surface softened to shades of rust and gunmetal and lavender, Makatu teased Waipuilani, saying he knew about something that she didn't know. Then he'd lead her to the reddest torch ginger flower with the tallest spear she'd ever seen. Sometimes they scavenged plumeria flowers to make lei for visitors from other parts of the Kahālāwai. They threaded the blooms into garlands to pile on the aunties' shoulders. On mornings when a pig was put into a pit for slow roasting, Makatu woke Waipuilani early to chant the blessing of gratitude and aloha. In every way they lived the old ways: they wove long slender spears of the *hala* tree to make hats and mats; they helped beat the mulberry bark into pliable tapa cloth while chanting and telling talk story about the ancestors.

Waipuilani was so used to Makatu that she hardly noticed his thin arms filling out with biceps and his chest forming contours. "You'll be bigger than the uncles," she said, rubbing her fingers against the stubble sprouting from his chin. They spoke to each other in Hawaiian, though Makatu told her they should be practicing English, even a little, because things were changing, and they would need to know it. He'd heard the men talk as they toiled with their shovels. As sweat ran down their backs, they said not to complain: this work was hard but better than working on the plantation. Makatu wondered how plantation work could be worse than what they were doing: moving clods of dirt, shovel by shovel, so water would go somewhere away from where they needed it. He did not think this work was what in Hawaiian they called *pono*, meaning righteous. The chiefs of the old days and the elders of his ohana had always made sure that everything they did was balanced for the common good, so being pono was not something he had to think about. Now, with the chiefs and many of the elders gone, he had to think on his own. He had a sacred duty to be pono, but he knew that soon he'd have to go below, following the others to work in the cane fields, so how could he help anything be pono? The plantations weren't pono. He'd heard the rumors that the plantation managers, the *luna,* forced Hawaiians to keep working even when the sun was hottest. They made kānaka work straight through, ten hours at a time, no matter the heat.

Sitting with Waipuilani, eating the food she'd brought him and watching the twilight colors, he pointed to a soft patch of pink spreading over the surface of the sea. He'd been telling her about the ditches. "But it is *kapu* to move the water," Waipuilani said, using the Hawaiian word for something that is forbidden because it will displease the gods. "We must take gifts to the *heiau* altar. We can take the mango just picked, and dried fish Auntie took off the line today."

"You go. Not to old heiau up top. Torn up already. Rocks used in ditch. No respect." Makatu hung his head as Waipuilani sprung up with alarm.

"You must come too. Now. Or gods will punish us."

"No, just punish me," Makatu brooded. "The ʻāina does not like what I do." He spread out his palms and studied his calluses. The blister between his thumb and forefinger was infected. Waipuilani ran her own work-worn fingers across the leathery surface of Makatu's palms, avoiding the raw places where the blistered skin threatened to crack and bleed. "The ground, is hard, does not want to be cut apart," he said, withdrawing his hand. "Does not want plantations, to make sugar to send all over. Does not want to give plantation this water from Kahālāwai. We say 'yes, we do it' and dig to make it go over there, to sugar, to mill, then far away on ships. Nothing here for us, and water is gone."

Waipuilani looked out over the flat land a thousand feet below and then out to sea, as if ships of their sugar were steaming away in that very moment. She was frightened and could feel that he was too. Every year since their parents had gone off the mountain others had followed. They always went at the end of harvesting, after seeing the fruit dry and puckered, the seeds withered, the promise of new life shriveled in their hands. Everyone promised to come back to visit and to help the others move when their time came. But no one had come back for Waipuilani, which was just as well, because she did not want to go.

Makatu had been working on the ditches for close to a year when the luna sent him to another dig site to the east. He would have to live there in a large tent with other workers and get meals from the camp kitchen. They would take money from his pay for his mat in the tent and the food they made for him. This would be the end of his life as he knew it, but he promised Waipuilani that this would not lead to a life in the cane fields. The aunties threw themselves into making a farewell feast. They sent down to the ponds for mullet to roast over hot rocks, and they brought okolehau liquor from the stills.

Sticky stalks of sugar cane were cut to chew during talk story and gossip about plantation life down on the flat lands. He'd heard these things before: men living in cabins, many to a room, sleeping stacked over each other. They would receive money for every day they worked, but a portion would be taken away before it was even given to them, to pay for their bed, shelter, and food. There was no barter, rest breaks, or time to visit with ohana. They worked for many days in a row, morning to dark. Food arrived in a box, made far away by strangers, with bits from the many countries that made up the work groups. They could buy what they needed at the plantation store, and what they spent was taken from what they earned. It was the new way: paying to live in a place, getting wages, using money for things they'd always traded for or had made themselves. Isolated in the plantation towns, they often lost track of where the people they loved had moved or when they could see each other again.

    A chorus of the Hawaiian lament *auwē* sounded through the dark. Makatu looked around for Waipuilani, who was helping the aunties. He saw her moving from the fire to the tables, bringing fresh fish from the coals. He hoped she was not hearing this talk, but she didn't seem to be listening. He turned back to hear what people were saying about living in Lahaina. Everyone knew someone who'd said something, and they pooled all the stories into one long talk story. One had a friend who worked supplying the ships that came to port to restock provisions and visit the prostitutes. He took note whenever one of their own men joined the crew and went to sea. Another who lived in the plantation camps kept track of any kānaka coming into their fold and sent news of their whereabouts back up the mountain, though it often took weeks or months to find a messenger to take it. Makatu wanted to hear how kānaka like him made their way in Lahaina. If it was so terrible, and it was not safe to speak up, how had some protests resulted in permission to grow food on tiny patches of ground outside their shacks? There were tales of people trading with each other, even though they didn't speak each other's languages, and there was talk about the strange greens and beans and types of sprouts they were learning to grow and eat. Another said there was no poi in the box lunches because all hands were needed for the cane, with no time to pound taro. They ate rice and pickled cabbage flavored with vinegar and hot peppers, and the dark brown, salty liquid the Asians liked, made from fermented soybeans. And never mind that the kānaka wanted to work with other kānaka, to help hold onto each other and their traditions. They knew that was exactly what the lunas did not want.

    At dawn the next morning Makatu whistled the signal for Waipuilani to meet him behind the giant agave's twisted, striped spears. She scrambled awake, knowing something was amiss. He shushed her questions and pointed to the flame-orange sun rising over the canopy of kiawe trees. As it lifted into the new day, he told her that he'd thought all night about the talk around the fire. He said that what they said was their future was not his future, and he would not be cutting any more waterways for the mill. He would go to Lahaina to find something more pono. He promised to come back to get her, then he rose and moved toward the Honokowai Beach trailhead, the first leg of the path to Lahaina.

With that, their childhood together was pau. She put her head on her knees and keened "auwē, auwē." By noon, after telling her tearful story to the aunties, she was getting used to being teased about Makatu: hadn't all the kāne gone, all vowing to come back? They had stayed behind, waiting for them, but no one had come back to stay and resume the old ways. Soon the last of them left on the ancestral lands would go too. It was their time.

TALK STORY: *Waipuilani in the 1880s*

Waipuilani pulled the brim of her lauhala hat low on her forehead. It was early but the morning sun was already blinding. She wiggled her toes in the cool, ankle-deep mud and felt her feet press against the sturdy taro corms supporting stems as thick as her ankles and leaves wider than her torso. Like every other day, she'd waded into the taro patch as the sun rose and would be there until it crossed overhead and fell toward the blue Pacific. She liked the sameness of these days, especially when things around her were changing. Everyone talked about it and no one knew what to do about it.

The aunties worked a few feet away, grunting as they stooped to tug and thin the plants. They plunged their wrinkled fingers in and out of the submerged jungle that crowded the pond bottom. They worked without talking until someone called for rest, complaining about "aches and pains." Auntie Kailani, who looked older than her 34 years, half of them spent in the taro ponds, was the first to hoist herself upright. She was already stiff, and it was not yet mid-morning. Around her the others unfurled their backs and stretched, humming agreement that it was time to loosen their joints. Waipuilani tossed aside the weed she'd just yanked out. The nimbler women were already clambering up the bank, resuming the threads of chatter, remembering each other's news, woes, and the worries that tore at their souls.

Waipuilani looked up. Her eyes were clear and bright, unclouded by the cataracts the older women acquired after years of working in the sun. She took her time joining the women. It was hard to listen to their complaints. She was only a few years into her teens, the youngest among them. Three young girls her age worked in the potato patch further up the path, but they too had complaints. As water was diverted, the soil was dryer and harder. They all longed for the days when it tumbled clear and cold into ponds they could jump into when they were hot. Waipuilani remembered watching the torrents, trying to imagine what it was like where the stream originated, which was also where she and her family had come from, in times before any of their memories. They'd followed the water down, following the contour of the valley, working through the deep gully, to end at this clearing where they'd settled and dug the taro ponds. She'd joined her mother and aunties in the taro ponds since she was seven and the water reached above her knees. She liked wading in and brushing through the wide leaves, licking the rainwater droplets that collected in their span.

Now, as the aunties trudged toward the pits to relieve themselves, Waipuilani fell behind. She fussed with her limp muslin skirt, annoyed at the muddy hemline that would never come clean. With little else to do now that Makatu was gone, she ended many of her days at the washing pond rinsing her garments, beating them on the lava rock with the sharp ridges that broke down the fibers and released reddish particles of dirt hugged by the threads. She hung them on the twine the aunties had woven of vines and coconut fibers and stretched from the post of one shed to the next. Watching her skirt dripping, knowing it would get dirty all over again the next day, and the day after, she would indulge in thinking about Makatu.

She wasn't sure how long he'd been gone, maybe over two years. She thought about Makatu all day long, through the heat and tedium of taro tending. She thought of him through the nights as she lay on her pad on the open platform, listening to the rustling palms, the pests scuttling about, and the creaks and murmurs from the huts around her. She could not form a picture of him in any other place than there, because she herself had never been to another place. The aunties said that maybe he went on a boat, or worked in the mill, or on the docks, or went to those places the whalers went for ale and food and women, but Waipuilani couldn't imagine any of that. She only knew him for the ways he was with her.

Joining the women behind the pandanus thicket, lining up for a turn in the pit, she tuned into their teasing in pidgin Hawaiian. "Eh, Waipuilani Wahine," Auntie Laka said, tossing her words over her shoulder, heaving her square, thick torso a step closer to relief, "You so quiet. You want to say: Where Makatu now? Same, every day. Ya?"

Waipuilani knew that every one of them pined for someone who had left. They all doubted that their beloveds would ever come back, though they'd promised that they would.

"Makatu?" Auntie Makanui scoffed. "He gone. Long gone."

"He is not long gone," Waipuilani said to Kamea, who was closer to her age than the elders. Kamea's belly was beginning to swell with the child conceived when her kāne returned to tell her he would go whaling and be gone for many months, but would return with money to make a new beginning for them in Lahaina. Knowing he was at sea, Kamea looked up many times every day as if she might catch a glimpse of him in that ocean that spread out toward the horizon.

"He say he come back. So, he come back," Kamea said, matter-of-factly. Then she lifted her skirts and stepped toward the pit, leaving Waipuilani unsure if Kamea meant that her Kimo would be back, or that Waipuilani's Makatu would. She decided that she meant both.

"He better hurry," Auntie Laka said, switching places with Kamea. She swished a palm frond to chase off the flies that clustered near the hole despite the scoops of dry dirt the women tossed over their leavings. "Maybe he come back and we be gone."

Waipuilani thought back to when her father had lived with the family. One day the last chief of their ahupua'a had called together the families who'd stayed to farm after the land divide of the Great Māhele, which was twenty years before she was born. Waipuilani was just six years old, but she remembered everything about the day of that meeting. Her father went but her mother stayed in the taro pond and the children ran about nearby, where the aunties kept an eye on them. Later that night, her mother hushed and settled everyone so her father could tell them what the chief had said.

Waipuilani had seen the chief only a few times. He was an old man. His skin was the color of *koa* tree bark. His feet were crusted with rubbery callouses, thickest at the heels that slipped over the edges of his woven grass sandals. He spoke in Hawaiian language interspersed with pidgin because, like the rest of them, he was trying to learn English. Her father, a great storyteller, told them how the chief sat beside his wife on the tapa mat. She wore a blue *pareo* twisted under her armpits, leaving her shoulders bare in the old way, and creamy yellow plumeria flower blossoms in her hair. Everyone had waited, looking down, while the elders took a place on the ground around them and settled. Then the chief raised his arm and pointed to the sea. "I will follow the others who have gone down," he said. "My time here is finished."

Everyone knew this day was coming. The chief's sons had moved off the land soon after he'd sold their water to the haole and watched the ditches being dug to carry it away. The chief told the people that he would give each family a plot of land, and they would then own it. They could stay to grow something to eat or sell, or they could sell the land to agents who would give them money for it. He couldn't say how much, and no one knew how much to ask for, or even what to do with the money. Those were things they would have to learn about. It was their decision, he said, but the water was going away, and life would be hard without it.

Waipuilani remembered her mother's tears as her father described the sad silence among them. They were being pulled along by change and were helpless to change the course of anything. Their chief had always kept them safe, and now he was abandoning them. They didn't know what to do.

Many, like Waipuilani and Makatu's families, chose to stay on the mountain and live the way they always had, for as long as they could. Others sold their land to whoever offered something for it, wrapped their belongings in a *pareo,* stuffed their cash into its folds, and trudged off. "Chief says 'go,'" they muttered. "He gives this land, then says 'go' because this land of no use."

Each time a group left, the aunties keened auwē and made offerings at the heiau. Without their chief, the gods were the only place to turn for help and guidance. One went with her fist raised in the air, clamped around the deed to her small, rocky parcel. "We burn this at heiau, we give the gods back what they give the chief, and the chief give away." But she was restrained. "No, no. Listen to our chief." They did not understand money or land exchange, but the gift from their chief was not to be thrown aside. "He knows. We listen. Keep the paper, take to Lahaina, give to get money. Do this. Our chief orders this."

As months and then years wore on, the resolve of the ones left on the mountain dissolved with the decreasing waterflow. They no longer believed the gods were with them. After a year of indecision, Waipuilani's father said he would leave the Kahālāwai to find work in Lahaina. "Water stopping, taro dying. I must go." His departure began with a trip to the heiau to give thanks for the life of plentiful food and safety the mountain had given them, and to petition for abundance in the unknown life that lay ahead. Waipuilani helped her mother and the kupunas gather taro and collect wild apples to lay on the elevated platform of the heiau. They formed a semi-circle around the altar as one of the aged uncles led the chant: *"Ke mauna o ka hāliu kua, I kū au aloha me ka mahaloaloha, aloha e* - now may I turn my back and travel. I bid you farewell and gratitude, with love."

Waipuilani's family lingered. They did not want their father to leave, even though they knew that he must. She scouted for a feather or a fallen blossom to add to their offering. But the clearing yielded little besides dried red *'ohelo* berries, already picked over by the birds. Finding nothing more to scavenge, they repeated the chant before returning for a last meal with ohana. In the cool night air, with the light of the moon, her father lifted his pack of a few tools and garments, the *aumakua* talisman of the owl that he always carried, and started down the path to Honokowai Point. Waipuilani remembered the quiet of that last meal with father. She remembered how everyone went to their mats earlier than usual that night, after he'd left. She watched the moon cross the sky, then laid still on her mat and listened to the swaying trees and scavenging rodents.

The morning after her father left, Waipuilani glumly padded to the taro patch. It was all she knew to do, the only place to go. The aunties argued their usual issue: whether to plant more for later times, because they'd need taro no matter what, or to harvest what they could because soon they'd all be gone and have no need for it. One of them insisted on keeping their pond tidy so whoever came after to buy their land would behold a patch that had been well tended to the end, while another scoffed that it would not matter, that the days of taro were over. Waipuilani worked with this talk going in one ear and out another. She was used the ways they tried to find courage to move forward and do what had to be done. She had been through it with her father. She would go through it again a few months later when her mother and sisters left her behind and followed him to their new life in Lahaina.

Chapter 8

Lots of Jobs, Women, Beautiful Beaches

With so little known about Waipuilani, it was tempting to let her lay in the obscurity where she'd rested since her death in 1941. But a few years earlier I'd abandoned a draft book about another fascinating woman because of a similar lack of records and data. I refused to do it again. The Hawaiian tradition of talk story offered a culture-based tool that helped me imagine her young years and the forces pressing on her. Using the memoir technique of "imagined truth" helped me to weave the bits I knew into realistic situations. Expanding those situations into imagined but believable – and maybe even probable – outcomes helped me to see how what had happened to them could have had an intergenerational influence on me. For example, I saw that the women of my family, going back to Waipuilani and extending through to my mother and her sisters, all chose and settled with men who'd come from other places, rather than marry men from their own culture and places of geographical origin. There were tens of thousands of such men to choose from among those who'd arrived in Hawai'i in the 19th and 20th centuries. Most of them, like Waipuilani herself, hand landed in Lahaina seeking work and relative stability from destitute situations in their homeland. In

Waipuilani's time, they came to work the sugar plantations. A generation later, in Grandma Rosa's time, they came to work the ranches and small businesses. In my mother's years they came to build tourism, and over 25,000 U.S. military came as part of defense operations in the Pacific. Had I been brought up in Hawai'i, I would probably have selected someone in a role catering to the droves of tourists or to the U.S. military that continue to dominate the island economy. In other words, I'd have fallen onto the very path that my mother was adamant that I should avoid. She'd known, and I can now see, that Hawai'i is a class system where people tend to stay in their caste.

The evolution of partnering from pre-contact Hawai'i through my mother's time was fraught with challenges. Chief among them were the many alien influences that came into play as people of different cultures arrived and infused their own practices into the ways Hawaiians had always mated. The initial sexual role of island women was formed among the original South Pacific voyageurs who muscled their way across the open Pacific in canoes in which priority for space went to the male paddlers. The few women and pigs they could squeeze into the boat shared the remaining space with food and seeds. Arriving on land, presumably at Ka Lae at the south point of the island of Hawai'i, the women's approach to copulation and reproduction was practical. They accommodated as many partners as they could and procreated as much as they were able. Those women knew their role in everyone's survival. Perhaps the concept of ohana that welcomed all keiki, cherishing even those of uncertain paternity, evolved from the early practice of fluid partnering that was required to continuously populate the islands.

Captain Cook's journals describe arriving and anchoring near the shores of what he'd named Sandwich Islands, after his English sponsor the 4th Earl of Sandwich. Despite his claim to have discovered the islands, the hundreds of men and women who paddled and swam out to meet Cook and his crew obviated the fact that the islands had long since been discovered. Cook was aware that many of his crew carried venereal diseases and he wrote in his journal of his efforts to keep island women off the boats. But sailors who'd been long at sea without sexual contact ignored his orders and helped the Hawaiian women and girls climb on board. When they left, hours or days later, many had contracted syphilis and other diseases for which they had no immunity. Likely, many also left impregnated with the first hapa haole babies.

Evolving from these circumstances, Hawaiian women felt no shame about sexuality and expressed it freely as a natural part of everyday life. Plural relationships were normal, and homosexual and other "queer" liaisons were accepted. They did not feel antipathy toward mating with foreign laborers as a moral issue, although the Christian missionaries wasted no time in trying to change the norm to monogamy. Contrary to moral strictures and laws against interracial partnering on the United States mainland, Hawai'i was not yet a state and was not bound by them. Hawaiian religious and business leaders tolerated people of all races laying together and producing multi-racial children with a "don't ask/don't tell" approach that was practical and even economically advantageous. The plantations needed foreign workers willing to move to the Hawaiian Islands and stay for a long time. People with brown skin seemed to be more amenable to accepting harsh work conditions for little pay.

Hawai'i's need for cheap plantation labor saw no sign of abating, so if interracial marriage and procreation induced workers to stay in Hawai'i longer, or permanently, it was an acceptable means to an end.

Representing Hawai'i's melting pot as a socially beneficial outcome of color-blind tolerance whitewashed the colonialization of the Hawaiian Islands and the eradication of Hawaiian culture. During the years from the War of 1812 to the U.S. acquisition of Alaska in 1867, the same years that the Kānaka Maoli were adjusting to the influx of foreign laborers and the transition of their sustainable economy to plantation agri-business, Americans were using the doctrine of Manifest Destiny to morally rationalize taking Native American land as part of the process of "civilizing" them. The historian John Seward wrote that "the belief in American Exceptionalism...undoubtedly influenced and justified the American takeover of the Sovereign Nation of Hawai'i."[16] Attuned to their image, and with astute public relations acumen, Hawaiians were portrayed one-dimensionally as a magnanimous, simple-minded population. Marketing slogans like the catchy, alliterative "Hawaiian Hospitality" and "The Spirit of Aloha" reduced the perception of islanders to one of easy-come, easy-go largesse that amounted to "Take our land. Come over and enjoy it. We'll get out of the way because what's ours is yours." Hawaiians would even put on grass skirt and greet you with a flower lei. It was in their job description.

TALK STORY: *Waipuilani — mid-1880s*

> One morning Waipuilani arrived at the taro pond and saw the aunties sitting on the bank. They

pointed to where the water had once dripped downhill and had, that morning, dried up fifty feet short of the ponds. Waipuilani had known this day would come. She went back to roll up her mat, help collect their pots and pareos, and bank the cooking coals. By the time all the aunties arrived, she was tidying things up so any who might later need shelter would find it hospitable. The aunties finished removing all traces of their lives there. This did not take long. By noon they left, stopping to make an offering of a taro leaf at the heiau. They did not expect to return.

Trudging along behind the lumbering aunties, Waipuilani imagined that Makatu would meet her when they got to Lahaina. She couldn't work out how he'd know when or where she'd be coming. She left that to the gods. Glumly they followed the dried-out stream through the ravine and abandoned clearings that had once been alive with people.

After a few hours, wilted from hours of sun on her face and the hot dirt on her bare feet, Waipuilani felt the first waft of the heaving ocean. She'd been at the beach only once when she was a tiny girl, but her nose recognized the smell and her skin felt the wisp of moving air. Heading toward it, remembering playing in the waves with her father, she picked up her pace. A mile later, arriving at the shoreline, she dropped her bundles, ran across the sand and into the lively, lapping water. The surging and retreat of aerated foam rejuvenated her. The sunlight sparkling on the surface, flicking back flashes of color, dazzled her. The water was not bluish green, nor still and flat and solid, like it had seemed all those years she'd looked down upon it. She lingered at its edge while the aunties scattered through the encampment trading taro and breadfruit for guava fruit and dried octopus.

Finally, as the sky turned pink and lavender, Waipuilani shook water from her ears, twisted her hair to wring out the saltwater, and followed the scent of fish roasting over lava rocks laid in the cooking fire. She hadn't had fresh fish since the farewell dinner for Makatu. She was hungry, but she paused with the others to thank the sea and earth for their bounty, and then waited for the elders to have the first portions. Many of the aunties stayed late around the fire to talk story, but Waipuilani was tired. She rolled out her tapa mat at the base of a coconut palm, after looking up to make sure no nuts could fall on her as the tree swayed in the night. She laid down and the fronds' rhythmic swishing lulled her to a sound sleep.

The poi pounders woke Waipuilani early the next morning. The thud, thud, thud of the broad-bottomed, cone-shaped stone working the taro was familiar, though everything else she awoke to was alien. The taro being worked was from their patch on the mountain, brought in the Hawaiian tradition of arriving with gifts of food. She felt sand in her ears and a few bites from insects she didn't want to think about. She heard boys shouting and saw them knee deep in water, fishing for the morning meal. Untangling the pareo wrapped around her legs, she raced to the beach. She wanted to learn how to fling the net into the arc that unfurled and flattened across the surface, before disappearing below. She wanted to help drag it in, heavy and alive with silvery, flipping creatures struggling against captivity. But the boys waved her away. "This our job. You pound poi, peel mango."

Disappointed, Waipuilani shuffled across the sand to the aunties squatting around a mound of papayas. She flicked away bees crawling over the sugary drips and the pile of peels. One of the aunties gave her a basket of mangoes to wash in a nearby freshwater stream where others were rinsing sand from watercress and guava. "This water coming from home?" she asked. "Home," she repeated, pointing up toward the mountain. "Not so much water left, to get down this far," an elder tutu said. "This water here, from springs. Comes from under, not down from up there. Good to have this cress, yeah?" she said, pulling the crisp green leaves with their delicate white roots grasping the soil around the rocks. "To eat with fish." The morning catch of *opah*, called moonfish, was already sizzling on the fire.

Waipuilani took her washed mangoes back to be peeled and piled over washed ti leaves, alongside the pared lilikoi, mango, and breadfruit. She settled on a pandanus mat and sucked juices from the peels set aside to throw to the chickens that roamed about, pecking and clucking. After the monotonous mountain fare of poi, potatoes, and mealy wild apples, her taste senses were coming alive. The fish was steaming on the open coals, wrapped in ti leaf. She'd never had fish two days in a row. She was in a trance of flavors and fragrances broken by an auntie giving her the mangoes she'd washed. "You peel this, then mash," she said, pointing to coconut shell bowls. "Put here, cover with ti leaf to keep bugs off."

Waipuilani was happy to help, and she was happy to be there rather than toiling at home in the taro pond. The air was brighter at the ocean, it seemed. Colorful pareos, pinned to twine lines stretched between the palms, fluttered like flags in the breezes from the sea. Children kept the fire burning with foraged palm fronds and bits of dried driftwood. Men coming back from setting the nets scooped up toddling keiki on the beach and brought them back for feeding. Setting aside her hope to see Makatu in Lahaina, Waipuilani imagined herself making her new life there on the beach. But Auntie Kahana, handing her a wood plate piled with fish and fruit, dashed her thoughts. "You eat plenty," she said. "Long walk all day later. You eat this fish, poi, coconut." Waipuilani pushed away the mangoes she'd been peeling, giving them to another auntie to finish, and accepted the food. "We go soon. Eat now. Little bit later we eat more, but not so much as here." Others were already rolling their mats and gathering their damp clothes from the line. The ones still at the fire talked of a new food, rice, that the Oriental traders had brought to the area. "Too much cooking," one of them pronounced. "Need pans, long time on fire. Has no taste. You will try in Lahaina."

It was no use for Waipuilani to ask to stay a few days at the beach. She wanted them to leave her behind for awhile, just as her mother and father had left her behind on the mountain. But like the others, she had family in Lahaina and was eager to get to them, so she had to be ready when they said it was time to go. Her belongings smelled of the sea and smoke from the campfires, and she put them to her face and inhaled, memorizing the smell of the place. A short while later, after tidying where they'd slept and stowing packets of coconut meat, toasted seaweed, and dried fish to eat along the way, they began walking the distance they only knew as *aloaloa,* which means "far." They felt enlivened, full of chatter and eagerness, but soon the aunties' thick, swollen feet slowed to a shuffle and Waipuilani, despite the strength of her youth, slackened her pace to match theirs.

Approaching Lahaina, five hours after they'd started out from the beach, Waipuilani noticed people staring at them. Strange men ran their eyes up and down her body. She felt the new sensations of defiance and shame. She noticed that she was darker than most of the onlookers, and that her long, loose hair was thicker, with more coarse curls. Her clothes were simpler than the white high-neck, buttoned, tucked, belted, full-skirted garments of many who stopped to stare at them. She dropped her eyes and focused on the dusty brown ankles of the aunties walking ahead in line. Their shredded *pareo* skirts were dusty and dragged against their dark calves. The old men walked crookedly, leaning on walking sticks they'd cut and smoothed from ironwood branches growing on the mountain. Their hairless legs were bowed and looked too spindly to carry them much further.

Moving from the outskirts into the town of Lahaina, they passed shanty houses built on stilts, food stalls, and shops hawking everything from soap to tools. They pushed past crowds gathered around the crude, rickety structures, falling quieter and drawing closer together. Waipuilani was overcome by the unfamiliar sounds and smells, but most of all by the many, many people. They looked strange with eyes, noses, hair and skin of different shapes and colors. She didn't understand their languages and didn't realize that there were so many languages. She saw no welcome in their eyes. She looked about for Makatu – surely, by some act of the gods, she would find him among the curious crowds or hear him, above the hubbub, calling her name.

The voice that Waipuilani heard calling her was her mother's, a voice she hadn't heard in four years. She embraced Waipuilani, exclaiming over and over that her little one had grown so tall but was too thin, too thin. Did the aunties not feed her? She fussed and wept, then turned Waipuilani over to her brothers and sisters – five of them, aged six through eleven, and one infant half-sister who had come along in the years since they'd been separated. Her siblings had dim memories of Waipuilani from their days in the Kahālāwai. Now Waipuilani was more a grown-up than a girl. They looked at her shyly and took her hand to lead her to their home.

Waipuilani was confused and disoriented. She didn't understand how these young ones could navigate through so many muddy, crooked streets. They led her away from the town hub and toward the edge of town leading upland, opposite the harbor and wharves. They stepped around the open sewage, rotting fruit peels, stinking fish heads, and animal excrement without seeming to notice it, a skill Waipuilani noted and resolved to learn. They turned into a crowded alley and walked past a dozen colorless, windowless shacks. Stopping in front of one built of rough-hewn planks on a raised platform, Waipuilani's mother said, "We here." She glanced at Waipuilani and saw her disappointment but offered no explanation as to how and why they'd come to be in that place.

Waipuilani bit back the questions she'd stored for so long about why they had not sent for her to join them. She looked around and was grateful that they hadn't, though she'd felt abandoned. She'd looked forward to a feast where long-gone cousins and neighbors from the ahupuaʻa would bring something to share and they would sing songs and talk story in their own language. But a quick glance across the room dashed her hopes. She tried to hide her disgust at the reek of baby urine and rotten fruit breaking down as flies crawled over their brown-yellow rinds. She hadn't seen nearby streams for washing and collecting water to drink, nor gardens to pluck from when it came time to cook.

Waipuilani's mother spoke in pidgin, matter-of-factly laying out how life there worked. "You hungry, yeah? Not so good food here. Rats eat, or go bad, cut too long from vine. No place to keep. We buy in town, go see what selling, get what can. Others pick and bring to market. Pay money to get. No trade. Can get food at plantation store but take too much from *makua kāne* pay."

Waipuilani was relieved to hear her mother use makua kāne, the Hawaiian word for father. But the rest of what she said was a lot to grasp, and for her mother to explain, in their faltering English. "This from Auntie Kala," her mother said, holding out a sour-smelling pineapple that was beginning to ferment. Waipuilani accepted the gift and tried to remember who Auntie Kala was. But she was distracted by a few giggling children peeking in the open door, curious to see the new girl from the mountain. Their thin muslin shifts were colorless and unwashed, and their feet were caked with mud, but their eyes were bright. One of them, taller than the others and closer to Waipuilani's age, reached out to offer her a greasy packet of dried fish. Waipuilani took it, murmuring *mahalo*, the Hawaiian word for thank you, wondering if that word was still used and understood. More than the fish, she was grateful that the tradition of food sharing had carried on in this strange world. She wanted to sit on the stoop and talk to these girls, to ask the many questions arising that she was pushing back until later. Even without a feast of welcome, she longed to talk story, even with these girls. She suddenly understood that everyone – not just the elders, but the young ones too – had stories, not only of the ancestors, but also of people from their own short and present lives of people who were already slipping out of reach and memory. Even she, Waipuilani, was creating a story that could be told if anyone wanted to hear it.

Chapter 9

Adrift in the Āina

In the late 1880s, by the time Waipuilani had settled into Lahaina, the level of shipping traffic had declined from its heyday from 1830 through 1860, when it was called the "Whaling Capital of the World." In 1846, Lahaina's busiest season on record, 736 whaling ships came through on their way to Alaska, where the actual whaling occurred. Ships would stay in the Lahaina port for as long as three years, primarily for provisioning, repairs, and to wait out weather patterns, before embarking on the return voyage around the treacherous Cape Horn back to New England. While in port those ships spewed rowdy seamen onshore in search of good times and available women.

By 1871, the year Waipuilani was born, kerosene was replacing whale oil as the nation's primary illumination fuel, so the whaling era in Lahaina had peaked, though it'd left its impact on Lahaina as a center for shipping and commerce. She'd have arrived in Lahaina long after the first Chinese arrived in Hawai'i in 1852, and after the Japanese arrivals in 1868 and the Portuguese in 1878. By the time Waipuilani settled in Lahaina those ethnic groups had tightened into enclaves. The Japanese had their own schools where children wore uniforms and adhered to the tenets of their culture. The Chinese had cohesive labor unions. The haole missionaries were educating everyone they could at every level, from rural one-room schools to the Lahainaluna school, a Protestant missionary boarding school for royal Hawaiian children. Established in 1831, Lahainaluna was the first high school west of the American Rocky Mountains.

It is hard to imagine the tumult of Lahaina's transitional social upheaval during the 19th century and the challenges of one like Waipuilani to find her way within it. She did not know English, have any but the most primitive schooling, nor any sort of counsel or guide for reference. The ways that foreign-born men and women interacted was ruled by customs and formalities that were alien to her, while the ones of her own people were disparaged by the missionaries and enacted away by their royalty. But she had this one thing in common with everyone who'd arrived a stranger and had chosen to stay: she had to dig in, learn the ropes, and reach deep for grit and resilience. That meant learning the ways people were the same, as much as the ways in which they differed. Their food may have seemed strange, but she had to try it. They wore strange clothes, but she had to be open-minded.

Even with the breakdown of mores and courting practices, many of the islands' men had no access to women who might be suitable wives. They often saved for years to accumulate enough money to use the "picture bride" system to bring over a bride from their home country. In arrangements brokered by liaises, they selected a bride from photos and used their savings to pay for the bride's one-way ship passage, a cash offering to her family, and a commission to the matchmaker. Books have been written about brides who arrived looking hardly recognizable from their dolled-up photos, and about grooms whose circumstances were far from what had been represented. But the savings had been sent, the oceanic voyage had been made without recourse for return, and they had no choice but to find their way as a couple. The co-existence at which they arrived, as rosily embodied in the metaphor of the melting pot, was too often a hard-fought necessity.

AGAINST THIS BACKDROP, AND WITHIN THIS CHAOS, Waipuilani met the Chinese man who would become my great grandfather. I've pictured how this came about. Perhaps she was out and about in Lahaina's food markets, procuring food at her mother's behest, trying to learn the alien ways of the vendor transactions. Young and unworldly, she probably attracted stares imbued with the accumulated loneliness of men awaiting their arranged bride, or of men who still hoped to find one. Perhaps they knew that Hawaiian women of earlier times were more accessible than the women of races ruled by the Christian codes of celibacy until marriage.[17] Perhaps they figured Waipuilani was an easy get. She was at the lowest rung of Hawaiian society and had few ways to elevate her stature.

Waipuilani was probably streetwise enough to know that marrying a kānaka, even though she was one, would make things harder in this new world. She faced a complex and counter-intuitive dilemma: it was in her best interests to avoid the attraction of like to like. She would be better off striving to enhance her standing by marrying someone unlike her. This contrivance around marriage, with the cultural mores of so many nations to be considered, was a dramatic departure from the traditional way of Hawaiian mating – freely, because they chose to, without legal and ethnic considerations. That was the model that Waipuilani had grown up with, but she had learned enough about her new world to know that the old ways no longer served.

TALK STORY: *Waipuilani in 1890*

> Settled in Lahaina by the late 1880s and wanting to make the best of it, Waipuilani saw that she could be most useful by helping her mother find food. She was adding another mouth to feed, and there were barely enough coins for everyone already there before she arrived.
>
> Going to the market and paying for food was entirely new to Waipuilani. They'd always fed themselves by growing, foraging, or trading. Now she had to learn about money – one *dala* was equal to 100 *keneta*, just like American money. She had to learn to stretch her keneta and to recognize a bargain, which meant knowing the worth of something. She learned that getting to the stalls early in the morning meant getting best quality, and that going back at the end of the day meant she could pick over what would otherwise be tossed to the feral chickens. She did not mind going twice, and she never missed a day. She liked getting away from the dank and smelly shack her family crowded into.
>
> Waipuilani also used her time in the market to look for Makatu. She hoped to see him by chance in the food or fish stalls, where he'd probably be working were he still in Lahaina. But she had no sighting of him, nor had any of the aunties heard what had happened to him. After she'd learned how life turned out for island-born men like Makatu, Waipuilani began to hope he'd gotten far away. If he hadn't, he was probably working in the plan-

tation fields under the whip of a luna. She would rather think that he'd gone to sea than to imagine that, even if it meant being apart. Everyone told her "You find another kāne while you young, not wait for Makatu. You find one here, that you like."

But how to find another one was something Waipuilani would have to figure out on her own. The old bonds and connections were breaking down. Most of the advice she got was cautionary. She should avoid plantation workers because they were low caste, and she should avoid the seamen because they came back diseased after boozing in faraway ports with prostitutes. Waipuilani saw many wahine like herself setting out with men who were alien to their customs but hoping for the best. She was getting close to twenty years old, past when wahine married, but she was holding out. She wanted the obvious and most basic thing: a simple man who understood their tradition of fishing, tending the taro, repairing the nets, someone she could trust and who would treat her well.

Waipuilani was lonely and overwhelmed by everything she had to figure out. She had enough on her mind without thinking about finding someone to love. Every day in the market put her brain in a spin. She tried to make sense of the languages of the Japanese fish mongers, the Chinese vegetable stalls, the Portuguese bakers, the island traders with their mounds of stacked coconuts and lauhala hats and mats. Usually, she just pointed at what she wanted and guessed whether the cost was good value. She tolerated the pushy Chinese women who elbowed her aside, spat on the slimy ground, and shook their fists to drive down the price of a fish head or press for an extra inch on a cut of meat, because from them she was learning the names of foods she'd never seen before, how quickly they spoiled, portion sizes, and what went with what. All this was knowledge they'd not known on the Kahālāwai where fresh food was abundant, though always the same. Old women sometimes pushed her aside to snatch the larger winter melon or eggplant. She looked for bits of extra fat, when she could get them, for her father who was growing thin on the plate lunches the plantation delivered to workers in the fields.

Waipuilani loved the hubbub and strange ways of town living. She left early every morning for the walk across Lahaina, passing fishermen coming from the docks with handcarts of their silvery catch still flapping their tails, their gills weakly flaring. Sometimes there were baby octopuses in writhing pink piles, and slabs of red, glistening ahi tuna cut into chunks she longed to take home but never had enough coins to buy. Carts from the upland areas brought the Hawaiian staples Waipuilani had grown up eating, but also a fragrant array of new vegetables: bright green spring onions, snow peas, curly cabbage, and red chilies. She discovered water chestnuts and bamboo shoots, and spices like star anise and the hard, rust-colored curls of cinnamon bark that she liked to carry in her hand and inhale as she walked through the foul-smelling alleys. She had a sharp eye for scraps like fish gills and heads, or chicken feet, that could flavor a soup. She was learning to like foods with new textures like rice and noodles. She asked to sample exotic dried plums, fermented beans, ginger, and tiny hot red peppers, and made snap decisions whether they would be to her family's liking. She was like a hungry cat ready to pounce on anything that she could take home to give them a sense of plenty.

Walking through the market had an unpleasant side that Waipuilani detoured around but couldn't always avoid, like skulking dogs pawing through rotted garbage and rats gnawing on what the dogs left behind. She hurried past hovels with scantily clothed, rail-thin Chinese girls leaning against the doorways, their lips smudged with crimson, as diseased-looking men held out greasy wads of dala to pay for a few minutes behind the grimy curtains with them. To Waipuilani, the seamier parts of town were hardly worse than the compound of sheds where she lived with her family, though the aunties made order of the little they had. She missed living in the open air and tried to draw her mother and stepsisters outside to walk in Lahaina's parks and shoreline, but they resisted. Her mother preferred to stay inside because it was easier to keep track of the little girls, who had several times lost their way in the maze of tightly clustered shanties. The once-easy banter between families, and their system of watching out for each other's' children, had broken down as fewer and fewer spoke the Hawaiian language. Their men were beaten for speaking Hawaiian on the plantation, so they whispered the familiar words in the night, as endearments or when telling secrets. But in the open they forced themselves to use the strange sounds of English with a bit of Chinese, Portuguese, Japanese thrown in. It was a potluck of words and phrases, a spoken mélange that the haole ridiculed yet made no effort to improve. It served the elemental interactions between the various populations without enabling speech that could feed dissatisfaction and unrest.

There was so much more to learn about all these strange people. Passing the doorsteps of the humblest shacks, Waipuilani had seen tiny altars of icons or images of deities with an offering of a blossom, fruit, or cup of tea made when entering or leaving. Waipuilani liked to watch the altars change from day to day and noticed that they were often taken down on the days the Christian missionaries came to teach everyone to pray in English. These ways of worship were so different from the massive Hawaiian heiau built of the volcanic rocks that Hawaiians called pohaku, which they believed were alive and able to convey messages of wisdom. She clung to her spiritual roots though her mother and most of the aunties had gone over to the god who hung on the wooden cross. "Gods not here in this place. Auwē," her mother said, advising as she often did that it was easier to forget about the old ways. Waipuilani understood that many Hawaiians felt forgotten and abandoned by their gods and ancestors. Her own father seemed more defeated every time he came back from the plantation for his day of rest. She too felt unanchored in this turbulent new world where every piece of their lives seemed molded by the men they called haole.

Waipuilani saw many of those haole. They were easy to spot. They had white skin and white hair over pink scalps and were always hurrying along in their pale linen suits. From the looks of them she couldn't see how they could have changed everything. But she learned important lessons from watching them and comparing them to men of other races. She saw how they kept themselves clean, and she noticed that clean people were treated with more respect, so she began taking care with her looks and hygiene. She borrowed needles and thread from tailors she'd befriended to repair her clothes and take up her hems so they didn't drag along the filthy streets. And, necessary to being presentable, she began to want things, like tools to tame her hair and slap-slap sandals to keep her feet out of mud. She took interest in things in the marketplace she'd always considered out of her reach and figured out a way to have small amenities without sacrificing what she took back to her family. She had learned enough Chinese language to buy in bulk and enlisted a younger sister to help cart the heavy sacks back to their compound, where she took what her family needed and sold the rest to neighbors. She kept the few pennies of profit. She thought this was fair, though she kept it to herself. Above all, she enjoyed delivering the vegetables, eggs, and the novel new Chinese and Japanese ingredients that Hawaiians were beginning to work into their diets: soy sauce, mung bean sprouts, lychees, and peanuts.

Waipuilani's awakening to having what money could buy, besides food, was her doorway to adulthood. She began wandering through the tailoring stalls, watching the artisans' needles flying in and out of cloth in rapid but precise stitches, transforming the fabric into embellished garments. They liked her curiosity and taught her to appreciate the rough cottons as much as the silks they kept in the back of the shop. She learned about dyes and drape. She watched them lay out the patterns, cut into the bolts of fabric, and run the pieces through clacking, whirring machines. Their hands darted here and there, shifting the cloth, tugging and pulling it under the needles, producing dresses and skirts, shirts, and slacks. Sometimes she sat on a low stool and watched customers select silks and be measured for custom garments or choose one of the ready-made Chinese *cheongsams* that hung at the entry, fluttering like colorful flags. Waipuilani had never seen anything like the frog buttons and braid clasps and trim. The Hawaiian *muʻumuʻu* that hung loose from the shoulders lacked this finery, but she learned to see the advantages of both ways of dressing.

The few pennies Waipuilani set aside for herself barely covered the cost of a hair clip or a pearly button, but they were noticeable and aroused suspicion. Her mother and aunties questioned where she'd gotten them. Waipuilani knew they were insinuating that she'd been compromised by men in the marketplace – the usual way girls like her came to own a string of beads or piece of ribbon. She had seen girls her age escorted through the stalls by natty men who stood by, ready to pay, as they picked out a length of silk. She'd noted how they looked to those men for a nod of approval, then handed the goods to the merchant to wrap while their escort paid. Most of those young girls were on the arm of older men who knew how to wear a suit, whose feet were encased in narrow, shiny leather shoes, who had a wallet rather than a pocket of grimy bills. Few of them, either the girl or the man squiring her, were Hawaiian. She tried to imagine Makatu as a man who could smoothly manage the purchase of a length of silk for a lady on his arm. She couldn't conjure that picture, nor the opposite, of him as a man who hissed and leered at girls in the market alleys or plantation camps. She could only picture him as a decent man living simply on the land with ohana in the old ways. Trying to imagine herself on the arm of one of those men with the wallet so readily pulled out, she knew she could not put herself in such a situation. She could not be anything but Hawaiian, but it was dawning on her that being Hawaiian doomed her to living in a narrow band of island life that would always be one of struggle.

With no one to guide her, Waipuilani observed, drew her own conclusions, and relied on her own instincts. Everyone flowing through the streets of Lahaina seemed separate and different from the one next to them. But whether Hawaiian or from some other country, she saw that every one of them was trying to claw their way into someplace better than where they'd come from. Just as she was. Something new was stirring inside her, an interest as much in her future as in the moment. The most specific thing she could say was that she was ready to get away from her family of origin and start her own.

Chapter 10

Teapot to Melting Pot

My initial inquiry into how Waipuilani came to marry a Chinese man had little to do with how her choices affected the women of my lineage, nor their ultimate impact on me. My primary interest in her was building her story: fleshing out her character, the trajectory of her life, the "and then, and then, and then" sequence of how one thing led to another, all of it bringing her to the threshold of adulthood, ready to choose a life partner. My fascination centered on how much she considered Sun Akana Wong's race and age, and how much her choices were narrowed because she was a low-caste kānaka. Perhaps Sun Akana Wong's race and age were advantageous, considering that the Chinese were well-regarded as shrewd and hardworking? Did she consciously weigh the pros and cons of marrying a Chinese, or did this relationship evolve organically? It is possible that she and Sun Akana Wong had passion and love, contrary to my speculation that she was forced by circumstances to marry outside her racial and ethnic community. Had she married a Hawaiian, our family would have avoided the pot for another generation or two, though who can say that would have been a good thing? Whether she'd have done this or that differently, history has shown that the scales were tipped toward most Hawaiians eventually ending up hapa.

Their cultural and racial differences aside, the age difference between Waipuilani and Sun Akana Wong was remarkable. He'd arrived in the Hawaiian Islands five years before Waipuilani was born. After his youth in China, he lived on three Hawaiian islands, compared to Waipuilani, who'd never ventured beyond a small area of Maui. I picture them meeting in Lahaina's markets or in church, two of the few places a young girl like her would have gone. He would have made the overtures, since Waipuilani would never have approached an older man whom she'd have politely called "uncle." The language barriers might have been passable, since Sun Akana Wong had been in Hawaiʻi long enough to know English, and Waipuilani was by necessity having to learn it. He was experienced with women – he'd had a wife and family in China, and a Maui-born son from a liaison during his first years in Hawaiʻi. Perhaps he approached Waipuilani with an offer to taste an unusual fruit from his country, or to repair her sandal, pointing at it and gesturing for her to come to his shop. Whatever gate I can conjure being opened, some of them quite fanciful, through the lens of my current time, the picture of such an older man engaging a young girl seems a bit predatory or opportunistic.

But let's say that there was a spark, that she'd accepted whatever enticement he'd held out. What then? The usual courtship rituals: a sunset stroll along the harbor, or a meal at a cafe she'd longed to dine in but could not enter alone, even if she'd had the coins to spare? Perhaps she began stopping in his harness shop where he'd offer her a cup of tea from the pot that he kept brewing. This might have been new for her. Hawaiians of the time were not tea drinkers – the warm bitter liquid was not suited to the island heat, nor did Hawaiians light fires to cook if they could avoid it, as there were few trees to burn, and fuel was costly. Sipping slowly, she'd listen to him tell of arriving in the islands penniless and making his way. She'd shrug off the fact that he'd already had four children, some as old as she was. She'd grown up with the loose configurations of Hawaiian families, so she might have been undaunted by anything except that he could get her out of her family's overcrowded shack and into one of her own.

TALK STORY: *Sun Akana Wong in the 1850s*

> The hardest thing for Sun Akana Wong was the ridicule from villagers he'd known all his life. They mocked him for living in a hodgepodge lean-to of corrugated sheets and boards washed up by the sea. They tsk-tsked that he could not feed his woman and three sons, though most in the village had only a meal or two more each week than he did. Most of all, they laughed at his plan to leave the Tong'An District, a place along a finger of water pouring into the bay of the South China Sea, and go to the faraway place called Hawai'i. He was foolish to believe the rumor that these islands needed workers, and to spend the few coins left from his wife's dowry to get there. This Hawai'i was a place of half-clothed savages, they'd heard, where missionaries had to teach the natives to make clothes and cover their bodies. And what would he, a cobbler and harness maker, do in this place where no one wore shoes?
>
> Sun Akana Wong did not answer. They were all hungry, same as him, and none of them knew how to make things better. He was the only one

with a plan. He let them rattle on while he held in his mind the image of men riding horses on cattle ranches, all harnessed with reins he'd made. He hadn't made anyone in his destitute village a pair of shoes in a very long time. The few who had shoes ground them to shreds over the rocky fields and shell-strewn shoreline, then passed what remained of them to others who wore them because it was better than having nothing. Sun Akana Wong argued that going barefoot was better than wearing the useless lashings they bound around their feet and called shoes. But few paid attention to what he thought best.

The day came when Sun Akana Wong bade farewell and booked passage for the miserable voyage in the hold of a ship going to the Hawaiian Islands. He suffered every heave and roll through the weeks of storms and swells, the boat threatening to split into pieces with every surge. Like other vomiting, retching immigrants in the airless hold, he was too sick to eat at sea. After three miserable weeks the boat arrived in Lahaina. Sun Akana Wong walked down the gangplank in the blinding sun, weak and thin, touching the solid ground so improbably far from his village. He was a nameless, faceless arrival amongst a hoard of hundreds just like him.

But Sun Akana Wong had a trade. He'd brought his tools and wasted no time plying his skills. He spread a cloth on the hard-packed dirt street near the wharf, covered it with samples of his shoes and harnesses, and crouched beside it while Lahaina's throngs flowed past. Few stopped to examine his wares, or even glance in his direction. He was tempted to give up, to take work gutting fish in the

Chinese stall in exchange for something to eat, when three teachers from the elite Lahainaluna school passed by. They picked up the shoe samples and turned them over in their hands, passing them back and forth. Then they took measure of Sun Akana Wong, who was pale, slender, and cleanly shaven except for a straggle of light brown hairs that came together in a V-shaped tangle below his chin. After months at sea, his hands had softened and lost the purplish brown dye stains that normally colored his cuticles and finger pads. His tools were laid out in an orderly array: an assortment of awls, hammers, knives, and pinchers he'd kept wrapped in felt against the salt from the sea and had since oiled until they gleamed with readiness for work. He'd brought heavy threads and the beeswax with him in case such essentials were not available in Hawai'i, and a half dozen leather pelts to fill the first orders that would establish his reputation.

The teachers left but returned later with a Chinese interpreter to discuss their need for shoes for boys coming to board at their school. Most had never owned shoes but would be required to wear them on the campus. The teachers requested, and paid for, a sample shoe line for the school administrators to recommend to their students, who would then be sent to the stall for fitting. Sun Akana Wong had never made shoes for children. The ones in his village were too poor to have them. But he set to it, using the pelts and materials he'd brought with him from Tong'An. The Lahainaluna people liked his work and appointed him the recommended cobbler, making him one of the Hawaiian boys' first stops after arriving in Lahaina to begin boarding.

Most of them returned again and again, as their feet grew during the years of their education and into their adulthood.

Sun Akana Wong knew that he was lucky, and he did not take this for granted. He took care to make skillful shoes until word got out and adults began ordering their own custom-fitted shoes. He began trading shoe repairs for the ecru-colored linen pants and cotton shirts he wore at the cobbler bench under the thick, stained leather apron he'd brought from China. Bartering with other vendors helped spread his name across the marketplace. He was off to a good start, and things continued going well. He'd even struck up with a woman from the Maui up-country and had a son with her, but she'd taken the child and left no word of their whereabouts. He did not mourn the loss – he had plenty of sons, with the three back in China, and was grateful that they and the one on Maui had caring mothers. What he needed next in Lahaina was someone steady, practical, and of good heart to take care of him. He was almost fifty and beginning to feel it.

Chapter 11

Anything Else?

The second time I was present when the family chart was brought out, at my cousin's Thanksgiving gathering, I was prepared with questions about the stories behind the names. I wanted a conversation that shed light on the lives of our ancestors. But I'd held back, so everyone could settle into the moment. At the first lull I jumped in. "So, it looks like Sun Akana Wong died about thirty years after he met Waipuilani," I said, pointing to where his name was boxed in and tagged Husband #1. "Were they together that whole time? I read in the 1930 census that she had Makatu's name. So, they reunited and married." I pointed to his name, penciled next to Sun Akana Wong's, but not labelled as her husband. "How did Makatu get back in the picture, after all that time, after she had four – five? – kids with Sun Akana Wong?"

"Makatu came back," my chart keeper cousin said.

Sometimes my cousins' responses were maddeningly simple. Maybe I was being too nosy. Maybe they weren't into discussing our ancestors' lives. They already understood, in a way I was learning, that Hawaiian liaisons often were not linear, monogamous, nor sanctified in marriage, as they were in the 1950s Christian world of my upbringing. Maybe just seeing the lineage on the chart sufficed to show how everyone stood, relative to each other, no details needed. As I'd anticipated, teasing out bits of Waipuilani's story would require some delicacy, which is not my strong point.

"Makatu came back from where? Came back because Sun Akana Wong left? Or did Sun Akana Wong leave because Makatu came back?"

The questions hung in the air. No one jumped in with an explanation or even to say they didn't know. Were my questions impudent? Or was there something here to hide? My insecurities and vexation went into overdrive, as did my belief in the importance of family transparency. But did they consider me enough of a *bona fide* family member to open up with? I wanted to say, "You guys. Give me a bone." This had all the elements of a grand yet relatable drama: an innocent girl whose true love, the boy from her youth, had been swallowed up by life, who gave up on his return too soon, and succumbed to courtship by an older man with a wife and sons back in Canton, or Szechuan, or wherever – taking note of one more detail I would have to Google. I wanted help exploring the endless maybes: maybe he gave her a few strands of braided red silk threads that mean "I wish you good luck" in China. Maybe he liked her because she didn't speak English well and he could be quiet with her. I could rattle off maybes for days and probably would, in the absence of anything more concrete to go on.

But the conversation wasn't happening. My questions, once again, would have to wait. I left the chart and went to the kitchen to help the aunties. They were scraping sticky remnants from the serving platters and cinching black trash bags full of disposable dinnerware. I offered to start in on the pots and pans, but they said I should be going home. The Kamehameha Highway could be dangerous in the dark, they said, so winding, with all those blind curves. Did I bring a dish I needed to take back with me? Did I want leftovers? "Plenty, plenty" they said, so I helped myself to a few guava rolls that were easy to grab but which I knew I wouldn't eat. After the customary hugs all around, I stepped outside into the profusion of brown, green, and black rubber flip-flops left at the kitchen door. I found mine which, like me, didn't seem to belong there. They looked too preppy, from L.L. Bean, khaki with navy blue mallard ducks woven into the cross strap. I slid into them and started toward the carport, passing a whining whitish-gray terrier tied to the downspout. It lifted its tail and head as I went past, then dropped both with disinterest. Three aunties sat at folding tables in the driveway, fanning flies from an array of desserts, waiting for everyone to come back outside for pie or *mochi*.

"Goodbye, Auntie, goodbye," I said, giving each the customary two-cheeked kiss. "See you, see you."

"Where you going so soon?" one asked. "You sit and eat."

"I'm going to try to find Tutu Wahine," I said. "I mean, I am going someplace quiet so I can imagine her."

"OK. See you, see you." They waved me away like one of the flies hovering over the carrot cake, no more interested in my quest than were the cousins inside.

I drove the Kam Highway back to my house, going the opposite direction from the flow of cars coming down from holiday on the North Shore beaches. At Kahana Bay, a mile from my house, I slowed for the picnickers who were lugging coolers across the road to their cars. At my driveway I made the hard, abrupt turn through the tall wood gates, grateful the caretaker had left them open. I eased through, disrupting a few feral chickens that clucked and scattered before they resumed scavenging. I parked at the end of the long red dirt drive, still thinking about Waipuilani, and walked across the grass to my place of contemplation, the sea wall. The waves surged forward as if to greet me, then drew back and came in again in their eternal cycle, as black crabs scuttled across the rocks for bits of food delivered by the surf. I looked toward the reefs where I often saw little red triangular flags bobbing along, a signal to beware that there was a spear fisherman below, but there were none. They were probably taking the day off for Thanksgiving, I thought, or perhaps it was too late in the day to see the octopuses they hunted in coral crevices. Further out a lone paddler moved toward Kahana Bay, creating a dim silhouette against the encroaching twilight.

This quiet moment at the sea at the end of day was my idea of a quintessential Hawaiian experience. But it was not typical of Waipuilani's experience of Hawai'i, nor was it my Grandma Rosa's, nor even my mother's. This was an American haole experience of Hawai'i, a privileged place with its gated entry, long set-back from the highway, and stretch of private shoreline. Perhaps my relatives perceived me as disingenuous. Perhaps they saw my set-up as a presumptuous incursion into a getaway world I'd made on my own terms, apart from the culturally authentic Hawai'i into which I would never assimilate.

I shook myself, resolved not to let my feeling of dejection get in the way of unearthing my great grandmother's story. I would find it through research and historical milestones and intuition laid against dates and places that I could verify. My guide would be what was going on in her world laid against a matrix of the basic human needs and desires on which humankind base their choices. Of those, I'd already felt deeply into the sorrow and confusion at having to leave one's home. We have all felt that. I could believe in the loneliness and insecurity of finding one's place in a new world. That is universal and relatable. And I could feel into the pull to bond and mate and procreate. I could follow this emotional roadmap as it led Waipuilani to follow her instincts, from gateway to gateway, while the ticking of her biological clock grew insistent. Thinking of her in this context, I can reframe Sun Akana Wong's age, race, and worldliness as positive assets that might have been, not a capitulation, but a smart choice.

Chapter 12

Don't Ask, Don't Tell

Once I'd imagined a plausible way for Sun Akana Wong to enter Waipuilani's life, I began to think more deeply about the circumstances that drove the partner choices the women of my family tended to make. For the most part, the men with whom they mated had come to Hawai'i from another place and had established a foothold through hard work. Like so many American immigrants entering the U.S. though our many borders, the people who heeded the call to opportunity in Hawai'i arrived with the hope that their labor would improve their lot. My female forebears aligned with such men as one of the few options they had to escape their place in the island caste system. This strategy had worked for my mother. In turn, she would take it a step further by keeping her own daughters out of Hawai'i entirely and steering us toward places with young men she would deem more suitable than we were likely to find in the islands.

Elevating their daughters' prospects by way of a propitious marriage is a universal parental goal, I might add. However, many cultures with elaborate systems of matchmaking aim to fortify existing cultural and familial connections by making choices within them, rather than looking to potential partners from outside their milieu. I've come to appreciate my mother's ambitions for me, though I have deep sadness that circumstances drove her to ensure that her daughters would never consider men from her own culture.

Because my mother had grown up with the cross-racial marriages and sexual liaisons between the many races who had populated the islands, she was comfortable and accepting of the everyday reality of it. She did not question the "don't ask, don't tell" approach to these relationships by Hawaiian officials and Christian missionaries, and the ways that multi-racial partnerships served the plantation owners' interests. But she also knew that they were taboo or outright illegal in many states that still had enforceable anti-miscegenation laws on their books. As she set her sights toward getting to the American mainland, she knew she'd have to tread carefully.

In 1891, the year that Waipuilani married Sun Akana Wong, Queen Liliʻuokalani ascended to the throne. By 1893, the year that haole businessmen overthrew and imprisoned the queen, Waipuilani had begun bearing children. Stretched thin by children and domesticity, the outside world of politics and power may have seemed distant to her. But over time, without the voice of their queen and without the means to remain close with their scattering ohana, Hawaiians like Waipuilani accepted the decline of the Hawaiian ways they'd grown up with. They learned to get along in the polycultural mash-up their islands had become.

When I was a child trying to process my mother's rages, I was struck by her vehemence whenever she saw someone prey on the weak. "Take take take," she'd say, her voice hard with bitterness. Once, during an argument with her, she accused me of being a taker. I saw how quickly and irrationally she could be triggered to that refrain. I did not understand what she meant, but there was something in that "take take take" that always made me want to weep. I can now see the taking in a colonialist context, which makes it more wrenching, because it was about more than my mother's experience. It was about what had happened to an entire society.

American history is thick with the kind of taking that drove Hawaiians from the āina they revered. Native Americans endured similar travesty, though the United States used more violent and aggressive tactics to steal their land. Hawaiians' isolation had made of them a trusting people. They did not see the dangerous implications and threat of U.S. interests, even though it was clear by the mid-1800s that the United States considered Hawai'i essential to trade and their defense of the Pacific region. Hawaiian kings and queens governed with vision and good intention, but they were vulnerable to manipulation by American businessmen and politicians. As the history of native-born peoples has shown, land that the United States considers valuable it takes for its own.

Although many Hawaiian islanders supported annexation and the potential for Hawaiian statehood, there were factions that lacked the language skills and political will to express their grief about the loss of Hawaiian land and sovereignty. Future generations of Hawaiians inherited this anger and sorrow, which cohered in the 1970s into the Hawaiian sovereignty movement, a vocal grassroots campaign that advocated for some form of redress for the overthrow of the queen and Hawaiian autonomy. Generations of my female forebears did their best to adapt to what was left for them, which could be described as the dregs and leftovers after the colonialists had skimmed off the *creme*. My mother's refrain of "take take take" reveals her bitter understanding of having been robbed.

Thinking back to how, as a child, I'd loathed hearing my parents and our Hawaiian visitors tag other islanders by their race, I realized that my thinking about the practice had become more nuanced as I came to know the islands better. For example, for Hawaiians during the past two hundred years who found themselves outnumbered by foreign people, the ability to identify newly arrived factions by their race helped the local population to sort out and appreciate newcomers while holding onto their own identity as Hawaiians. It had an intentional bent toward goodwill and cooperative relationships. But the practice had no such useful function in our homogenous little Midwestern community in the 1950s. There, it was not used to get along, to promote peaceful co-existence. Its use by haole townspeople was purely racist, which in those times we called being "prejudiced." Even were the epithets and injurious slurs directed at people of color who were thousands of miles away, I could see that racist thinking in any context was harmful to all sentient beings. I remain ambivalent about the racial labeling then, and ongoing, in the islands, but I can see that it could have been helpful to Hawaiians who were being forced to rapidly adapt to the multi-racial population foisted upon them.

By the time I was able to fully grasp the displacement and deracination of the original people of Hawaiʻi, I was also awakening to the mass extinction of animal species. Mass extinction occurs when a species disappears much faster than it can be replaced. The usual cause is loss of habitat, which means that the animals are victims to forces that they cannot control. I hadn't set out to compare what had happened to the indigenous Hawaiians to the mass extinction of animal species, but since I happened to be learning about them simultaneously, I couldn't help noticing that they had a frightening dynamic in common. Both had been pushed to the fringes by invaders, whether human or floral/faunal; both had tried to survive by accommodation and adaptation. In both situations the casualties, the shrinking of their numbers, were dramatic. Hawaiians had become an ethnic minority in their own country by 1898, the year the United States annexed the Hawaiian Islands. By that time indigenous Hawaiians like Waipuilani had dwindled to just twenty percent of Hawai'i's population. They could not have been oblivious to their threatened extinction. In reconsidering the way Hawaiians parse out fellow citizens' racial backgrounds and label their components, I want to think that the practice helped them to figure out where to find societal shelter at a time when the extinction of their race felt possible and even probable.

THE DEGRADATION OF THE HAWAIIAN CULTURE AND THE creation of a new one that was diffuse and diluted resulted in the creation of a caste the Hawaiians called hapa. This caste is the fundamental ingredient of the vaunted melting pot.

The word hapa is complex. I heard the term a lot when my Hawaiian aunties came to visit us in Wisconsin. The word wove into their gossip and memories. To me, listening in but never directly witnessing their referents, it seemed like everyone they knew must be hapa. We kids were hapa.

Virtually every Hawaiian person they mentioned was hapa. Nowadays we can say that most of our worldwide population is hapa. My mother tended to use the word for specific persons, but I tend to see that it applies to the entire Hawaiian population. The word describes the outcome of an evolution. Having grown up with the word – hapa was one of the handful of Hawaiian words that my parents used between them and that we kids understood, but rarely used ourselves – I have always seen the word as reductive: a person is racially pure or is not. Thinking of it that simply, I understand why this Hawaiian word would never have been used outside our home, where there was so little racial diversity. (Parenthetically, when I think about the Hawaiian words used in our house, all were generally negative: *nuha* to describe sullen and stubborn; *lolo* to describe someone crazy or acting stupid: *kāpulu* for people who were sloppy or places that were cluttered and slovenly.) When my parents described someone as hapa it was usually a neutral, matter-of-fact descriptor of reality. There was no racial disparagement, except when a hapa stood beside haole. In that case, haole was superior. This was not said, but it was implicit.

On the mainland United States, in my experience of the way we think about racial groups, the ones who are hapa haole, or half white, tend to be included with the ones who are not white. In Hawai'i, the ones who are hapa haole can fall into either camp. Which side they land on depends on personal and complex nuances of context and value. When my parents attached racial labels to groups or persons they knew in Hawai'i, their pride in specificity eventually gave way to the generalized labels the people of the insular Midwest could picture. Korean, Samoan or Tongan, Japanese, Chinese, or Filipino were lumped together as Orientals.

Over time they were further sorted into classifications like Asian and South Pacific Islanders. In recent years, many within those groups, even those from tiny nations like Palau or from a distinct region of a larger country, like Okinawa, are insisting on their specific identity. Growing up with this range of nationalities floating in the air was natural and never piqued my interest in those cultures or in the people behind the labels. Perhaps this is because my parents didn't talk about the racial breakdown of the people of our own region, the Midwest. Their parsing was reserved for the people of Hawaiʻi, who I didn't know and couldn't see, so I really didn't know what they were talking about.

The distinct memory I have of the word hapa, besides how my mother used it to describe people they knew in Hawaiʻi, was how she used it to describe us, her kids. That our mother thought of us, referred to us, in terms of our race illustrated how she had pigeonholed us. It was an indoctrination that I took in at deep levels. I was being "carefully taught." Although I grew up living fully as haole, I never dove into the psychological implication of my mother labeling me as something that wasn't *whole*.

To be half can signify half full or half empty. I embody the duality, living as half full, but carrying the shadow of the half empty, which is the part that was lost. I don't know specifically what was lost but I have always felt that something had been. I believe that deep-seated sense of loss lives in people of Hawaiian blood as part of our genetic inheritance. The loss can be measured as diminishing percentages of one's Hawaiian blood as one melted into the pot. It can be felt as the vacating of a sense of wholeness and integration, a necessary loss incurred during the process of assimilation. The word hapa is grossly reductive of all the decisions, compromises, conflicts, and heartbreaks comprising the intergenerational halving of the half, and the next halving of the quarter, over and over, until race is parsed into barely discernible slivers. To be a literal half, racially, is to be uncommonly whole, paradoxically.

For individuals who are hapa, how they think of themselves – their self-concept – determines their path forward. We can fragment our components, emphasizing one or another, and relegate parts of ourselves to the shadows. This is an automatic reflex or can be a pragmatic calculation that one makes in self-serving situations, which is most situations. In my case, I called myself what seemed palatable to whatever crowd or conversation I was engaged in, which was typically skewed toward the haole/white. I had no allegiance to the Chinese or the Hawaiian, since I wasn't brought up to attach to either of them except when doing so served a purpose. It was a mixed blessing to be able to what we call "pass." The good part was being able to blend in; the other part was that I failed to form a crisp identity and attachment to any of the components of my makeup. People of my Wisconsin childhood called us Hawaiian. We were okay with that, although I am only one eighth Hawaiian. Though I am a much higher percent Chinese, I never called myself Chinese, partially because I hadn't realized how much I was, and partially because it hadn't seemed a safe or advantageous label to hang on myself. Mostly I've said that I am white, which I could legitimately claim, because being hapa haole means one can emphasize the white and the leave the hapa part obscure unless there is interest in defining it.

By contrast, many I know who grew up in the islands tend to identify far more with the hapa than the haole, even though many of them had Caucasian fathers. They think of themselves in terms of their racial makeup, rather than keeping it in the shadows as some quality they could pull out and use if needed or if useful. Visiting a friend at her Honolulu high-rise apartment, I came across a book called *Part Asian, 100% Hapa* by Kip Fulbeck,[18] which features facial portraits of persons of mixed race. They reflect the full global spectrum, going far beyond the interracial pairings of the major racial groups that came to the Hawaiian Islands. The persons shown, who are Japanese/Mexican, Chinese/Iranian, Korean/Nigerian, and other seemingly unlikely mixes, have written statements about how they see the hapa part of themselves as "half full," but in a different way than I'd personally grown up thinking of half full. For me, being half full meant I could claim to be white. The persons in this project are asserting bold appreciation for the range of cultures and the races they embody, irrespective of whether there is any white in the mix. They are expressing that as a value into forward-leaning media, fashion, and artistic initiatives that herald the expansion of creative expression. Lacking such models of hapa pride in the 1950s, and being the only mixed-race people on our block, the path of least resistance was to identify with the haole part of hapa haole and reap the benefits of all the advantages that are conferred on white people by a white society.

With so many young people now celebrating their Asian and Pacific Island makeup, and with so many online channels and social media available for their expression, I indulged many hours in reading their testaments of hapa pride. They awakened me to a way of seeing oneself that I'd missed out on: an appreciation for oneself as a whole person that is the fully fused sum of its parts, rather than the cobbling together of disparate parts desperately seeking integration. For one of my generation, coming from my scripting, this was the ultimate conflict resolution. I wanted to experience myself as a fully blended, fully realized amalgam of the Chinese, Hawaiian and haole. Leaning into the concept, trying it on, I felt an instant cessation of tension. I felt more spacious and magnanimous, able to make attributions I'd withheld, fearing they'd pigeon-hole and stereotype me. I could openly ascribe my defining characteristics to the ambitious grit of my mother's Chinese will, to the fluid adaptability and sensorial appreciation of my Hawaiian forebears, and to the safety net of white privilege that undergirds my self-confidence.

AS THE WEEKS SPOOLED INTO THE MONTHS OF MY HAWAIian hiatus, Waipuilani's pull felt insistent. I was unable to procure a photo of her nor to build on my paltry store of anecdotes about her. I wanted to bypass the cousins who might have helped but didn't. I wanted to conjure her, to reincarnate her for a day or two, to go back in time and beam myself over to where she lived in Lahaina. We'd sit on her stoop watching gecko lizards grab at insects with their long tongues, and plumeria blossoms release from their leafless limbs and drift to the patch of matted brown grass. She'd talk in Hawaiian language-infused English, and I would understand her perfectly. I'd tell her how much it meant that she was Hawaiian, that I had often heard her described as the last "pure" Hawaiian in our family. I'd tell her that I had struggled to feel and embrace the Hawaiian in my blood, and that only three generations later, it did not have a hold on me.

The Hawaiian in me seemed like a trickster, I'd explain, because when I searched for it, I kept finding the Chinese. I'd ask her how she'd felt looking at her babies and realizing they were half pākē, then how she'd felt looking at her grandchildren, including my mother, and realizing they were three-fourths pākē. She'd tell me she hadn't seen them as anything but beautiful babies, and wasn't that how I saw my own babies, whatever they were. I would tell her yes, but I'd never liked the Chinese and I didn't want to be one. I'd tell her how my mother had not drawn attention to herself as a Chinese and so it took until after her death for me to fully see how much she was. If I couldn't see her as Chinese, how could I accept myself as one? Waipuilani would laugh, letting it roll up from her tobacco-ruined lungs, a rattling sound. She would ask what my mother had said about all that. She'd never said anything, I'd tell her, except that we were hapa. Half. And Waipuilani would say that we are all beautiful and should not let all that matter. Then her eyes would grow distant, and she'd be in a memory. "But the most beautiful was Rosalie," she'd say. "Your grandma. Like a rose bud. Roses, not so many here, ya? So, I name her Rosalie."

TALK STORY: *Rosalie — 1901*

> Waipuilani awoke in pain and cried out. Her belly seized and gripped the infant curled within, grasping it tight then releasing. She moaned. This was just the beginning. She'd been through this before. She knew how it would be. She sat up, her hands splayed across the curve of her mound, wondering why Sun Akana Wong was never there when this moment arrived, when the passion they'd had for

a minute so far back boomeranged to her in this searing seizure. The roosters down the road crowed and the wild chickens clucked and flapped their useless wings. By the end of this day, when Sun Akana Wong returned for supper, they would have another child to feed.

She looked at Margaret, her first born, breathing peacefully in her cot in the corner. She was sorry to have to wake her. "Margaret Aliona. You get up." She stumbled through the English that Sun Akana Wong said she must speak to the keiki, hating this language that would, if she did not learn it, force her to the outside of her own family. "Take sisters to Auntie Manuela. Baby coming, tell Auntie."

Aliona stirred and sat up. She was nine years old, but she knew what lie ahead. She remembered the other times when she had crouched outside the curtain as her mother howled new life into their midst. She ran to her mother, but Waipuilani's eyes were shut. "Go, go," she said.

Aliona ran to the outhouse and then to the clothesline stretched between a hook on the house and a branch of the flowering poinciana tree. She tugged at her dress until the pins flew off and it fell free. She pulled it over her head. Across the road two white ibis perched on the back of a bony cow. Pigeons cooed from the rusted tin roof of Uncle Tanaka's shed. The red hibiscus was opening after closing its petals in the night. But Aliona had no time for the magic of the Maui morning. She rushed inside and rummaged through the clutter to find a brush, then tore at her thick waves, trying to tame her hair into the tidy braids the school required. "Mama, my hair," she said, aiming her voice to the bed where Waipuilani lay on her side, her knees pulled up toward her shoulders. Ah Lee and Julia were awake and had climbed into their mother's bed, whining, and crowding close on the narrow mattress.

"Go, go. I keep Ah Lee, you take Julia. Go," Waipuilani panted. She rolled onto her back. Her belly was dark and taut, and sweat covered her face. Her eyes were fierce, opened wide and then sliding back under the ridge of her brow. "Go. Tell Auntie baby coming." Her voice slumped to a groan.

Aliona pulled Julia toward the door. She was wiry and agile, like their Chinese father, but had the bronze skin of her Hawaiian ancestors. She wore the pale-yellow shirt from the day before, soiled but passable, with a few buttons undone. She fumbled with them while Aliona grabbed a banana from the brown-spotted bunch on the table. "Here. Eat," she said as they scurried out the door.

The minute they were gone Waipuilani got on the floor and squatted in the old position. She would not endure this for one extra minute if she could get it over faster, even without Auntie Manuela. She pushed and fell back, close to unconscious, then rose again and pushed, clenching her teeth and straining until her eyes felt like they would burst blood. She worked her agony, holding the bedframe while the pain took her to the edge of blacking out. But she'd shake herself back, pant harder and faster, until she lurched forward and caught the infant's head as it slid and separated from her.

Another girl. Sun Akana Wong would not be happy. She would have to try again for a son. He already had three sons in China, and one somewhere on Maui, and Ah Lee, the one they had together who would start school this year. How she could love this baby when she already had to think about another one later? Exhausted, the adrenalin of birth deserting her like the backwash of a tsunami, she blacked out, only to awake a few seconds later. How long had she been out? She looked between her blood-crusted legs to find the baby. She saw that Auntie Manuela had come and was cutting the cord with a machete she'd put to a flame to sterilize. She turned the baby upside down like a Peking duck in a Chinese grocery store. She patted the baby's back until it wailed, then wrapped her in a soft, clean cloth, and put her in Waipuilani's arms.

They both fell silent as they gazed upon her, fair and pink, delicate and translucent like the petals of that sweet-smelling flower the haole had brought to the islands, that rose. *Lokelani*, folks on Maui called it. Waipuilani ran her coarse finger across the baby's forehead then drew back her hand, feeling like she'd touched a delicate silk in Hamamoto's kimono shop. Her hands were still thick and rough, hands accustomed to digging sweet potatoes and trimming breadfruit, hands unused to anything as delicate as this baby's skin. Waipuilani surged with pride that this child was the color of the dolls the haole children prized. She was like a porcelain teacup on their crude board shelf. Waipuilani would name the baby Apina, but she would call her Rosalie, like the flower. This one – more than her Aliona, with her smash-nose and skin the color of koa wood, or her Ah Lee or Julia with their monolid eyes – with her light Chinese skin, would have it easier when she grew up.

Auntie Manuela heated water on the small brazier Waipuilani used for cooking. She dipped the baby into the warm bath, shushing her squalls as she swaddled and handed her back to Waipuilani, who remained in a reverie, looking back and forth between the mess she'd made of the bed and the miracle of the baby. She'd lost track of time but knew the day had passed, and school was out, when Julia and Aliona peeked through a crack between the curtains. She said "You tell my girls baby ok. Yeah?"

Auntie Manuela said. "I take baby, show her to sisters."

"Auntie Manuela, I born in cave," Waipuilani said. "I call this baby Rosalie. She hapa in a better way. Good for her. Yeah?"

Chapter 13
Hiding in Plain Sight

I've heard my cousins describe our Grandma Rosa as having been a beautiful woman in her youth. Studying the photos of her in her later years, I can see that she must have been. She had high cheekbones, a wide and sensuous mouth, and a strong jawline. In the images I've seen of her, she holds herself regally and is usually gazing into the distance, as if harkening to something unseen signaling to her, something that she alone hears.

Because I loved her, I want to imagine her always and everywhere beloved, even as a baby girl with a Chinese father who may have devalued girls in favor of sons. Whether Waipuilani and Sun Akana Wong peaccably integrated their cultures in their home is hard to say. I doubt that Rosalie had much help in sorting out her world of multiple ethnicities. The melting pot was drawing them in, inexorably, and there were no guidebooks for how best to assimilate into its engulfing stew. Within one generation, from Waipuilani's childhood to Rosalie's, the islands' Chinese population had burgeoned tenfold. By 1901, the year of Rosalie's birth, over sixteen percent were Chinese. This may have helped her find her footing.

Still, it was a tumultuous time in the evolution of Hawaiian and Chinese co-existence. There was only one Chinese woman to every seventeen Chinese men, which set the stage for many Chinese men to marry island women. Though the first Chinese were brought to Hawaiʻi specifically to work the sugar plantations, and they were considered exemplary laborers, they were less than twenty-eight percent of the plantation labor force by 1900, the year that Hawaiʻi became a U.S. territory. Many Chinese plantation workers had walked off their jobs when their contracts under the Masters and Servants Act were voided, after the Act itself was abolished as unconstitutional. Some returned to their homeland and others tried to go to the mainland, despite the restrictions of the Chinese Exclusion Act of 1882, the first and only federal legislation that suspended immigration for a specific nationality. The Act prohibited both skilled and unskilled Chinese laborers from entering the United States and, as later amended, prevented the return of Chinese laborers who'd been in the U.S. and had left.

But thousands of Chinese workers who were no longer contracted to the plantations remained in Hawaiʻi and were the first of the islands' many ethnic groups to flock to urban areas. Hard working and opportunistic, they opened shops, ran services, and cultivated agriculture ventures like growing rice and vegetables. Many Hawaiians resented their rising presence and influence in Hawaiian commerce, although their clever skills and tireless work ethic were much admired. While the Chinese numbers and their impact increased, the Kānaka Maoli population dropped precipitously. One hundred years after Captain Cook's arrival, when there'd been over 300,000 indigenous Hawaiians, their number had dwindled to under 30,000.

Born in 1891, Rosalie grew up in a world without a reigning monarch, a world in which the United States was taking over island commerce and government, a world in which the increasing presence of Chinese small businesses empowered them in island affairs. As half-Chinese in a ubiquitous subculture, she'd have seen Chinese everywhere, in their wide range of roles. By contrast, the Hawaiian Kānaka Maoli were diminishing in numbers and struggling to adapt. Their attempts consisted of grand and minute conquests made at the expense of sad and irrevocable surrenders. Among their adaptive strategies was miscegenation, which resulted in new levels of interconnection that generated new configurations of community.

The pendulum for Hawaiians had been swinging from isolation into the limitless possibilities of globalism since the early 19th century. I believe the women of my family embraced that transformation and sought to take advantage of the opportunities it offered. This was probably more practical than visionary, but often the one drives the other. The Chinese who'd come to the Hawai'i were thriving while the star of the island-born Hawaiians had long since dimmed. That Rosalie had a Chinese father surely predisposed her to marry a Chinese man. That once-alien population was now infused into her very blood, and she was of its culture. Her marriage to Clarence Young made their children three-fourths Chinese, a dramatic tip of the scales toward the Chinese in our family. With more Chinese blood came more of the epigenetic inheritance that I have perceived within me and has been the underlying driver of my inquiry into my identity. The Chinese who'd come to Maui during Waipuilani's era were opportunists driven by desperation. They carried the intergenerational scars of centuries of starvation and war not only to the Hawaiian Islands, but directly into the psyche and soul of my lineage.

Clarence Young and Rosalie had five children and, as Waipuilani had in the prior generation, Rosalie spent many years raising them in a fatherless household. Just as Sun Akana Wong had left Waipuilani and their children on Maui and moved back to China, Clarence Young had left Rosalie and their children on Maui and moved to Oʻahu. There, he started a new business and family. I've heard no talk story about why he left, no revelatory tales of blame or justification, no excuses, or explanations. Nor have I ever heard any sweet memories of him. About him my mother was inscrutable, personifying the cliché about the Chinese. She never accorded him an anecdote or a remembrance to give any hint of what kind of man he was or her feelings toward him. I asked my eldest Hawaiian cousins very directly whether they had any story, description, or piece of data, about Clarence Young, and they responded that they did not. The walls of silence closed around him and were sealed shut. The presence of this grandfather in my life, however superficial, might have helped me align with, and perhaps even attach to, the part of me that is Chinese. Lack of his verifiable male grounding as a kind of certification of my Chinese lineage is key to the ghosting of it in my self-concept.

Though Clarence Young's abandonment and the family silence about him keep him relegated to the shadows, his surname was a thread I noticed wending here and there throughout my early memories. I often mused, superficially, on the many surnames that showed up in records of Waipuilani, Rosalie, and my mother. Following the trail of their names would lead to questions about the nature of the men who'd come into and exited their lives, in many cases after fathering their children. It took me until my adult years to be ready to explore those realms and when I dove in, it was not easy. In many cases their surnames in public records are the only evidence I have of a pairing between them. With only those names to go on, I was once again forced to extrapolate what I could and use that tiny piece of data as a springboard for imagined truth.

Even as a child I loved that Grandma Rosa's name was poetic and floral, and for a long time I assumed that Rosa was a derivative of Rosalie. Learning that Rosa was the Portuguese surname of her third husband, I was charmed that in her happiest years she had the lovely name Rosalie Rosa. She'd carried on being Grandma Rosa to us after George Rosa had died, though she'd married again and had legally taken the name of that husband, whose name was Henderson. Of that man the only thing I know is his surname. My mother never acknowledged Henderson in any way except to put his name after Rosalie's on the envelopes she sent to her mother, and it is the name in the return address corner of letters Grandma Rosa sent to us. We never asked why we weren't calling her Grandma Henderson. Did we call her Grandma Rosa because my mother loved her stepfather George Rosa, or because no one cared about Henderson enough to want his name in the room?

It saddens me to be so reductive about Grandma Rosa's life, paring it down to the faceless men whose names she'd used in succession throughout her life. As children, we were not encouraged to be curious. Our parents drew a hard line in front of things they said were "not your business" so we didn't know what we didn't know. We were Catholic, so divorce was unthinkable, and it was shameful to be labeled as a "broken family." The surnames from my mother's family pointed to the serial marriages that were commonplace amongst our Hawaiian family but socially taboo in our haole world, and thus unmentionable. Perhaps learning something about those men in those lives could have illuminated things about my mother and the forces that had shaped her.

Had Grandma Rosa lived longer after my few visits to her in Honolulu, I'd have gone back and invited her to reminisce about the men she'd loved. I was at that stage in life where I was taking lovers, so would have been interested in her experience and counsel. I'd have asked her about Henderson, but I'd not have tarried on him. I'd have wanted to move on to George Rosa, who my mother loved so much that she christened her first son George. It was always George Rosa who Grandma Rosa planned to lie beside in the cemetery beneath Diamond Head in Honolulu, and it is there that she is buried. Though I have no blood relationship with George Rosa, I lay a flower on his gravestone when I visit Grandma Rosa's grave, with gratitude, because he made Rosalie happy.

But most of all I'd want to learn about my grandfather Clarence Young, because I carry his genes. His personality no doubt determined my mother's, and so ultimately helped shape mine. We were never encouraged to follow the tendrils of our ancestry back through time to help us know ourselves better. Clarence Young was a non-entity to me, so when I finally accepted him as an ancestor, I was forced to recalibrate my dominant racial identity from Pacific Islander to Asian. Even here, putting that on paper, I am averse to embracing the Chinese in my blood, but I give myself a pass for coming so late to this seemingly obvious realization, and to resisting it. The men who brought Chinese blood to our line were not revered. I was brought up as Hawaiian and haole. Once I realized that my mother was seventy-five percent Chinese, the next and obvious realization was that I too am less Hawaiian than I'd believed. That the full complement of our racial mix was never explained, or that we were expected to figure it out without being walked through it, is like the way adults don't explain sex to children and trust that one way or another they will learn it on their own.

As dominating as Clarence Young's genetic input may be, it at least is something I can quantify. What I cannot measure is the emotional residue of this man who's been "ghosted" by his family. His legacy is abandonment. My mother couldn't tell us about Clarence Young without having to disclose the disgrace of that legacy. My parents were very strait-laced Catholics and would have never seen the value of transparency. Did my mother suspect that, as we grew more worldly, we'd begin comparing our grandparents Clarence and Grandma Rosa, and her grandparents Waipuilani and Sun Akana Wong? Did she fear that we'd realize how closely Clarence Young's serial monogamy and progeny maps to Sun Akana Wong's? I've always believed she feared that we'd accept it as a cultural and family pattern or take it as a model for our own behaviors. Or, just as bad, that we might let the story out of the shadows, which I would do here, were I privy to anything more concrete than my speculation.

Whatever my mother felt about her father, she used his surname name Young until her marriage, when she assumed my father's name. After that she still occasionally squeezed the name Young between her baptismal name

Mildred and her married surname. I was never curious what the Young represented and didn't realize that it was a Chinese name – that in fact Young is as common a name among Chinese as Smith is among haole. Children go with what is accessible to them. In our town there was a family with the name Young who were decidedly not Chinese. Bob and Jean Young played bridge at our house, went to our church, and had a stocky, bespectacled son in my sister's class. I identified the name Young with them, not with a Chinese man who was my long-lost grandfather.

Among the Honolulu-based Youngs related to Clarence, my mother kept in touch with a few. She referred to them as "uncle," which I'd assumed was a generic honorific, in the way that Hawaiians call adults "uncle" and "auntie." I knew that she had brothers, which meant I had actual uncles, but I only knew them as names that appeared on her Christmas card list: Larry Young and Valentine Young. I don't recall seeing that we got cards back from them. If we had, they'd have been taped across a mirror with all the others – Christmas cards were a process in those days, and lists were cultivated based on who returned cards, so we scanned the array of new arrivals every day and inventoried them.

Staying in touch with faraway friends and family was challenging in those times. In the days when I was traveling for business my mother insisted that I call or visit anyone to whom we were remotely acquainted, were I nearby, but she never suggested that I visit anyone with the name Young during my trips to O'ahu. I learned that when my parents went back to Hawai'i they regularly got together with her brothers Larry and Val. I wished I would have too, but I did not have enough background about them to know that I should.

One of those Youngs, my Uncle Larry, died when my mother was in her eighties and deep in her own struggle with cancer. I felt the poignancy of her losing her brother while her own death loomed. It was my first inkling of the mortality of our family, that a whole line of interrelated persons would take with them a trove of shared experience that was theirs alone, never to be remembered by anyone but them. I realized that forces beyond their making had kept them from being close, but that those same forces had also kept them close.

*O'ahu, circa 1970: My Grandma Rosa,
whose floral name Rosalie Rosa I found so charming*

The one with whom my mother remained closest was her mother, Grandma Rosa. I loved my mother most when she was talking about her mother, so I loved Grandma Rosa too, immediately and unreservedly, from the minute I met her. She came to visit us in Wisconsin in 1963, when I was sixteen. She taught me how to knit and I was thrilled to be learning something from her, in the way my friends had learned sewing or baking from their grandmothers. I would always have this skill, I promised myself, and I still knit sweaters to this day. Shortly after she left to go back to Hawai'i, President John F. Kennedy was assassinated. Like everyone across our nation, we spent five days crammed in our family room around the television, back in the days when most households had just one. It was perhaps the only time when all seven of us settled together for more than a meal. Through those dark hours watching the funeral in black and white, I knit away, producing a sweater for my youngest brother Dennis, who was in kindergarten. I made it of a hideous pistachio-green yarn that I cannot imagine having had any part in selecting. He wore it with nonchalance, the way little kids do, unaware of its ugly color. The memory of Grandma Rosa's leathery brown hand laid over my clumsy fingers, guiding the needle point into the loop, wrapping the yarn around and pulling it through, was knit into every stitch.

Looking back on my childhood without grandpas and grandmas, I feel cheated in not having had them. I want to believe they would have steadied my thoughts and given me ballast in when I felt lifted off center, like a boat that is listing. Despite Grandma Rosa's physical absence, I was informed and molded by my mother's everyday honoring of her. This was not nothing, but it wasn't the warm presence of direct experience. I could have benefited from time with my grandmother Elizabeth, who was only seventy-five miles away, but my mother's hatred of her precluded discovery of her as a comforting, nurturing presence. Of her I recall only the stress of getting ready for her arrival and the rage my mother unleashed after she'd left. Elizabeth died when I was in my thirties, years before I realized how much I'd wanted to know her.

But the grandmothers of our family were at least somewhere where we could, if we wanted, get to them. The grandfathers were gone. Whether dead or alive, they were not accessible. My father's father Hugo disappeared during the Great Depression, when my father was a child, deserting his wife Elizabeth and their four young children in the worst of times. He was like a stone that dropped in a lake and sank, leaving no trace. Thus, my father's father was as much an unmentionable as my mother's father. What happened to these men can now be ascertained on the internet, but what is revealed is data without dimension. They hadn't been in my parents' sphere, nor in mine, when they could have meant something, so I have chosen not to so belatedly invest in trying to sense their humanity.

Chapter 14

Aloha in a Bowl

My appreciation for grandmothers, and realization of my need for them, began emerging in my late twenties. I'd had my first child and wished I could offer him the kind of intergenerational nurturing that I'd so longed for. As yet unaware of the family pattern, I unknowingly fell into perpetuating it for another cycle: my son's grandparents were geographically and psychologically distant on both maternal and paternal sides.

Up to the time I had settled into mothering, I'd lived large in New York City, Los Angeles, and San Francisco, after a stint in Turkey in the Peace Corps, a year hitchhiking through Europe, and van-camping through Spain and North Africa. I'd been skiing in Vermont, biking on Nantucket, and hiking in the Rockies. Finally, after settling into the San Francisco Bay Area, I'd befriended a Hawaiian family who helped me to get hired in the San Francisco office of a historic and prestigious Hawaiian company with operations in sugar, shipping, and resort development. I began learning the basics of Hawaiian history, beyond what I'd gleaned from Michener's novel.

Though I was communicating with my company's Honolulu home office many times each day, I wasn't communicating with my family there. I hadn't seen Grandma Rosa since she'd come to Wisconsin in 1963 and I felt sheepish for going around the world but not getting to Hawai'i. Though flights to Honolulu had become affordable and convenient, I still felt constrained by my childhood scripting to avoid going to the islands. But when my company suggested that I go to Maui to look at their resort developments and sugar operations, and then to Honolulu to meet home office managers in their historic building on Bishop Street, the door to time with Grandma Rosa swung open. I packed my bags.

ARRIVING IN HAWAI'I IS INSTANT IMMERSION INTO everything you were enticed to expect. You feel it even before disembarking the plane, after the long flight over the Pacific. It is the glimpses of topaz ocean edged by the white froth of waves as the plane lowers itself. It is the elation in the cabin, the collective sense of the dream of a tropical getaway about to come true. The beauty of Hawai'i arrives in layered sensations: the fragrant air, the lilting music, the feel of the soft breeze, the realization that everyone is relaxed and smiling. It is so true that to say it is almost trite. Why had I gone to Russia and Morocco instead of rushing here, I wondered. Walking through Honolulu airport's roofless terminals, I sponged up the happiness of fellow passengers, many already festooned with lei, their sandaled feet showing off fresh pedicures. I came to the taxi queues where a driver in a salmon-hued aloha shirt held up a placard with my name. This gesture from my company disarmed whatever residue of my haole diffidence not yet dissolved. Arriving at my beachfront hotel, I took a lift to my fifteenth-floor room, slipped out of travel clothes, ordered fresh pineapple spears from room service, opened the sliding doors, and stepped onto the balcony. The sounds of ease and enjoyment wafted up from tourists bobbing in the fabled ocean swells while poolside loungers sipped on drinks delivered from the bar. It was picture-perfect, just as the brochures had depicted.

I spent the next few days in my company's headquarters, a stately building that is listed on the National Register of Historic Places. I liked being in a space that had been so conscientiously designed to meld Western and Asian cultures, starting with the circular Chinese symbol of good luck over the main entrance portico. The building was constructed in 1929, a few years after my mother was born, and a few years before the start of the Great Depression. I'd learned during travel through Europe to apply historical time markers to where I was on the map, and I began cross-referencing Hawaiian milestones with what my mother and grandmother – I'd not yet "met" Waipuilani – were doing during those events. I'd already begun exploring their experience relative to each other, and relative to me.

After a few days in the office, I checked out a company car and took a day off to visit my Grandma Rosa. She lived at the home of her eldest daughter in Pearl City, a sprawling flatland of about fifty thousand people in an area that had once been rice paddies. Driving there on the West Oʻahu freeway, I passed the Aloha Bowl, the airport, and signs to Pearl Harbor. I glimpsed the grand, pink Tripler Army Medical Center commanding the hillside, an icon of military patronage. I turned into an area of cookie-cutter homes, most built in the 1950s, many lifted off the ground on stilts. Each was hemmed in by driveways along the sides and fronted with rectangular patches of prickly, yellow-greenish grass. I found the place, a beige bungalow on a street crammed four or five cars per house, reflecting O'ahu's claim to having the nation's highest percentage of three and four generations of family living under one roof. I found a place to park half a block away and walked back.

At the doorstep, as I raised my hand to knock, Grandma Rosa emerged from the rear of the house. She'd been picking mangoes from the neighbor's tree and cradled two fruit in her cupped hands. She wore a soft dress patterned with pale yellow flowers in the muʻumuʻu style introduced to Hawaiians by missionaries. Her gray hair was gathered into a loose bun. She greeted me as if my coming were a regular thing, but her eyes were warm and searching, taking in everything about me. She ushered me past the screened-in lanai to a small kitchen that smelled savory with a simmering pot of long rice soup made with chicken and rehydrated shitake mushrooms. I wondered if this was the homecoming meal that she made for my mother when she came back to Oʻahu. I told Grandma Rosa that my mother made this same soup every time she returned to Wisconsin from Hawaiʻi, as though trying to keep the islands close for a bit longer.

Grandma Rosa shuffled about the tiny kitchen, ladling the soup into a bowl, and chopping scallion greens to toss over the top. Her low voice rasped from years of smoking unfiltered cigarettes, but in the inflection of her speech I recognized the Hawaiian lilt my mother occasionally slipped into, usually when she was talking about Grandma Rosa. I watched her, I listened to her, and I melted in a wash of love. I told her how my brother and I had recoiled from the squiggly transparent noodles the first time our mother brought them back from Honolulu. Those "Chinese vermicelli" and the waxy red anthurium flowers atop their spindly, leafless stems were our evidence that Hawaiʻi was alien and exotic, a place we'd have to experience if we were ever to understand our mother. Grandma Rosa passed the bowl of soup to me, then served herself, sat down, and we ate together.

My plan to ask Grandma Rosa about her childhood fell to the side as I let the singular simplicity of having a bowl of soup with her settle into my soul. I took refuge in her questions about my children and work and travel, letting our conversation skim here and there like a water strider on the surface of a pond. If I'd kept to my agenda, perhaps I'd have learned about Waipuilani years earlier than coming upon her by chance in my sixties. I'd hoped Grandma Rosa could segue from her young years to my mother's, which would hopefully lead to the marriages and divorces, the children of many fathers who'd lived under her roof, and how they'd all managed. But I remained in the spell of the precious present until she stood to serve us seconds. I nudged myself to probe for what I'd come to discover, but then I melted again, watching her lift her bowl to her chin, work her chopsticks, and slurp the broth. I noticed that her fingers were shaped like my mother's, as were the planes of her face. That visual information, and that soup, was enough for that day.

Knowing my auntie would be home before long, I rose to be on my way. I wanted to remember this time as just mine with Grandma Rosa in her kitchen. Before I left, she pared one of the mangoes, showing me how to peel and slice the fibrous, syrupy pulp, and we ate it with our fingers. I promised to come back another day and we could go to the Pali. I wanted to hear her stories, layer upon layer of them, the details I sought emerging organically, without my list of questions. She would see that her stories lifted my confusion. I would hold them in a way that was clean and clarifying, free of the 1950s Catholic moniker "broken" for families like ours. She'd coped, found her way, as an intermittently single mother without the paycheck or career that my generation expected as a woman's birthright. Perhaps she'd crossed certain lines, as I'd overheard when I was too young to understand what that could mean. I would never ask her about that, or about anything that would cause defense. I just wanted to watch her ladling soup into my bowl while I melted in unconditional love, making up for all the years when I hadn't had her.

Carrying the second mango back to my hotel, after Grandma Rosa had pressed it into my hands and reminded me how to peel it, I felt my mother's love for her mother flow through me and blend with mine, like two rivers joining in confluence. Slowed by the rush hour stop and go on Honolulu's H-1 highway, I had time to reflect on how spontaneously the love had flowed between Grandma Rosa and me, and how awkwardly I felt stuck at the periphery of the rest of our ohana. My mother had tried to shield us from aspects of this culture that she understood well. Despite her isolation and homesickness during all those years in the Midwest, she'd never been sentimental about Hawai'i. Sitting there in Honolulu traffic, inching along, I experienced that there was love in her attempts to protect us, attempts I'd always seen as darkly secretive and small-minded. She'd continually curated what to share and what to withhold about practices that she called "island style," and at the core of that was Grandma Rosa. She had loved my father and us children, but above all she had loved her mother. Everything she said about Hawai'i was, at root, to safeguard the dignity of her mother.

My mother longed to be with Grandma Rosa on the Other Side and often said, in the months before she succumbed to cancer, that Grandma Rosa was talking to her in her dreams, guiding her home. On my mother's last day, I tucked the phone on the pillow behind her ear when Auntie Jan called to say farewell. In fluid Hawaiian, the language of their youth, Jan was telling her dying sister that their mother was waiting to take her home, and that Jan would be not far behind.

IN THE YEARS BETWEEN VISITING GRANDMA ROSA IN 1973 and learning about Waipuilani in 2012, I had entered full-fledged adulthood. I'd passed through the phases of marriage, motherhood, career, divorce, empty nesting, and had negotiated the groping passages between each stage. I'd lived enough life to be able to see the arc and dominant themes of my existence.

Realizing that if I were writing my life story, the half-dozen trips I'd taken to Hawai'i by that time would be significant in the narrative scaffolding, so I resolved to go back and delve deeper. I wanted to write essays about the islands with an external, expository focus. Shaping anything more personal would require help from people who desired to see the stories told. At the time, in the 1990s, interest in talk story was avid, a result of Hawaiian cultural awareness and activism. I longed to sit around the proverbial fire, talking into the night, feeling ohana bonds tighten in the ways of tribes and kinspeople, getting lost in the exchange between open-hearted telling and appreciative listening. The essence of story plays to an ancient drive to archive our legends, to our longing for enchantment, to our hunger to be lifted into another's experience, and to be transported into another time and place. It is a kind of spell casting. In its artful thrall everyone, even if momentarily, surrenders. I had fallen into the talk story spell, for example, when we were gathered around the family chart, and it was said that Grandma Rosa had been one of the most beautiful women in Lahaina. I hadn't heard this before and had no way to know if it was true, but I wanted to believe it, so I chose to believe it, and then fell under the spell of her fabled beauty. This is how it works.

Having grown up with so little family lore, I hoped to discover and give it voice for descendants who'd grown up on the mainland, far from a felt sense of what it means to be Hawaiian. Given context, these tales might shed light on ancestral experiences that influence our present-day behaviors. I went to Oʻahu hoping for talk story to illuminate this inheritance, despite what I called the Family Firewall. I was able to unearth only a few verifiable bits and pieces, all of them commonly known. Nevertheless, I appreciated each of them to validate or disprove my body of conjecture. And, though frustrating, the lack of discourse and fact checking with my island ohana, apart from sessions with Auntie Jan, allowed me much imaginative freedom. In deep obeisance to our ancestors, I reined in that freedom by sifting and winnowing what I could access across intuitive, digital, and analytic planes.

This I know for sure: the Hawaiʻi of my great-grandmother's time, though remote and seemingly unworldly, was already global. My grandmother was born into a cosmopolitan world, and my mother lived in the midst of the international collaboration and conflict called World War II. Globalization opened the door for young Hawaiian women to marry men outside their caste, though it was not a free-for-all. For many, miscegenation between the Kānaka Maoli and the caste of haole missionaries and entrepreneurs remained *kapu*, forbidden. There were exceptions, sometimes at the highest levels, such as the 1850 marriage of Charles Reed Bishop, an American businessman, and Bernice Pauahi, an *aliʻi* from the Royal Family of the Kingdom of Hawaiʻi. But women of Waipuilani's caste had few opportunities to cross paths with haole men who might be inclined to marry them. However, there was a plethora of Chinese men who seemed ambitious, determined to elevate their standing in the island economy, and eager to marry island women.

Having made a rational case for why a Kānaka Maoli woman would partner with a Chinese man, based on practical and situational imperatives, I began to wonder whether, *a priori*, they'd felt an innate impetus to strengthen their bloodline through miscegenation. The plausibility of this arose during a wide-ranging discussion with Micah Kamohoaliʻi, who longtime friends in the Kohala district of the Big Island had arranged for me to meet over lunch. Micah is a Hawaiian scholar, artist and designer, a teacher of Hawaiian language, and a renowned *kumu hula* (master of the hula arts). We hoped that Micah could give insight into why Kānaka Maoli women, going back to the original Polynesian voyagers who'd landed on Hawaiʻi Island between 300-600 CE, had moved from there to other districts or islands.

Micah is a mesmerizing storyteller and I quickly fell into his spell. He told of how when he was newborn his grandmother had claimed him to be the bearer of, and to carry forward, their clan knowledge of rituals, arts, lore, and genealogy. She'd taught him to chant the names of hundreds of their lineage back to the first arrivals on Hawai'i Island. I asked Micah, whose clan has deep roots in the sacred Waipi'o Valley, what had prompted the ancient mothers to go elsewhere when Hawai'i Island had abundant water, land, and conditions to grow food?

He let the question settle while our server brought plates of locally sourced produce and seafood that had been caught that morning on the boats at the nearby Kawaihae harbor. We took a moment of pause for appreciative silence imbued with the Hawaiian reverence for food, a pause of gratitude that I'd noticed seems to arise naturally over Hawaiian meals. After a few bites, he put down his fork and began telling of how the Kānaka Maoli lived, attuned to what came up from the earth and fell from the sky. They were completely self-sustaining, which is both a strength and a vulnerability. Living so intimately with the elements, their instincts were astute. The mothers left one Hawaiian district or island to go to another, Micah suggested, to strengthen their bloodline. That they were driven to do so is a mother's instinctual imperative.

IN THE MID-1960S, AROUND THE TIME I WAS A WISCONsin teen fancying myself a student at the University of Hawai'i's East-West Center, a movement called the Hawaiian Cultural Renaissance began advocating for the return and preservation of the Kānaka Maoli language and traditions, much of which was near extinction. Their call was urgent and strident, coming on the heels of Hawaiian admission to statehood in 1959. At twelve years old, from so far away, I would never have heard the anguished voices of the Renaissance. The celebration of statehood was all that was conveyed to us mainlanders. The newsreels that came across our black and white television were the first nationwide media attention I remember being paid to Hawaiʻi. The brouhaha over statehood enabled me to see Hawaiʻi as something beyond the narrow context of my mother's origins, or the site of the bombing of Pearl Harbor. Watching the statehood celebrations with their surfeit of lei, speeches, and parades, I never questioned that this was anything but a good thing. Much was made of the challenge to reconfigure the American flag to work in that fiftieth star. Businessmen who'd lobbied hard for statehood began planning investments. The only holdouts, a group of southern state politicians who'd held up statehood for over a decade, feared giving Hawaiians, who were not considered white, the right to vote. They worried that this would trigger agitation among people of color in the American South who'd been denied their constitutional[19] right to vote.

Although Hawaiian statehood would come with advantages like representation and equality under American law, many Hawaiians believed that Hawaiians were trading away too much for too few benefits. Others welcomed the end of the ambiguity of U.S. territory "protection" and the chance to vote for Hawaiians to represent their interests in Washington. Through all the ambivalence was a practical and widespread hope that statehood would bring more prosperity for all Hawaiians. Though the arguments of those opposing statehood were drowned out for a time, their enduring fervor helped pull Hawaiian language, music, crafts, dance, beliefs, and rituals back from the brink of extinction.

Chapter 15

Why'd He Have to Go?

Waipuilani gave birth to her fifth child, a second son named Amana, in 1905. Their first son, Ah Lee, was ten years old when his little brother Amana arrived, and Sun Akana Wong was approaching sixty. He'd been a Hawaiian citizen for nearly forty years, and the auspicious birth of this latest son signaled his time to return to his homeland. He'd left behind sons who were young boys when he'd departed for Hawai'i. He'd promised to return and wanted to honor that intention, even so many years later than he'd expected. Until his sons with Waipuilani were old enough to take with him to China, he established a home apart from her so he could raise their sons in the traditional ways of his homeland. Perhaps other factors played into his separation. We know from public records that Makatu and Waipuilani married in Lahaina in 1907, when they were both thirty-five and Amana was just two years old. Grandma Rosa must have reminisced about her father, because Auntie Jan told me that Sun Akana Wong was a loving presence for Rosalie and her sisters. He died in China in 1923, two years before my mother was born. Records show that Amana Wong lived most of his ninety-plus years in the Hawaiian Islands. My mother must have known him as I have a wispy recollection of her mentioning an Uncle Amana. In the Hawaiian language *amana* means crosspiece, or connection, a fitting moniker for this boy who may have been his father's last direct tie between the Hawaiian Islands and China.

Considering how little I know about Sun Akana Wong, I have many opinions about him. Though they are complex, I hold them loosely, aware that they are based on sketchy, unverifiable information. I judge that he took on too much, with three serial monogamies – two of them Hawaiian – and fathering the nine children that I know of. He stayed with Waipuilani until their older children were adolescent, which is a tick in the plus column. But the resources that he would have expended taking his sons to China would have deprived Waipuilani of access to their savings, a share of income, and the myriad other ways that having men and boys supports a family. I do not doubt that the lives of the women and children that Sun Akana Wong left behind were harder because he'd left them. In those days before family support laws and entitlement programs helped abandoned women, Waipuilani would have had no recourse except asking any ohana who was willing to extend a hand.

I have struggled with resentment over the abandonment of Waipuilani and Grandma Rosa and their daughters. They were left in intractable poverty while the sons were given a path toward prosperity. I remind myself that these things that supposedly occurred took place long ago, yet I feel them as acutely as if they were recent. I believe that the intergenerational impact of abandonment affects me and my children, to this day. The residual effects of ancestral trauma often show up in the form of baffling behaviors and unexplainable patterns seen repeating in our children's lives.

Without knowing our origin stories, are we doomed to live as endless permutations of what happened to our ancestors, unaware of the invisible forces that keep infusing them into the present as inexplicable hot buttons, senses of *deja vu*, biases, and mental illness? I have no doubt that Sun Akana Wong leaving with the boys left an imprint on Rosalie – they were her father and brothers, after all. Consciously or not, she'd have passed emotional residue from their departure on to my mother, who likely passed some of it on to me.

I admit to having much antipathy toward the Chinese. It seems always to have been in me, but I do not blindly acquiesce to it. I've tried to trace it back to a memory or an early negative experience. There were no Chinese people or communities in my Midwestern childhood. My mother was the only Chinese person I'd been exposed to, but I didn't perceive her as Chinese until I was grown. I've found that most individual Chinese persons with whom I've interacted – generally in Chinatown markets and other commercial situations – were rigid and charmless, but I did not actively dislike them. My dislike is directed toward the Chinese political and military leadership that I've been exposed to through reading and media.

After watching the 1972 televised arrival of President Richard Nixon in the People's Republic of China, I read everything I could about this nation that had been sealed off in iron-clad isolation since 1949. Nixon's breakthrough exposed the Chinese Red Army's cruelty to Chinese citizens: the soul-destroying suffering and starvation of "re-education" camps, the destruction of literary and artistic treasures, and other wanton acts of human and cultural annihilation. I understood that terrified people without enough to eat do not develop charm or a proclivity toward niceties. As a Buddhist practitioner, I was deeply affected by the Dalai Lama's narrow escape from Tibet in 1959 as his homeland and countrymen were tortured and subsumed into the boundaries of Chinese proper. Images of the 1989 protests in Tiananmen Square, the 2020 student demonstrations in Hong Kong, and the persecution of twelve million Uyghur Muslims, have fortified my abhorrence for Chinese transgressive behaviors. I've tried to resolve my aversion by making brief stopovers in Beijing, Guangzhou, and a few other Chinese cities as part of other itineraries, but I was disturbed by the robotic compliance and aura of fear that seemed to propel workers in the hotels and airports. What was the fear: of the return of hunger, of surveillance, of being caught at something forbidden – a word I heard a lot in China – and disappearing? I was so sensitized to this ambient unease that, during a three-day layover in Beijing with my son, I stayed in the hotel rather than accompany him on tours of the Bird's Nest stadium, the Great Wall, and other attractions.

From what deeply shadowy realm of my psyche came this animus? When it slowly began revealing itself, it seemed easy to ascribe it to my mother. But I could not remember anything toxic about her feelings for the Chinese, nor any bias akin to things she'd said about Hawaiians. The only thing she consistently mentioned about the Chinese was their acumen with money – specifically, their skill in penny-pinching. She was proud of her own ability to snag a bargain that others had missed. She often left tags dangling from a rock-bottom-priced article she'd found, pointing out how one price after another had been crossed out in red pen, each one lower than the one before. She'd leave such tags attached to gifts to convey how cleverly she'd acquired such a treasure at such a reduced cost. She saw it as outsmarting everyone, rather than that she'd settled for something that everyone else had rejected.

Looking back, realizing that my mother's sartorial choices for herself and us children were always a bit more fashionable and unique, against the bland midwestern aesthetic, I ascribe those markdowns as the gift of people too timid to take the style chances that my mother considered fresh and forward-leaning. And I see that much of the frugality that embarrassed me, like her packing our school lunches in (then rare) plastic bags, then washing and hanging them on the clothesline for reuse because she thought it wasteful to toss brown bags, were recycling in the way we now support to mitigate climate change.

In my argumentative adolescence, when I wanted to be indistinguishable from the other kids at school, I urgently wanted my mother to be like the other mothers. Midwestern women were frugal, but they didn't wear the trait as a badge of honor like my mother. I wanted her to take it off. I pointed out that obsession for the lowest cost didn't signify greater intelligence, but was merely an adaptation to the fact that the Chinese had always been starving. We heard this cliche when we didn't like food put before us: "think of the starving kids in China." But she would never engage in the whys of any situation. This was one of the few contexts in which her defenses about being Chinese relaxed, but only within our family walls. She was well aware of American distrust and negativity toward the Chinese. Though Wisconsin was one of only nine states without active anti-miscegenation laws at that time, the Chinese Exclusion Act had been repealed less than ten years before she'd arrived in Wisconsin, and she understood that she was one of the 'undesirable elements'[20] the act had intended to bar from entering the United States.

CONTINUING MY IMAGINED CONVERSATION WITH Waipuilani, reaching over a century of time to sit on her doorstep at the edge of Lahaina, I would tell her that I liked what she'd said about us all being beautiful, no matter what our make-up, but that I'd had a hard time figuring out where I fit in. I'd always wanted to feel that I belonged somewhere, though I'd loved my life going here and there to experiment where that might be. She would say that she never had the freedom to go places, as I had. She'd only gone one place, but that was like going to a different world. She'd had to adapt to survive. I would tell her that hearing her name for the first time was like getting a key to the treasury that held all the things I needed to keep alive. I'd spent so many childhood hours listening in on my mother talking on the phone to her sisters. They were all trying to keep something alive. I believe what they were keeping alive was their memories of home. And their linkage to their home was their mother, Grandma Rosa.

Calling Grandma Rosa, in the days before transoceanic cables and digital rates, was as expensive as calling Europe. My mother would calculate the long-distance charges and call Grandma Rosa at odd hours when the rates were low. It was still a hefty chunk of her budget, but she scrimped (the word she always used) where she could. She baked bread rather than buying it, and she reused tea leaves until they barely flavored the hot liquid. She slaved in the August heat canning peaches and home-grown garden tomatoes over boiling hot water baths, all to save a few pennies toward another call to Grandma Rosa. She was the touchstone, the anchor to what was slipping from my mother's and her sisters' grasp, a loss they had consciously set in motion and could never undo.

If you'd walked through my childhood home, a classic white, two-story clapboard Wisconsin house on a shady street of towering elm trees, you'd have seen few Hawaiian artifacts. Considering their source and significance, they did not seem precious to us. There was no consecrated altar where they could be admired and protected, so they landed almost callously on a shelf or in a cupboard. The treasures that were too highly valued – Grandma Rosa's hand quilted spread of red anthuriums in a mass of green stems, and a 24-carat gold bangle bracelet with tiny green jade insets – were hidden away and rarely brought out. The other more mundane artifacts were not protected or elevated. On the floor at the foot of an armchair was a steel-gray, lava-rock poi pounder that was special to my brother George and went to him when our parents died. We had a few long-playing records of Hawaiian songs that grew dusty until my mother needed them to dance hula at a church bazaar or school fair, which was also when her cellophane "grass" skirts and red satin tube tops came out of their trunk, smelling like moth balls and mildew. A dried lei, with its string nakedly exposed as its once-vibrant blooms dried and shrank into a uniform shade of ecru, was looped around a sepia-toned photo of my parents on their wedding day. We propped the Christmas cards that arrived from Honolulu, posted weeks in advance to get to us on time, on a side table in the living room and laughed at their images of snowmen under palm trees and hula girls with Santa hats surfing in the waves. Everyone knew the song Bing Crosby and the

Andrews Sisters recorded in 1950 about *Mele Kalikimaka* being "Merry Christmas in the old Hawaiian Way," so folks understood the meaning of Mele Kalikimaka my mother wrote in red lipstick across the living room mirror. For years I assumed this was a Hawaiian custom because no one else I knew wrote on a mirror with lipstick.

Apart from those few icons and festive gestures, my mother let out something about "home" only when some annoying thing about Wisconsin contrasted with how much better they did things in Hawaiʻi – a universal impetus for people who've relocated from one country, or even town, to another. During the years when I practiced piano scales and Bach Inventions over and over, she spoke wistfully of the Hawaiian way to make music spontaneously, without lessons, everyone strumming ukulele and singing, as if they lived inside a Rogers & Hammerstein musical. To me these observations implied criticism and were discouraging. But they also were a glimpse into her memories and provided starting points for imagining what Hawaiʻi was like. Ever present in those pictures was Grandma Rosa. Missing her mother was probably worse because my mother needed her. She had no help in Wisconsin. She was exhausted by five kids, loneliness, culture shock and, I suspect, depression.

But my mother always had my father, a gentle man who was steadfast. He must have seemed a paragon of virtue to her after growing up in a world of absentee fathers. My father put in the vegetable garden, mowed the lawn, and changed the storm windows as the seasons changed. He wallpapered rooms and installed paneling and added a carport to the back of our house. He did his chores cheerfully and conscripted my brothers to help. He was emotionally distant, though I never felt that he was uncaring. My parents had strong convictions about sticking it out and breaking the pattern of fatherless families. Yet I never heard her blame Grandma Rosa or the men who'd abandoned them. She accepted the instability of Hawaiian families as an endemic characteristic rather than a moral shortcoming, a response and adaptation rather than a capitulation.

Chapter 16

What's in a Name?

My mother was born in February, 1925 to Clarence and Rosalie Young. Like their other children, Rosalie baptized her Catholic. I would like to know how Catholicism came to our family, and when its hooks were set hard and how they maintained their grip. My mother was a practicing Catholic to her grave, as are my Hawaiian cousins. My father was also raised Catholic, meaning that our household revolved around the Catholic routines of Saturday confession, Sunday Mass, Holy Days of Obligation, and Lenten sacrifices. My mother asserted Catholic beliefs and practices with more intention than she presented her Hawaiian and Chinese heritage; Catholicism was our culture.

My parents contributed more volunteer time and tithing to the church than they could probably afford, particularly toward a new roof for the church and the construction of a parochial elementary school so we could be educated by nuns. A years-long parish dream realized, the school opened when I was in sixth grade, a most inopportune time for a young girl to have to change schools. I went with resistance. I felt like someone had pressed a searing iron into my forehead, another branding mark to keep me from integrating into the worlds I wanted to enter. I fully hated the nuns with their self-effacing garments, groveling deference to priests, the institutionalized gender inequity, and that being in a Catholic school caused friends from public school to pull away.

But Catholicism also left me with a lifelong penchant for mysticism, ritual, and appreciation for Latin, choral music, and sacred iconography. I still attend Christmas Eve Midnight Mass if there is a nearby cathedral that will stage it with the pageantry that is the Catholic Church's grand performance art. I still wish I'd been able to wear a white surplice, as my brothers did, and carry a tall candle down an aisle clouded with incense while everyone mumbled prayers in Latin. Nevertheless, I shed the dogma of Catholicism as soon as I left home and have never had an urge to return. Lately, however, when people ask about my background, I include that I grew up Catholic. It seems as dominant a formative force as saying I am Chinese. I wince to have to own both identities. I have as strong an antipathy to the Catholic church as I have to the Chinese government, but I accept the seen and unseen grip of both as integral to who I am.

AS MY CHILDREN APPROACHED ADOLESCENCE IN THE MID 1990s and I began thinking about how they would navigate the minefield of multi-racial identity, I came across the author Amy Tan's novel, *The Joy Luck Club*, published in 1989[21]. I was wholly unprepared for the ways the author's tale of conflict between China-born mothers and their American-born daughters described my relationship with my mother. Meeting those fictional mothers with the same harsh, abrasive traits as my own mother, I realized that my mother was a stereotype. I was overwhelmed with recognition and revulsion mixed with sorrow and compassion, knowing I'd tried since childhood to reconcile those

"Chinese mother" traits with the flowing, lilting Hawaiian personality that occasionally floated to the surface of my mother's persona. I loved that Hawaiian side of her, the part that had charm. But just as often she'd flip into the off-putting personality Tan describes as hyper-critical, controlling, unaffectionate, manipulative, and devaluing. From this book I learned about the generational hunger, fear, and cruelty dominating centuries of Chinese poverty and autocratic leadership. I learned that Chinese culture does not traditionally value girl babies. Because they are not sons, they are a disappointment from the moment they enter the world. Often, throughout history, the family goal was to find a way to off-load them.

Putting down the Amy Tan book, I felt wedged in the deep schism between my mother's two dominant cultures. The Chinese part of my psyche was critical of myself that it had taken until so late in life to understood all I'd learned from this book. The Hawaiian part of me felt sorrow that I'd never felt precious in the way of Hawaiian children, regardless of their gender or parentage. Feeling this sadness settled something within me, and eventually led to a sense of integration.

AS THE CENTURY CHANGED FROM THE 1900S TO 2000, my children were in high school and looking forward to leaving our home. Our society greeted the new millennium with what seems, by hindsight, a laughable fear of a worldwide "Y2K" meltdown because computers would fail to convert 999 to 000. We laughed it off, but my kids had grown up with other real traumas that we have now normalized, like the first major school shooting at Columbine.

From that point on, they told me years later, they'd lost faith that there were any safe places. I wondered if I'd prepared them with skills to cope with and assuage trauma. I'd been so busy raising them and making immediate memories for them – creating birthday parties, planning excursions to ski and to camp in the Utah Red Rock that was our regional treasure, and trips into cities so they could experience diversity – that I hadn't formulated an ancestral offering that would enrich and fortify them. There'd been a costume day at their Montessori school when they'd gone as hula dancers. Did that count? Every year we'd commemorate St. Patrick's Day by raising the green, orange, and white Irish flag on our deck to honor their father's Irish roots. Did that help them to know who they are?

Two of my children have Hawaiian names, though they'd been chosen more for their poetry and symbolic meaning than to bind them to their heritage. Over time their names were associated with other cultural hooks – Malia's with President Barack Obama's daughter by that name, Aja Ariel's with the Steely Dan album *Aja* and the Disney movie about a mermaid named Ariel, and my son Keone often triggering mention of the actor Keanu Reeve. Ethnic names became more commonplace as they grew into their teens, but in their childhood their names were as awkward and burdensome as my name Moana had been in mine. I was surprised that I'd not chosen plain and generic names for them. I witnessed that popular icons often deflected association of their names with their Hawaiian heritage, but I was comforted that my children had the internet and other tools to help them go deeper into their roots when they were ready. My role was to encourage curiosity.

One day, after returning from a trip to Hawai'i, I began mapping out my mother's many names. I had reached the limits of available concrete data about my ancestors, so I was looking for a new way into their story. I'd always been intrigued with how many names my mother had used. Each one corresponded to the timeline of her life's milestones. By the time I was born in 1947, she was Mildred Lillian Young Macheel, though everyone called her Norma. I'd never heard her called anything but Norma, though she signed papers and checks as Mildred. People occasionally noticed and asked her about these names, mainly because they were such unusual names for a Hawaiian. She'd explain, her face softening with a sweet memory, that during World War II Hawaiian girls made up names so the G.I.s they'd met at Honolulu's wartime social clubs couldn't trace or stalk them.

Honolulu, early 1940s: My mother, center, with her sisters (to her left) and cousins (to her right), and a cute puppy.

My mother had settled on the alias Norma, after Norma Shearer, who was a popular actress of those times. She introduced herself as Norma to the G.I.s at the skating rink, including the one she'd fall in love with and marry. He, my father, continued calling her Norma long after learning that her actual name was Mildred. Perhaps he'd just become used to calling her Norma, or perhaps this alias eliminated confusion with his older sister, who also had the name Mildred. I've often lamented that, given all the choices, my mother hadn't chosen a more lyrical name, like her childhood name Lillina.

Yes, *Lillina*. Not Lillian, as shows up in my mother's official string of names, probably the result of an uncorrected typo. This small transposition of an *a* and an *n* directly affected me, since she christened me Nina, a derivative of Lillina. I did not learn that my official name and my mother's childhood name were entwined until I was in my fifties. It was revealed during a phone call when my mother was getting her affairs in order, which is how we got onto the subject of names. She began reminiscing about her childhood name of Lillina, which the other children had trouble pronouncing, so had shortened to Nina. I was so stunned by this revelation, so off-handedly delivered, that I grabbed a pencil and began scribbling down what she was saying. I was afraid that later I'd think I'd imagined it.

Flabbergasted, I chided her. "Mother, if I'd given my daughter my name, she'd have begun hearing about it while still at the breast. She'd have grown up hearing me croon, 'Mommy loves you so much that I gave you my own name.' It would have been part of her known heritage, her felt sense of value, from Day One. How could you never have told me this?" She couldn't register that she hadn't told me, nor appreciate how the discovery had rocked my world. I was certain that, had I known this, it would have changed the course of our relationship, as it did from the moment that I learned of it. From then on, so late in my life, I began looking for the ways my mother and I were similar rather than all the ways that we weren't.

Hawaiians born after 1860, the year King Kamehameha IV signed the Hawaiian Act to Regulate Names, have had to manipulate and compromise their naming practices. Specifically, the Act took away their right to give their babies Hawaiian names and it required them to give Christian names. The Act did not spell out what made a name Christian – a mention in the Bible, or a saint with the name? Absent this, the people of Hawaii interpreted Christian to mean English. For over a century, until the Act's repeal in 1967, generations of Hawaiians went forth with alien-sounding names like Elizabeth, the one given to Waipuilani. Before then, a child's name would have been more lyrical, poetic, and imagistic, originating in the Hawaiian language and chosen by a Hawaiian kupuna based on auspicious traits, stars, and other portents surrounding the date of birth.

Even so, considering that there were some Christian names, such as Anna or Helena or Emma, that sounded somewhat Hawaiian, I am baffled that Grandma Rosa chose awkward, unseemly names (to my ear) for her daughters: Winnifred, Mildred, and Augusta. The name Mildred, for example, has two ds and an r, neither of which are in the Hawaiian alphabet. Even if Grandma Rosa had chosen the name from a book of saints, could she have found one more obscure than St. Mildred, a seventh century princess from Kent, the daughter of an Anglican ruler named Meerwald and his wife Ermenburga?

Given that the Christian name was often a throwaway name to comply with the law, when the family planned to use a Hawaiian name, perhaps it didn't matter that Mildred was an alien name. The key name was Lillina, the name bestowed by a kupuna in the old tradition. The child may not even have known that she had the other Christian name. Perhaps she'd only learn of it when her records were called up on her first day at school.

TALK STORY: *Lillina — early 1930s*

> Lillina could finally go to kindergarten. She'd turned five in February. Waiting so many months until September was hard. Every day her sisters went to school and she had to stay behind. On her first day she walked with her mother Rosalie to the plantation schoolhouse. Her older sister Winnie ran ahead while Rosalie took Lillina to stand in line to meet the teacher sitting at a wooden card table on the school's sagging porch. Lillina fidgeted. She reached out to pull curling, yellowing leaves from the leggy poinsettias growing wild against the weather-beaten rails. She could hear Winnie bossing the other children in the play yard.
>
> Lillina had never seen anyone like this person they were waiting to see. The woman's head seemed held to her neck by the stiff collar of her bright white blouse. Lillina tried to count the mother-of-pearl buttons arising from a place below the tabletop, climbing up and over the mound of bosom and ending at the waddle hanging from her chin. Lillina had never seen so many buttons. She'd never seen clothes that covered every inch of skin except hands and face. She stared and pulled back, but Rosalie squeezed her hand. It was their turn.
>
> "And this little girl is?" the woman asked, scanning her list without looking up.

Rosalie said their last name, "Young."

"Ah, Young. You must be Mildred."

Lillina froze and Rosalie glared. She'd written the forms to show Lillina, not Mildred, even though Mildred was in the registry.

"You. You are Mildred?" the teacher repeated. She looked up and fixed her eyes on Lillina's small, nut-brown face. She placed her hands flat on top of the papers on the table as though holding them down from a wind.

"No, I'm not," Lillina said, pulling back. She pressed against her mother's hip and rubbed the top of her bare foot against the calf of her opposite leg.

Rosalie nodded, unsure whether to appease the teacher or her child. She wanted to explain that Mildred was the haole name, but that " . . . this name is not right for her. Too big for this little girl." But she couldn't find the words to say that Lillina has never been called Mildred so could the teacher call her Lillina, even if it was not the name on her list? This child with tangles of wiry hair still carrying the sand and snarls of summer, this child who runs barefoot a quarter mile to the cane field ditch to collect water in a rusty tin to pour on the ti plants, this child who'd seen night watchers floating down from their cleft on the ridge to the swatch of light the full moon sprinkled across the ocean, this child was Lillina. But all Rosalie could manage to say was, "Her name is Mildred, but ohana call her Lillina, and keiki call her Nina."

"Mildred," the teacher said, looking directly at Lillina. "You can call me Mrs. Whimple. It says here your name is Mildred Lillian."

"No, not Lillian," Rosalie said. "Lillina."

Mrs. Whimple lowered her eyebrows into a frown that pushed a ridge of rubbery skin to the bridge of her nose. Lillina dreaded more fuss. A line of mothers and children waited behind them, and her sister Winnie had come back from the playground and pulled on her dress to get going.

"Lillian. Mildred Lillian." Mrs. Whimple tapped the roster, typewritten with smudging black ink and rough gray rub-outs. "It says Mildred Lillian."

The sun was heating up the day. Mrs. Whimple's face was beading with sweat. Her feet, stuffed into flesh-colored cotton hosiery, were swollen like boiled sausages. Lillina could see them under the table, sliding in and out of her leather pumps.

Rosalie did not have the will to cross Lillina's new teacher, to explain that the last two letters of Lillina had been transposed on the typewritten list, thus Anglicizing a Hawaiian name, or to point out that Hawaiian names usually ended with a vowel. "Call her Lillina," Rosalie said firmly, giving up on the rest of it. She met Lillina's eyes to let her know things would be alright. Mrs. Whimple swatted a fly from the roster and put a check beside the name Mildred on her list. She gestured for them to go inside and wait with the others.

They pushed through the screen door and stepped into the cool, dark hall. The maroon-colored linoleum floors gave off a waxy glare. A row of cubby holes lined one wall and a wooden bench freshly painted dark blue ran along the other. They sat next to another mother and her son, who scooted down to give them more room. Rosalie fanned herself with the registration form Mrs. Whimple had given her.

"We okay, ma? I not Mildred Lillian?"

"You are Lillina," Rosalie said. She fingered her daughter's dress, its yellow with pink flowers on green stems faded and soft from many washings. "Your cousin Vickie wore this on first day," she said. "Now Vickie first in her class, so this dress good luck."

Lillina sat swinging her legs, looking at the other children and their mothers as they entered the dimly lit space, peering uncertainly while orienting from the bright outdoors. She had worried that this school would be mostly haole kids and teachers like Mrs. Whimple. But the children they saw inside were like her – Hawaiians with a hapa dash of Filipino, Chinese, Korean, and Japanese. Their mothers were like Rosalie, proud and sassy in their worn, shapeless dresses. They were alike with their sun-leathered skin and bowed legs, in the way their thick toes gripped plastic slippers that slapped against their cracked heels with each step deeper into the school's cool corridor. They found a place to sit or stopped to talk to a friend with the pidgin that Lillina was used to: "Ey. You heah too? Crazy hot out der. Cool heah, yeah?" Except for Mrs. Whimple, school seemed just another gathering of people Lillina already knew from the store, the play yard, the church.

As the hall filled, the women leaned against the cool metal lockers and shushed their antsy children. They were all waiting for something – to go into the rooms, Lillina guessed. In time, the bell clanged. Mrs. Whimple stepped inside and clapped her hands to get everyone's attention, though she didn't need to. All eyes were already on her.

"Welcome to your first day of school this year," she said. "Children, look at the number at the top of your card and go to the room with that number."

She paused as the room erupted into murmurs and the rustling of papers.

"Mothers, you can help your child find the room

with their number. One through six. Point them in the right direction. And then, mothers, you can leave. We will keep them in that room until 2:00 this afternoon."

Lillina looked at Rosalie with panic.

"You go to number 1," Rosalie said. "And you find Winnie at end to walk home with. And you remember: you are Lillina, not let them call you Mildred."

Rosalie left with the other mothers and walked back to the tin-roofed Quonset hut at the far end of the cane fields where her two youngest children were waiting. The red dirt road was hot from the sun. Tall swaths of cane swished in the last of the morning breeze. Rosalie took her time, imagining her little girl standing up to that Mrs. Whimple, proud of her but hoping she would not make trouble. Her girls were afraid of nothing, not even cane spiders, some bigger than their hands. Except centipedes, she remembered, shuddering at the thought of them lurking in dark places, many as long and wide as a 6-inch ruler, ready to flip their fury into a bite that felt like liquid fire. Driving them from her thoughts, Rosalie thought back to how Lillina had held her ground with Mrs. Whimple: "I not Mildred. I am Lillina."

Passing Mrs. Yamamoto's gate, Rosalie waved at the old woman sweeping the dry, caramel-colored tamarind pods that had dropped from the ancient tree. She stooped to gather half a dozen and stuffed them into her pockets. Later she and the keiki would crack them open and work the tangy, sticky fruit loose from the fibers encasing the shiny black seed, puckering with the surprise of sour pulp. Then Lillina would go to the creek to fill the coffee cans with water for the *ti* plants. She'd still be her little Lillina.

The fictional teacher that Lillina encounters on her first day at school is a stereotype of the many descendants of missionaries who became teachers to Hawaiian children. They took their morality and pedagogies from their 19th century colonial forbearers. By the time my mother met them in the plantation school system, many were second and third generation residents of Hawai'i. They'd attended prestigious private Hawaiian schools like Punahou and had gone to university in eastern states like Ohio and Massachusetts. They'd returned to Hawai'i with the best teaching methods, primers, and lesson guides used by New England schools, and had set forth with the lingering zeal of Manifest Destiny. They imposed high standards and were effective, even if their rural Hawaiian schools had no glass windows, and their pupils spoke pidgin and had no shoes. By the mid-1880s, because of these efforts and the endorsement of the Hawaiian sovereigns, Hawai'i's literacy rate was ninety-five percent, thought to be the highest in the world.[22]

Given the few pathways to prosperity open to island-born Hawaiians, the boon of literacy was inestimable. The imagined interaction between Mrs. Whimple and Lillina reflects the awkwardness of both sides. The teacher hadn't known how to resolve what was on the page and the person before her claiming to be something else. The child, in her first interaction outside her ohana, had shrunk back with confusion. She'd heard herself tagged with the alien-sounding name Mildred and had witnessed her mother's inability to find the words to correct the misspelling of her name. The little Lillina, the nascent Norma, had begun her first day of school falling to the sidelines of an intimidating mash-up of cultures and languages and uncertainty.

Like my mother's name, mine is long and freighted with back stories. The individual components of my name are not harmonious with each other, though the string has a certain rhythm if you say it quickly. Nina Elizabeth Moana Macheel. This name evolved along my life's milestones, and it reflects complex geography and relationships, as names often do.

In the early 1950s, it was unusual to have a name that was hard to pronounce. Names tended to be safe and common, like Mary and Susie and Debbie. A name like mine triggered the question "What kind of name is that?" so my relationships always began with an explanation. Next came coaching in how to pronounce and spell my name, often requiring me to repeat the letters slowly and distinctly, then asking the person writing it to read it back to me, then correcting what had been put down. The disconnect between the human ear and the hand on the page, when it came to getting my name right, seemed a kind of mental sloth that soured the start of many social interactions. I envied those with simple names like Anne, or people who'd gone through life with a single, consistent name. Being called one of many set me up for identity confusion and made me a little suspicious: why are they calling me that when I wanted to be called this?

Nina was the discarded name that was never used or discussed before I was eighteen, after which time it came into its own and crowded out the others. My second name was Elizabeth, my German grandmother's name. My mother loathed her, so I evaded that name to avoid setting off my mother's temper. Much later, when I learned that the E. in the name Waipuilani E. Paki stood for Elizabeth, I wondered if that was the source of my middle name, and not the other Elizabeth who was the grandmother my mother hated. By then my parents had deceased so I'd never know.

I grew up being called Moana, which people of those times seemed constitutionally unable to pronounce or to spell. While correcting them, enunciating each letter slowly and clearly, I would throw out that Moana was the name of a grand and elegant hotel on Waikiki Beach. Today, after the Walt Disney Studios' 2016 release of a movie named *Moana*, the name is easily recognized by America's children and their parents, who seem to have no problem pronouncing or remembering it.

Beyond the difficulty of growing up with a name like Moana, I have an uncommon surname that is loaded with the same pronunciation and spelling issues. Each of my siblings pronounces our last name their own way and I too vary the way I say it, depending on what part of the country I'm in or who I'm talking to. It is a name that can be made to sound softly French or crisply Scottish or gutturally Prussian. The way the people in Southeastern Wisconsin pronounce it seems completely disconnected from the letters that constitute the name, but many from that region correct me on the pronunciation of my own name, if I pronounce it differently than they do.

The confusion and identity shift that come with the range of my names may be hard to appreciate by anyone with a single, simple given name, and possibly a nickname derived from it. I have experienced the ways names can help establish relationships and strengthen one's confidence, enabling one to show up as the most authentic version of oneself. We want that effect from the names we choose for our children. Otherwise, why not go with Baby X? We viscerally feel the faceless pain of one called "Jane Doe," the stripping of persona. But when endowed with a name, she becomes a relatable human being, like a paper doll that pulls itself into three dimensionality.

Both my mother and I had names that were used and then later not used. We had other names pinned over those original names. Then we had names that we chose and imposed over the interim ones. My mother had adapted the names she used to the situations in which she found herself, and then personified what those names signified. I grew up aware that my name shaped how my community related to me, but I never took the situation in hand until I chose to be called Nina for the rest of my days.

Until the moment I made that decision, I hadn't realized that I had agency to affect my identity so directly, nor that in doing so I had come full circle. I'd arrived in Wisconsin as the toddler Nina, a name that is common throughout the world and familiar to every school child that learns about Christopher Columbus' ships: the Nina, the Pinta and the Santa Maria. But somehow the "damned Germans," as my mother called them, were mispronouncing Nina with a long *i* vowel, as if it rhymed with Ina.

To eliminate this continuing travesty to her cherished childhood name (as I learned later it had been), my mother stripped me of the name Nina. But in an inexplicable inverse logic, rather than give me a name that was easy for everyone to pronounce and spell, she switched my name to Moana, an even greater challenge to get right. In no time everyone, including my mother, had shortened Moana to Mo. I hated being called Mo, but it's what I went with for sixteen years. I bristled at every reference to Moe of the Three Stooges and responded with tepid "heh heh heh, very funny" rejoinders to everyone who made the same tiresome joke. My baptismal record, which I'd seen, showed my name as Moana Elizabeth. Until I turned eighteen, I'd never seen my birth certificate, which showed me as Nina Elizabeth.

I ceased being Moana the day I registered at university. In those pre-internet days students had to personally go to campus to sign up for classes. It was a day-long process, often requiring going to professors' offices to get signatures to enroll, rushing from building to building, hoping to get in before the desired sections had filled. Amidst that pressure I was nearly stopped in my tracks when my records showed my name as Nina Elizabeth. Was that person me? For an instant I was not sure. How did the university get this name, and how could I undo it without jeopardizing my enrollment process? On the spot, in the dilemma of the moment, I decided to go with Nina and dump the name Moana.

Relinquishing this name was a choice for convenience, for something novel, a new identity. More significant was the shedding of the one and constant reminder of my Hawaiian heritage. Yet I felt the loss only of a burden that I wasn't aware I'd been shouldering. As Nina, I was treated as a full-fledged, plain-vanilla person rather than one who is racially ambiguous. For several years of overlap I answered to Moana, Mo, and Nina, but in my mid-30s, by then long gone from the Midwest and anyone who knew me as Mo, I asked anyone left who called me Moana to use my original name Nina.

TALK STORY: *Lillina — mid-1930s*

    Lillina was a little girl when her father went away. After that they were hungry and had to go out looking for food. They found fruit in the trees, berries on bushes, and small crayfish in the cane field irrigation ditches. There were tiny shells on the shore rocks with bits of meat in the curled furls that they could get out with pins, but it was never enough to be worth the trouble. Lillina's mother Rosalie took jobs in the big houses in Lahaina, and occasionally went off for an evening with one of the men who whistled at her as she swished through the streets. On those evenings the children went to their Tutu Wahine, who lived nearby on the outskirts of Lahaina. They never wanted to go there. Tutu Wahine was strict. But she made up for it with plates of dried fish and freshly pounded poi, and always had a pot of cold rice that they could stick together into little balls and eat throughout the day.

    Lillina hated seeing her mother go off with those men. Whoro was her father and why didn't he come home? Rosalie shushed her and promised to bring back something from the diner on Luakini Street, where she planned to order teriyaki beef skewers and miso soup and crispy, oily tempura vegetables. She always wrapped bites to take home for her keiki, and sometimes she came home with gifts that were just for herself, like the 24kt gold bracelet studded with bits of jade that the Chinese grandfather let her choose at the jeweler, telling her she could have anything she wanted. Sometimes she came back with money, usually just in time to pay bills or buy supplies. It seemed magical the way she could usually get what they needed. But she couldn't always, and those were the times when the Catholic Church helped them out.

Even with all that, Lillina and her sisters were often hungry. Sometimes they went to the edge of the plantation field and tore off a length of raw cane to chew on, though they knew it would rot their teeth. Rosalie would not listen to them complain. She always said things would get better.

One day, at a breakfast on the church lanai after Easter Mass, they met a short, sinewy cowboy from Moloka'i. He was a *paniolo*, a Hawaiian cowboy, and was telling talk story about herding cattle across the high pastures. He had skin like leather and silver streaks in the thick hair that was dented in the back from the brim of his cowboy hat. Without losing his story he looked at Rosalie sitting on a folding chair at the edge of the gathering, then looked away, then looked back at her. She sat balancing a plate of Portuguese sausage and scrambled eggs on her lap, flanked by her five children. Something about his look made her forget about a second trip to the buffet. She didn't want to miss a single word he said.

From that day on, things did get better. George Rosa married Rosalie and took her and her kids to the Moloka'i town of Kaunakakai. He had a son, Gordon, who was just a year younger than Rosalie's son Val, who came to live with them. They fit themselves into the three rooms of their apartment on the second floor of a weathered storefront in a weedy alley near the center of town. Everyone was delighted to be there, and to be with each other. The children snickered each time they heard their mother introduce herself with her new, improbable name of Rosalie Rosa. They loved watching her face wrinkle into a smile when George Rosa rode his dust-crusted horse through the gate. Gritty and sun-browned, his hat caked with dirt and sweat after days of herding on the Moloka'i Ranch, he reached his thickly calloused hands to grab whichever child got to him first. He tousled Lillina's wiry black hair, which Rosalie patiently braided into the pigtails she loved. He lifted little Augusta into the air and whirled her around. He swung his taut legs to the ground and boosted their brother Valentine onto the horse and led it across the yard to where Rosalie waited on the first step, lifting herself to his height to reach his kiss.

Lillina loved seeing her mother acting so silly around George Rosa. At the first sight of him riding up the alley, Rosalie ran to heat the rainwater she and the children had collected in their catchment tanks and saved for his homecoming. Rosalie helped him out of his dust-hardened clothes and led him to the galvanized tub behind the papaya grove. George called the children to him and splashed them when they got too close, a game they played merrily until Rosalie scolded that he was wasting his bath water and there would be no more. The build-up of red dirt loosened from the folds of his crinkly skin and settled to the tub bottom like sediment in a pond.

Inside, in the subdued light let in by the one high, small window, Rosalie rubbed coconut butter into her cheeks and wrapped her wayward, silvering hair into a tidy bun adorned with fresh plumeria from the tree in the yard. After George finished bathing, she'd *lomi lomi* out the knots in his shoulders, back and thighs. The children clustered in the doorway, shyly witnessing the transformation of George Rosa from careworn to teasing smiles.

Lillina loved the way Rosalie looked in her best linen dress with tucks in the bodice and pale blue ribbons at the neckline. They all loved the special food Rosalie made for George, knowing he'd been eating out of tins since his last meal with them.

After supper they'd sashay into the lively hub of Kaunakakai. The children straggled behind until they got to the shave ice stand, where they pushed to be first in line to pick their favorite flavor, pointing at its color – bright pink or orange or lime green – while George counted out change for the vendor. George and Rosalie stopped for a cold beer and drank it as they moved along the boarded streets. George carried one of the boys on his shoulders and let his arm drift around Rosalie's waist. He asked the girls how they were doing in school and their chores, and Lillina told him she had gotten an after-school job shelving books in the library. George Rosa winked at Rosalie. It was all turning out as they'd hoped: the children were fitting right into life on Moloka'i, and they were happy.

Chapter 17

Years of Respite

The young girl Lillina grew into a woman who was guarded with her nostalgia and allowed herself to indulge in it only sparingly. Her years on Molokaʻi were reserved for that category of sweet reminiscence. After their struggles as a fatherless family, their new stepfather, George Rosa, and Rosalie's happiness with him, gave their blended families a time of stability and peace. What I've heard described of those years gives the clearest image of Rosalie in her middle-age and my mother in her youth. Though most of the world associates this island with Father Damien, the saintly servant to the Hawaiian leper community, I think of it as a place where my mother was a happy young girl.

Hoping to visit the landmarks of my mother's years on Molokaʻi, my brothers, sister, and I took our teenaged children to Molokaʻi. We booked a house big enough to accommodate all of us and rented a few cars so we could all go on our separate desired excursions. We surely covered the island more thoroughly than Grandma Rosa and her kids ever had. Based on approximate directions from our aunties, we ambled through downtown Kaunakakai in search of a weather-beaten building in an alley with an upstairs flat where we think George and Rosalie lived. We found the library where my mother worked after school. The building was new and modern in her time, built in

1937. It was set back from the bustling Ala Malama Street by a patch of well-tended grass. We went inside and each in our own way imagined what it had been like for her there.

More than sixty years after her time there, Kaunakakai still had the feel of a provincial outpost. It was easy to imagine Lillina going about on those streets to Girl Scout gatherings, local fairs, or the many stores opened in the 1930s to serve the pineapple plantation and ranch workers. There had been a bakery, music store, meat market, and dressmaker lining one side of the street, and the large Misaki Store building had taken up most of the other. The Misaki Store had a sewing service on which some of the first aloha shirts had been made. It also carried everything from canned goods to fishing supplies to animal feed. There was even a Ford Model T for hire as a funeral hearse or delivery service for bulk purchases. The Kaunakakai Hotel, a restaurant, the Saint Sophia Catholic Church, and a poi shop occupied the rest of the street leading to the library. An open-air Kukui Theater opened in 1934 and Takata's Movie Theater followed in 1936, featuring Japanese silent films narrated by an unseen voice emanating from an unseen place.

Walking those small-town streets as a young girl, with freedom to go where she pleased, surely whetted Lillina's desire to explore the larger world. She chafed at her annual rotation of summers with Tutu Wahine on Maui followed by months in Moloka'i schools. It was hard for her to sit still, day after day, at school. She was not scholarly. She wanted to learn by direct experience. But where? She was too quick and clever for a life working in nearby shops and businesses in Kaunakakai, but nothing in her unhurried, unvaried life offered much else. She drifted along, meeting friends for a soda after work, doing the least amount of schoolwork required to get by. Unless she moved off Moloka‘i, her best prospect would be a job at the pineapple plantation shipping office. And this would be if she were lucky. Realistically, she'd wind up packing produce or sewing floral-patterned aloha shirts in the hot, clattering Misaki Store back-room. She knew her only escape from this fate was to get to Honolulu.

Lillina's opportunity to escape from Moloka‘i arrived unexpectedly, and sooner than she'd have wished, when she was fourteen. She was part of a plan announced by her estranged father, Clarence Young, who showed up one day and abruptly changed the course of the family life Rosalie and George had composed so intentionally. She was to move to Honolulu, a relocation that was orchestrated not for her benefit, but to serve the education of her brothers. She and her brothers would live in a bungalow Clarence had purchased, and Lillina would go along to cook and keep house while the boys attended the private Catholic school in which Clarence had enrolled them. The disruption to Lillina's schooling and to Rosalie's family was of no consequence to Clarence Young compared to the importance of educating his sons. Clarence may have rationalized the details and timing of his plan by news of Germany's invasion of Poland. A war was spreading across Europe and could cross the ocean and land in their midst. The U.S. military was aggressively expanding O‘ahu operations for the South Pacific defense, should the war come that far. Perhaps these distant upheavals had prompted him to bring his sons closer, though not under his own roof.

Rosalie had not heard about the faraway war and its possible implications for the islands, but she had other immediate worries. The paniolo life was wearing on George's body, and he'd need to find a new line of work. She had already begun thinking ahead, knowing their days as a tight family unit were numbered. Winnie had already left Moloka'i for O'ahu. Rosalie insisted that George's son go along to school in Honolulu, and Clarence had agreed, if George paid the tuition. That settled, Rosalie began planning that she and George, with her youngest daughter Augusta, would soon follow their children in moving to Honolulu.

TALK STORY: *Lillina — late 1930s*

> "Lillina. No lunch today?"
> Valentine spit saliva into his hand and slicked his wiry hair off his forehead. It quickly fell back to its usual place, hovering across his brow. He pushed against it in a futile, habitual pattern that would go on throughout the day until the priests at school would order him to get it trimmed. Then Lillina would settle him on a stump in the yard, near the tangle of green and maroon-colored ti plants. She'd sharpen the shears against a pitted lava rock and draw a torn pareo over his shoulders. He refused to let her put a bowl over his head to create the blunt bangs of the cartoonish Chinese stereotype. Lillina did her best to please him. Her job was to make their life easy so the boys could focus on their lessons. Their failure would be her failure.
> Though she was not yet fifteen, Lillina had full responsibility for their small bungalow. Clarence Young had taken them to Nuuanu Street, handed

Lillina the key, and came back only once a month to settle accounts. Lillina kept the receipts and her make-shift ledger in a brass-colored soy sauce tin, neatly organized by date. Barely looking at or speaking to her, Clarence would flip through them, inquire about anything unusual, and hand her cash for the next month. If the boys had other needs, such as a broken tooth or new shoes, they would transact with him directly, usually through the mail. They knew better than to ask for anything unless their need was dire. Lillina prepared meals with the meager allowance he'd advanced, apologizing that the soup was thin and tasteless. They all knew it was useless to complain.

"We still waiting for money. So cold noodles from yesterday. Bitter melon stewed. Avocado from tree by the park, pecked by chickens, but ok," Lillina would say. She often foraged from shrubs along the curbs and had once even retrieved something edible from a trash bin.

Their place lay amidst a maze of cul-de-sacs and alleys, wedged in a forgotten area between the back streets just above Chinatown. Their neighbors, toothless old bachelors and coarse hapa Hawaiian women in soiled, loose housedresses and with thick, flat feet that may have never been crammed into a shoe, lived in rickety structures that were perforated with termite pits and tracks. Lillina and the boys gingerly stepped around where the splintering floorboards seemed soft, afraid the supports might crumble. Their yard was thick with spears of aloe and tangles of gnarly *hau* tree branches. A towering breadfruit tree dropped enough of the starchy fruit for them to cook and eat for many days, until the boys complained that they were sick of it. After that Lillina traded what was left of the breadfruit with the neighbors for whatever they could offer – a papaya or a knob of ginger, or sometimes a piece of fish. What was offered was usually the parts they had discarded, but Lillina patiently pulled out the pin bones and simmered what was left – the bony tail and collar – into a broth.

    The boys spent most of their days at school and in sports afterward, leaving Lillina with long days without the company of family or anyone her age. She ventured out to attend Mass and Catholic catechism class with her brothers, or to buy food. She once asked Clarence Young where he lived and if they could visit but he said that was not possible. Her routine rarely varied. She had the boys' simple meal ready when they got home, usually broth and noodles with bits of greens or fish. They barely spoke to her, or to each other, as they raised their bowls to their jowls and slurped the warm liquid, stabbing their chopsticks at the last bits. Pushing their bowls aside for Lillina to clear from their study area, they pulled out their books and began homework. She could then eat what she'd set aside for herself. Then she went into the yard to wash dishes at the hose. She also hand washed the boxer shorts and button-up school uniform shirts her brothers had worn during the day. During the stormy season when the air was dank and humid it could take days for their clothes to fully dry. There were no spares in the closet, so it was pointless to complain if they had to put them on while still damp.

    At night the rains blew down from the Pali and beat on their rusted, corrugated roof. Rats scurried under the floorboards and cockroaches pressed inside, sometimes before Lillina had turned out the bare bulb hanging from a cord and settled onto her sleeping mat in the corner of the kitchen. She wondered what the scavengers thought they could get; she hadn't left a crumb or a peel or sticky drip to tempt them. The pests were part of island living, but their skittering nocturnal invasions set her on edge, triggering the thoughts she kept in the shadows during the day: resentment that her brothers' schooling was priority while her own was cast aside; loneliness for the friends and sisters she'd left behind; anger that her father had forced her to be a servant. She'd remind herself that she had wanted to come, that there'd been no future for her in Molokaʻi. And besides, these duties were required of her, given her place in the family. Who else was there? Her sister Winnie was too far along in high school to drop out, and Augusta was too young to leave Rosalie and move to the city.

When she wasn't itemizing her discontents, Lillina was trying to find ways to do all that needed to be done, to do it better, in less time, for less money. So many things were falling apart – the rotting porch posts, the screen door hinge that hung crookedly on one screw. They'd be easy to fix if only she had a nail or a screwdriver, or a friend who might have one to lend her. Her brothers were indifferent to their conditions and to her desire to free up time to get back to school. It would never have occurred to them to offer support, nor would she have asked. Though the nuns in her Catholic schools had urged her to keep up with her studies, finishing high school in Honolulu was no one's concern except her own.

Eventually, Lillina found time to get to classes at the President William McKinley High School in downtown Honolulu, and had managed to save a few pennies to buy books and pay the bus fare. She rose early every morning when the wild chickens started scratching about the dusty yard and the roosters crowed down the street. She eked out bagged lunches from bits of food and leftovers she had sealed against the armies of ants that marauded across the worktable at night. She hauled tubs of water from the courtyard pump and warmed them over their single burner, then called the boys to wash. She put out bowls of hot black tea poured over cold rice, and then hurried them along to get out the door to catch their bus. After they'd left, she tidied the house and herself, and ran to catch the bus to McKinley High School.

Lillina loved standing at the corner waiting for the bus. Surrounded by a cluster of riders who seemed to be headed to important places, she felt caught up in the life of the city. When her bus pulled up, braking with a screech, she climbed the grimy steps and dropped her fare into the coin cage. She looked for a seat in the back where she could study, but she was easily distracted. Winding through streets she'd never been on, she discovered places she could walk to from the bungalow, including the nearby area called Chinatown. She resolved to go there to look for fresher, cheaper food.

As the bus moved past South King Street along Honolulu's commercial blocks, more and more students climbed on board, all headed to the same sprawling, eight-acre campus with its gracious old building. As they all jumped off the bus, chattering and clowning, flowing toward the front entry, Lillina fell behind, savoring her daily passage under the school's imposing arches. She'd overcome obstacles to get back to school. She was proud to be there, even if no one was there congratulating her.

Once inside, Lillina ambled through corridors echoing with the chatter of students of every nationality, culture, and racial mix – a world of young hapas who looked and sounded like variations of her. As she passed clumps of giggling girls, she noted what they were wearing, how they painted their lips, made up their eyes, crimped their hair. Though she had little to spend, she had a flair for appearing to have more than she did. She observed how the others spent their money so that one day, if the chance came to join them or to spend a coin of her own, she would know what to choose.

Lillina never doubted that she was as pretty, smart, and talented as any of those girls, but she knew she would never have their freedom to linger, gossip, and flirt. They could loll about on the grassy campus after classes while she had to rush off to catch the bus to Chinatown. There, in the city's cheapest food markets, she dropped her girlish ways as she figured out how far she could stretch their weekly pittance from Clarence Young. She could appease her brothers' hunger but there was never enough for them to feel full. In the side alleys of Chinatown, she rooted through dark shops that smelled of dried fish, salted plums, and wilted roots she could not identify. She asked for samples to experiment with and could do wonders with scavenged bits from the day-old bins or discarded trimmings. She coaxed flavor from chicken feet and pig snout and organs she preferred not to know the names of. She learned how dried shitake mushrooms and limp watercress stems flavored a broth, and how a drop too much of fish sauce or an extra dash of Five Spice powder could ruin a dish, though her brothers had no choice but to eat it anyway.

She always concluded her monthly accounting meeting with Clarence Young with a request for a bit more, after tolerating his questions about why the boys complained about not getting enough to eat. Her only chance at culling out a bit for a small luxury, a hair pin or a spool of thread, lay in her ability to scout and salvage food that had fallen to the ground – an overripe mango or brown, bruised bananas – so she could deduct its value from the grocery allotment. She had to be resourceful and realistic. Relying on herself was the only way she'd get what she wanted.

Chapter 18

Nowhere to Run

By the fall of 1939, Lillina had morphed from an outer-island provincial to an independent, self-reliant city dweller. She was confident and practical, and held to her promise to keep as close an eye on her brothers as would a parent. But the lure of the world outside their spare bungalow beckoned Lillina. She was happy to at last be among girls her own age in school, but she also wanted to taste the fabled glamour of Waikiki Beach.

Everyone knew about the luxurious ocean liners bringing wealthy mainland tourists to vacation in Honolulu's beachfront hotels. Lillina had no sense that most of America was healing from the Depression and that the people coming to vacation at Waikiki were not reflective of the American mainstream. She imagined it was the prerogative of any American who so desired to book passage on one of the luxurious Matson Navigation "White Ships" – the Mariposa, Monterey, and Lurline – even though she knew that the Hawai'i of visitors was not the Hawai'i of the people who lived in the islands. She and her sisters had seen and scoffed at the Matson brochures with their idealized images of surfers riding the "stampeding white-maned stallions of the surf," of hula girls strumming ukuleles under Hawaiian moons (". . . and it's not a moon to be trifled with. It is potent . . . bewitching. . .just to look is an adventure," claimed a 1931 brochure put out by the Hawaiʻi Tourist Bureau).[23] And had these tourists heard the rumors that the U.S. Military was planning to conscript their beautiful transoceanic liners and use them to ship American soldiers to Hawaiʻi? Did they know that the Hawaiian Islands were being readied for a major role in a major war?

Though Oahuans witnessed, and participated in, the accelerated activity of their island's preparation for possible war in the South Pacific, they couldn't imagine it could materialize. The sprawling Hickam Air Force Base, activated in 1938, created a bonanza of citizen jobs serving its universe of barber shops, medical dispensaries, laundries, post exchanges, and cavernous, consolidated mess halls. Lillina longed to trade her servitude to her brothers for a job on the base, but she worried that she'd be funneled into the kind of dead-end work she'd hoped to transcend. The local economy, though burgeoning, seemed to predestine people like her to menial roles. She began to accept that the only way to achieve anything more would be to leave Hawaiʻi.

For Lillina to imagine herself anywhere other than Hawaiʻi was like trying to imagine war. They were both situations in which she had no experience, nor even thought possible. The enlivening, self-assured presence of so many servicemen, from so many places, helped Lillina to push the boundaries of her thought. These ordinary-seeming men, many not much older than she was, appeared not only prepared for war, but also ready to conquer the world. Their confidence attracted her. She liked the way they balanced good manners with an air of "come hither" playfulness. She began imagining herself going back with one of them to wherever it was that he'd come from. Surely one of them among the more than seven thousand U.S. Navy, Army and Air Force on her island would be right for her. Most of them were haole and came from the mainland, but she learned by listening to them talk that they, like Hawaiians, had distinct regional subcultures. They spoke with different accents and liked different foods. Subtle as it often was, it helped her to understand them.

Still, Lillina kept reminding herself that she was not yet sixteen. What did she, or any of the Hawaiian women who were surreptitiously eyeing GIs or blatantly flirting with them, know about their background, values, character, aspirations? Hawaiian men, historically accustomed to invasions of strangers and to the occasional need to step in and protect their women, found this group of men was different. They seemed entitled and cocksure of themselves, not impoverished and desperate for a job like the boatloads of foreign arrivals from generations past. This group came with the authority and aegis of the United States Armed Forces. Lillina was street smart enough to recognize that these men could help liberate her, but they could also lead her into a trap. She'd already heard stories of young women living in the moment, disregarding their long-term interests, falling into compromising situations that she was too Catholic and too self-protective to consider.

By 1940, as Lillina took on school alongside her domestic duties, she welcomed the news that Rosalie and George Rosa were pulling up stakes on Moloka'i and coming to O'ahu. Her brothers were in their own world and had no interest in her. She'd missed her sister Augusta and parents. They'd be living on Huna Lane, a walking distance from the bungalow on Nuuanu. George Rosa was able to get a job as pipe fitter at the naval shipyard that paid more than he'd pulled in as a paniolo. Best of all, he could return home every night, the first time since their marriage that Rosalie would have regular dinners with him. She was just forty years old. Their children were growing up and taking their places into their world, and all seemed perfect.

Until the day that World War II reached the Hawaiian Islands, and even as they were being attacked, Lillina had never understood why anyone would want to invade their sleepy isle. What did they have that was worth the effort of crossing the ocean to get to them? California, the place most Hawaiians aspired to visit, was over two thousand miles across the Pacific. Few Hawaiians could get to a neighboring island, much less anywhere on the U.S. mainland, just as few of the military stationed in the South Pacific could not, in other circumstances, have personally afforded a ticket there. The GIs stationed at Hickam felt like they'd drawn the lucky ticket at the lottery. If they had to be uprooted and shipped off to a possible war, what better place than the tropics to spend their time building facilities, transporting war machinery, filing administrative reports, and overseeing maintenance services? They'd been through combat training but were sanguine about having to use the full might and power of the United States Armed Forces to defend the Hawaiian Islands.

Despite their complacent sense of good fortune to be on a tropical island, the GIs got homesick and suffered "island fever." The U.S. military command tried to boost morale by bringing GIs and Hawaiians together in a social setting. Hawaiians were purveyors of products and providers of services to the military installations, so Oʻahuans and GIs comingled freely in the workplace and outside of it.

Fraternizing with each other was encouraged as a patriotic gesture, and few discussed the darker purpose of their presence, which was to make Hawai'i's the first line of defense on the U.S. western horizon.

THE JAPANESE ATTACK ON PEARL HARBOR WAS A LINE of demarcation that divided Hawaiian life into the time before December 7, 1941, and the time after. In one morning, Hawai'i was transformed from a hive of war preparedness to an intense center of active war operations. Hawaiians were shocked to discover how vulnerable they were. Lillina agonized over what they should expect and plan for, and whether to stay in school or drop out to join the war effort. Was it wrong to be opportunistic, to take advantage of the war economy? There was no one to counsel her. Her brothers never questioned that their place was to remain in school, and they refused to be distracted. But Lillina was more vulnerable to the diversions – chief, among them, the haole men everywhere she looked.

Lillina was aware of cautions against taking up with the servicemen stationed in their midst. There were strictures and social mores against Hawaiian women comingling with wartime military personnel. Eventually, being told that relaxing these taboos would help improve GI morale and diffuse angst, Hawaiian women let down their guard. They were attracted to the GIs' unique blend of opportunism, curiosity, and loneliness. These dovetailed into the contagious wartime attitude of "anything goes, because who knows what tomorrow may bring?" Both sides were tempted to push against traditional boundaries. Lillina and her sisters were at the peak of individuation, a natural time to take risks and seek independence. These GIs were the opportunity to get off "this damned rock" that they might never have again.

TALK STORY: *Lillina — early 1940s*

> Lillina had mixed feelings about being back in school, but she knew it was the best thing she could do. She was taking business and typing courses at McKinley High School. Though she was good with numbers, she found it hard to concentrate. Things on Nuuanu street almost ran on their own. Everyone knew their routines, and Lillina could ask for help from her sister Augusta when needed.
>
> Augusta was two years younger than Lillina, but she was clever and had spunk. She teased Lillina for becoming a drudge. "Go have some fun, the boys will not starve," she said, adding that Clarence Young would never give her a bonus or thank you, so she should start looking out for herself. Their older sister Winnie was already working part-time for the military. Everyone said there simply weren't enough people on O'ahu to fill all the jobs, so maybe Lillina could get one.
>
> Eventually Lillina gave in and went job hunting. She was hired on the spot to work after school in the vast, clamorous kitchens that delivered meals to the Navy mess halls. She wrapped an apron over her school dress and took her place beside a rack on wheels stacked with twenty commercial sized aluminum trays. On the table before her were hundreds of small white dishes and massive pans of orange, red, and green Jell-O cut into squares. Her job was to slide one quivering piece after another

onto a saucer, pump a dollop of whipped cream on it, put the saucer on a tray, and when the tray was filled, begin filling the next one. It was monotonous and her back ached from the repetitive motion, but she felt fortunate to get something that worked around her school schedule.

The challenge was getting to Hickam Field from McKinley High, and then home after work. The bus ride took up to two hours each way. She used the time for schoolwork but was often so exhausted that the material blurred, and she nodded off. The job came with meal tickets that she cashed in for food that she took home to her brothers. Whatever was going on in her life, they expected a meal and were waiting hungrily for her return every day. She was meeting everyone's needs, but she was exhausted and questioned whether she could keep on.

"Well, I'm not getting ahead, going from feeding the brothers to feeding the GIs back to feeding the brothers, day in and day out," Lillina said. She was on the porch with Augusta, her head tilted toward the cool twilight breeze sweeping down from the Pali. "I am going over to the War Office tomorrow, just to see what else they've got, now that I'm sixteen."

The next morning, she doused herself with the hose shared with their neighbors. She put on a dress with a delicate floral pattern and caught the bus, standing in the aisle the whole way to keep her skirt from wrinkling. The bus was packed with people of all ages, most in the uniforms of janitors, construction workers, or nurses, all going to their jobs at one military location or another. She held onto the overhead strop and swerved as the bus careered and screeched through half a dozen checkpoints and street closures. With a lurch that nearly pitched her into the lap of an elderly woman in a cafeteria uniform, the bus stopped in front of what had been a dilapidated warehouse. She looked uncertain, but others getting off told her that the interior had been cleaned out and outfitted for administrative processing. She went to a roped off area to fill out forms and wait in line. When her name was called, she handed over her clipboard and was taken to a room with dozens of young women clattering through typing tests. She easily passed and was hired as a typist clerk, starting immediately.

The woman overseeing Lillina's work was young and stout, with a shock of thick dark blond hair. She wore a khaki-colored uniform and brown oxford shoes over sheer hosiery. She crisply welcomed Lillina and led her down a long row of worktables fronted with hard wooden chairs, each in front of a black typewriter. She stopped at a place with a wire basket overflowing with papers and summarized what Lillina was to do: type supply requisitions, transportation passes, scripts for rationed food and fuel; pass them along the chain for approval and distribution; collect the carbon copies and file them into labeled folders in a wall of drawers. The woman pointed here and there as she spoke. Lillina took her seat, rolled a 5-part form into her typewriter, and began. Luckily, she'd asked Augusta to make dinner that night, as it did not seem the right time to tell the woman that she had to hurry home to cook for her brothers.

When Lillina started out that morning she'd had no idea that she'd repeat that day's routine five days a week for months to come: feeding the boys, tidying the house, laundering what needed to be line-dried during the day, making herself presentable for work, catching the bus to the base, and reversing the steps at the day's end. As with her last job in the mess kitchens, the schedule wore her down. She chided herself for once again postponing school, a decision made by default when she'd accepted the job in the typing pool.

But Honolulu was crackling with activity that energized her. The normally languid population seemed to have accelerated and she wanted to be a part of it. Since arriving in Honolulu she'd been going along day by day, waiting for something to happen, waiting for a rescue. She'd been a servant to her brothers and had entered McKinley High School as a friendless drop-in. She had never felt accepted and valued, had never been welcomed into a home – had never even been to her father Clarence Young's house.

Though her role at the War Department was miniscule in the giant machinery of war, but she felt important. Those forms made things happen: the requisitions she processed for the Army "KP" supplies resulted in the troops at Hickam getting fed. Feeling purposeful kept her going, hour after hour, under overhead lamps and ceiling fans that riffled the papers in her outbox as she cranked out more forms and reports to add to the pile. The rhythm of her keys tapped against the paper and echoed across the tiled floors. Every hour or so she looked up, resting her eyes on the trees beyond the ledges of tall, double hung windows pushed open to catch breezes. Then she began again, her typewriter bell cheerfully dinging as the keys hammered toward the right margin. She raised the palm of her hand and thwacked against the return lever, her eyes never leaving the copy propped on a board to read while the carriage rasped to the left and she mechanically resumed her key-clacking cadence.

Honolulu, circa 1943: My mother, in the floral-patterned dress, at her wartime job. The wall sign tells us that this gathering is for her, perhaps for her birthday.

Lillina missed having friends. She'd hoped to make some in the clerical pool, but there wasn't time for chatter. When she was transferred to the drafting department, she once again found herself in a pool of young, female, Asian and Polynesian coworkers, most of them unmarried. They dressed modestly in light cotton, knee-length dresses with soft prints in pale colors, belted at the waist, buttoned up the bodice, and trimmed at the collar.

They pushed their thick black hair behind their ears and secured it with black bobby pins, often tucking a plumeria or hibiscus plucked from a tree along the bus route. They worked in long rows of desks pushed close to each other, all of them supervised by pale, uniformed women from the mainland or career military men. Everyone rushed off at the end of their shift, just as Lillina hurried to catch her own bus.

Though she had made few friendships with co-workers, Lillina was elated to be able to go to social mixers with GIs. The prospect of going out to have fun changed their bungalow from a place of somber studiousness to the gaiety of getting ready for whatever the night ahead would bring. The boys kept their heads in their books and hardly noticed the complex dither of their sisters' work, school, and social lives. The girls vied to be first to the shower under the spout behind the monkey pod tree that pulled cold, sandy water directly from the Nuuanu stream that poured down from the Pali. Wrapped in *pareos*, their hair straight and dripping rivulets down their backs, the sisters swapped clothes and elbowed each other aside for a spot at the cracked mirror hanging on the wall in the kitchen. Winnie teased Lillina about her under-sized breasts and how they would never fill out, as her own had. Jan needled Lillina for being picky about things that wouldn't show up in the dim lights of the lounges or roller rink. She ignored them and continued rubbing out a scuff on the leather of her open-toed shoes, repairing the catch on her *faux* pearl necklace, discarding the wilted flower behind her right ear and plucking one to replace it.

Lillina knew that Winnie was right – the details she attended to would never replace the allure of a full, round bosom. But that sweet man she'd met from Wisconsin, Jim, didn't mind that she was tiny. She could tell by the way he looked at her. Augusta, too young to go along, took bets how long before Lillina would switch the blossom from the right to the left ear, meaning she was taken. Lillina smiled mysteriously but said nothing as she adjusted Winnie's hair clip and tugged at their cousin Cato's hem, scolding her for being too lazy to press out the wrinkles.

After inspecting each other and a final glance in the mirror, the girls headed out. Their favorite place was the roller rink on a downtown Honolulu pier surrounded by beer stands, shave ice and ice cream vendors, lei hawkers, and parked military jeeps lining the streets like a convoy. Lillina and her sisters headed there by bus, walking the last few blocks amidst a surge of other young people out to enjoy mixing in the balmy twilight. They made up names to use with any GI they met and quizzed each other so they wouldn't slip up and call each other their real names in front of GIs. They practiced saying the strange names of the states – Tennessee, Nevada, Iowa, Vermont – that the GIs spoke of with such nostalgia. They went over how they'd meet at a certain place at a certain time and promised not to leave until they were all there. They had rules about how to behave and assured each other they would not be too eager or too forward. They would play hard-to-get, use a fake name, and resist indecent advances. These men, after all, were strangers.

Those nights among the handsome, healthy young men stationed in Honolulu were the best amusement Lillina and her sisters had ever had, or ever imagined they could have. The crowds at the gaily lit parks, rinks, dance halls, and outdoor bars were a kaleidoscope of strangers, ever new and intoxicating. Occasionally they spotted their work supervisors and coworkers in the crowd. Lillina studied them, careful not to be caught staring, and later gossiped about how different they were after hours from their buttoned-up presence at work. The supervisors seemed less confident out of uniform, dressed in frocks, standing in clumps, smoking cigarettes and flirting with the GIs. Lillina took it all in, considering every behavior she observed a useful lesson.

But most of her attention was on the swarms of men. Everything about them was fresh and mesmerizing. She'd rarely seen blond men in her life, and suddenly they were everywhere. With the endless ways these men were both strange and familiar, Lillina saw them as a rare school of fish unexpectedly swept over the reef by turbulent waves and trapped in their lagoon, to be enjoyed while they were near and, once the wave drew them back, not likely to come again.

Afterward, back on the porch of the Nuuanu bungalow, Lillina and her sisters compared notes. Sorting out their realizations and uncertainties, they made up a scoring system to rank the GIs they'd met. They listed their traits: some were bold and macho, others were respectful and protective, some were shy and uncertain. The men were feeling the pressure of war but were also in the spell of the tropics, a combination that made them both forward and playful, a mix they'd have never enacted back home. Things between them and island women could build up quickly and dissipate just as rapidly.

But Lillina was still talking to Jim, the man from a place called Wisconsin, and something had settled in her heart. She wouldn't say it out loud, afraid to jinx it, but she already felt like she could stop looking at the clumps of GIs everywhere, and just look for Jim among them. She'd given him the name Kimo, the Hawaiian name for Jim, and she liked that he was comfortable with her calling him that. He'd told her about the Midwest and the town he was from, which seemed very far away.

"I don't think Wisconsin could be that bad," Lillina said. She and her sisters were on their way to the skating rink. She stopped to shake a pebble from her shoe. "Maybe cold, but not all the time, all year. I will not type forms for the rest of my days."

"You said you loved it," said Augusta, who was tagging along though she was too young to enter places with alcohol. "I want to get a job. You go to Wisconsin, work on a farm. I will take your job."

"You are too young. You stay in school. I can't stay in school, but I wish I could. Being sixteen, and maybe going to war, makes everything different," Lillina said, sliding her shoe back on her foot and rushing to catch up with Winnie and Cato, who had moved on. "We can only do this because all these kāne are here, just for a while. Otherwise, same old life. So, take advantage but keep your school."

The roller rink was alive with amber torch lights, the recorded calliope of the skate songs amplified by speakers that looked and sounded like megaphones, one lashed to the pavilion post at each corner. The smells of cigarette smoke and warm beer layered over the steamy sweat and the fragrant scents of plumeria and ginger blossoms the island girls wore in their hair.

Lillina skated in huge loops with her skirts flagging behind, wrapping about her slim legs. Jim caught sight of her and hurried to lace on a pair of skates and catch up with her. Lillina pretended not to notice his bumbling pursuit but was amused that any haole would risk broken limbs and looking so foolish, grinning at the jibes and whistles of his friends, just to be near her. Such a man deserved to be called by his real name and to know hers, but she'd gotten in the habit of calling herself Norma and stuck with that. She knew one day she'd have a hard time admitting to him that she'd been lying, and she knew that he would feel stupid for being duped. She longed to hear him say "Lillina", but she also loved hearing him say this new name, "Norma." It was special that he was the only one who called her that. It made her feel like a movie star, like the other Norma, who'd inspired her to choose it.

Jim was the first mainland person and the first haole, outside of work, that Lillina had spent long hours with. She was amazed at how much they understood each other though they came from such different places. He'd been brought up Catholic, just like her, and they both had three sisters. His father had walked out when he was a child, just as her own father had deserted her family. He told her how hard it was to be a boy without a father, and how his mother had struggled to feed them during the Depression. She told him how they'd had to pry the tiny *opihi* mollusks off the rocks and eat them when Rosalie had no money for food. He told her that he and his buddy had signed up for the U.S. Navy on a whim and had been put immediately on a bus to the East Coast, and not even given a chance to go home to say goodbye to his mother. They talked of how they'd both already come far past where they'd ever expected to go, and both knew they'd have to work hard for everything they'd ever get. They believed the military was their best path to avoiding what they feared most, which was being stuck.

Floating on a cloud of optimism and romance, fueled by the wartime sense of purpose, Lillina began imagining a life with Jim. She pictured a future with the military and the security of government work, reaping the benefits and perks of working on the bases. Eventually, Jim could adapt his naval mechanic skills he was learning to the civilian world. They wouldn't be pigeonholed into the Hawaiian Islands' prescribed future for locals like her, she believed, because he was haole. Their kids would be hapa-haole, and that would make things easier for them when they eventually moved to the mainland.

As they got to know each other, Lillina and Jim left off meeting at the social mixers and went to quieter places, often meeting in Chinatown. He took the bus from the Hickam base, and she waited for him on the bench at the bus stop. Sometimes she walked the mile from Nuuanu Street to their meeting place, saving the bus fare for a bowl of fresh ramen. Slurping the warm broth and dripping noodles, Lillina marveled that Jim was already adept with chopsticks, though he admitted that he'd never heard of such things before arriving in Honolulu. Happy to be away from the crowded mixers, they waved at the jeeps, buses, and convoy trucks with hundreds of servicemen heading to the venues. Throughout Honolulu the nights were lively with the voices, laughter, and recorded songs floating on the trade winds. GIs whistled and called out to the girls and facetiously offered them a lift, though both sides understood it was forbidden for civilians to ride in military vehicles.

Away from the flirting and striving couples in the clubs, hearing the far-off strains of the Andrews Sisters' lively song "Don't Sit Under the Apple Tree," Jim told Lillina about the apples in Wisconsin, their colors and varieties, the pies and German *apfel kuchen* (apple cake), and dunking for apples in a pail at Halloween. They talked about their different ways of seeing and doing ordinary things. They compared their hills and rivers, and their rainfalls and winds. They described what grew and what did not. Jim described the round juicy tomatoes he loved to pick off a vine and eat with a sprinkle of salt, and he wondered aloud why Hawaiians didn't grow them. Lillina had never had a fresh tomato but imagined a future in which she and Jim would make many things grow – things they knew about and things they had yet to discover.

TALK STORY: *Day of Infamy – December 7, 1941*

Lillina was struggling to stay in a dream. It was Sunday morning, the only day of the week she could sleep late. Something was trying to wake her up. She groaned, wanting the noise to go away. Was she was dreaming those booms in the sky, the neighbors' cries of auwē? But no, she felt the ground shake. She sat up. The drone of aircraft and sirens was close and real.

"Lillina. Something's happening."

Gordon Rosa was hopping across the room on one foot, pulling on his pants as he went out. The screen door slammed behind him. Lillina leaped up, grabbed her faded kimono and rushed outside, stumbling as she looked skyward. It didn't make sense: smoke on their island, if it came at all, should be coming from a different direction, from Pele, the goddess of lava and fire, spewing burning lava and black plumes into the sky. But this smoke was *makai*, over the water. The sea could not make smoke, she tried to reason, still half in her dream.

Outside, neighbors from their alley were gathered in clumps, craning their necks, shielding their eyes from sunlight, and pointing toward Pearl Harbor, seven miles away. Dozens of aircraft, low and thunderous, were flying below the radar. She spotted the red circle of the Imperial Japanese flag on their wings, and the black smoke billowing from their flight path. Her brothers Val and Larry dashed out and stood frozen on the steps, immobilized by the roar of the advancing and retreating bombers. Word flew through the streets describing the unimaginable: ships sunk at Pearl Harbor, many ships, ships full of men still sleeping. They had died. Many, many had died. Auwē.

Lillina instantly condensed and compacted the tragedy into one thought: Jim. He never told her where he'd be on the base. He couldn't. It was military security. But now she wished he'd broken the rules and trusted her with details. But why should he have trusted her when she wouldn't even tell him her real name? She would have to find him, since he would never find her using the phony name Norma Young. She'd let him walk her home from the rink and ice cream stands, so he would know where to come, if he could walk, if he were in one piece. If he weren't one of the men out there blown to bits, sunk to the harbor bottom in a bombed-out ship. She chastised herself for these wasted thoughts. She must be disciplined, must stay alert. She listened to news coming from the radio on a nearby door stoop, knowing that the military sanitized what information it put out to locals. She chafed against the probability that they would be placed under martial law and would have to stay at home. How could she observe curfews when she wanted to rush out and find Jim?

After a few days the military put out its reports, making excuses for how this could have happened. Crews got to work repairing the barracks, hangars, and mess halls damaged by Japanese strafing. Oahuans pitched in to help clean up what wreckage they were allowed to be near. They packed and delivered meals and stood on the curbside clapping as the military jeeps rumbled by. Lillina volunteered setting up makeshift shelters in schools and churches, working alongside Boy Scouts, ladies' church auxiliaries, and student organizations. They worked in darkness, fearing another attack. She threw herself into the McKinley High project to raise over $300,000 – which would be over $5,000,000 at today's monetary value – to fund a B-24 bomber that the students christened Madame Pele and presented to the 11th Bombardment Group. For days she carried a donation basket through the streets, driving herself to exhaustion to keep from worrying about Jim.

Finally, four days after the attack, Lillina's manager at work delivered a message from Jim. He was okay. Could she meet him at the shave ice stand in the park? She left work early and rushed to him. He held her and cried, traumatized by relief and remorse. He was both grateful and guilty that he'd survived, by pure luck, when so many of his buddies had not. He'd been in the underground bunker on routine switchboard duty, safe from the bombardments though aware there was carnage and destruction. But he was duty-bound to remain in his station though he wanted to break free and race to the barracks to find his best buddy Howard. Jim had last seen him polishing the saddle shoes he was so proud of, to look spiffy for a date with a girl he was falling in love with. The interminable pace of the minute hand had been tortuous to watch, but finally it had rounded to the end of his hours. Jim tore through the streets, choking on the smoke from smoldering debris and praying with each breath. He'd calculated that Howard would have returned for curfew, meaning he'd have been bunked down when the bombs hit. Clawing through the wreckage near Howard's berth, Jim came upon his leg, his foot still in its saddle shoe.

Howard was among the hundreds put to rest in the following week, and one of the eleven killed from Jim's own 11th Bombardment Group. Weeping, Jim told Lillina what he'd been through in the days before he could get a message out to her, and she told him how she'd been sick with worry, desperately pitching in to feel useful, to distract her from fear, and to help protect her island. All this they told each other as they sat on the bench in the park, just a few blocks from Waikiki Beach, bent over with grief and relief.

Chapter 19

War Bride

The second and last time I visited Grandma Rosa, again in the tiny, cluttered kitchen of the house she shared with my aunt in Pearl City, I pressed her to tell me what my mother had been like as a young girl. Grandma Rosa had prepared a pot of the long rice soup I'd so loved from our first visit. As easily as she ladled broth into my bowl, she spooned me precious bits about my mother.

She was a typical pākē, Grandma Rosa said, leading off with the racial descriptor with which Hawaiians so often began. At the time, I still thought of my mother as Hawaiian rather than Chinese, so this jarred me. She went on, adding that my mother was shrewd and had sharp instincts. She had intuition and could sniff out hidden things. I told Grandma Rosa that I only had a few memories of my mother being tender and loving, like when I was little and she'd come to my bed at night and trace a cross on my forehead, a Catholic thing. But mostly she was negative and didn't see the sense of getting help for her moods.

Grandma Rosa laughed her phlegmy chuckle. "Your mother had good sense when it came to choosing your father, the haole Kimo," she said. "It wasn't easy for her to live on the mainland. She had to protect herself." She did this, I believed, by steeling herself against missing anything too much, I said. Grandma Rosa said that their memories were so tainted by the war that it was hard to reminisce without running into a tragedy they'd worked hard to leave behind. My brother George had once observed that our mother was anti-nostalgic because nostalgia was not useful. He said that she took this position because she had so much nostalgia.

It took until their retirement in Florida, after they'd been together over half a century, for my parents to openly reminisce about their courtship in a Florida newspaper[24] article commemorating Pearl Harbor Day. My father recalled that he "first saw her rolling along at the rink. Nothing happened that time, but I saw her a second time and then again, before she got chummier with me." He thought she'd resisted him because she was shy and careful. He didn't realize that there was cultural pressure for island women to stay away from men like him.

"At the roller rink, where we met, it was about ten haole servicemen to every local girl. They would come over to help tie my skates," my mother chimed in, building on my father's recollection. "Jim was different. He just grew on me. But we weren't supposed to mix after social hours. There was a lot of prejudice." She explained that the local boys did not like their girls going out with servicemen. Island women who gave themselves to servicemen too easily were considered "loose."

Honolulu maintained a sanctioned system of regulated prostitution through the war years and tolerated brothels to meet the needs of so many men so far from home.[25] This reversal of what was considered decent for women, and what the islands felt prudent to provide visiting males, was a far cry from the way island girls greeted Captain Cook and his crew 150 years earlier. There was a practical reason for the recent caution: throughout history, untold numbers of island children had been fathered by men who'd just been passing through, men who'd often unknowingly left their progeny behind to be raised by single mothers and their ohana. Wartime added the additional risk that fathers of unborn babies could be shipped out to sea, to possible combat and death.

Grandma Rosa reflected that my mother was a "good Catholic girl," so she hadn't worried about her getting "in trouble" with Jim, even after Pearl Harbor had infused them with an urgent sense of "live for today." If anything, my mother felt even more cautious about risking her future without marriage. The attack blasted away the illusion that the U.S. military could protect any of them from foreign invasion. They'd all had a traumatizing introduction to mortality. Most, like my father, had never seen human death before. Witnessing it in its most brutal form affected him to the end of his days.

AFTER THE ATTACK ON PEARL HARBOR, HAWAIIANS were put under martial law. This meant immediate cessation of their civil and constitutional rights as citizens of a U.S. territory. The military gave themselves power to censor civilian mail, media, and telephone calls, to take over public transportation and hospitals, shut down schools, and conscript students to work. They imposed strict curfews, suspended trials by jury, and required Hawaiians to be fingerprinted and to carry identification cards. Anyone could be arrested and interrogated at random. Elected officials were told to stand down as civil courts, business, and community affairs came to a standstill.

I asked Grandma Rosa how Hawaiians felt about living under martial law when they'd done nothing to deserve it. She said that, by nature, the people of Hawai'i tended to shut up and do what they are told. This passivity went way back, I imagined, to the days when they lived under royalty and chiefs and a strict system of taboos. But Grandma Rosa declined going that far back into the Hawaiian psychology. Simply put, she said that they'd lived through the attack and believed that it could happen again.

Nor did my mother, when interviewed for the Florida newspaper, speak of those times with rancor. "When they tell you to stay off the street, you better stay off the street. They tell you, 'Lights out. We will shoot if we see any light.' There was a lot that was not right, but what do you do? If you step off the driveway you could be arrested by military police and taken before a military judge. People don't realize all the rights they have until they've lived under martial law," she said.

My mother, ever practical, had accepted martial law as a wartime necessity while I, half a century later, felt saturated with unexpressed anger I seemed to have sponged up from my ancestors. I told Grandma Rosa that it seemed I'd been put on earth to vent outrage that Hawaiian civilians had been so undeservedly constrained. I'd imagine myself taking a principled stand against this authority, making a statement about personal freedom – even by taking a simple action, like staying out after curfew. I'd participated in strident anti-war demonstrations in the 1960s Vietnam War era and still carried stores of residual aggression from those times.

Jim and Norma put off asking the military for permission to marry until October of 1944, nearly three years after the bombing of Pearl Harbor. Circumstances seemed to have settled enough and the wartime threat to the islands seemed to have waned. Still, they were denied and would have to wait until martial law was lifted. Their wait was bearable because Jim was an Oʻahu-based aircraft mechanic, so they could see each other regularly. He'd never been trained for combat, so they were stunned when he was suddenly ordered to ship off to Guam. This shifted Norma into high gear. She refused to believe that in these circumstances they would again be denied permission to marry. After all, she worked for the government, and Jim was putting his life in danger for his country.

"Being his wife entitled me to military benefits, so we went through the paces, seeking approval and talking to a chaplain," she recalled. Convinced they would prevail, she set a date which they had to change three times. "Every time we settled on a time, they'd assign Jim to something. And it had to be on a Sunday since military operations worked six days a week," she said. Still, just two days before Jim was to ship off, they got word that their request had been denied.

"OK," Norma said, "let's get married tomorrow." She took things into her own hands, summoning all the spunk and grit from that part of her that had run a household, had learned how to work vendors and manage expenses, and had navigated through prewar years into war years without parental guidance. That final denial from the military triggered her assertive resolve to shape her own future, beginning with the wedding that she put together in twenty-four hours. She enlisted a Catholic priest, invited all the guests, decorated the reception hall, and helped caterers prepare buffets of food. Photos of their wedding show Jim in his pressed khaki uniform looking a bit giddy that they'd pulled this off. Norma's ivory satin dress was floor length, and her diaphanous veil edged in embroidered lace flowed across dozens of rounded fabric buttons fastened with loops from her waist to the nape of her neck. She was grounded and erect and resolved.

*My parents at their wedding on the eve of
my father shipping out to Guam*

Their wedding celebration was bittersweet. They hadn't known how many guests would show up on short notice, but they were ready for a full house, because that is the Hawaiian way. The bride's family mingled with the groom's GI buddies, they had a few toasts, and a few swirls on the dance floor. Everyone kept their eye on the clock, mindful of the curfew requiring that Jim and his pals be back in their barracks by midnight. When it was time for them to leave, Norma remembered, "I stood for the longest time, in my long dress and veil, and watched him with his thumb out on the Pali highway, hitchhiking with his friends. Then I went back inside to the luau, a bride and a party without the groom."

My mother dove into her role as wife, even though she didn't know where Jim had been shipped or the nature of his mission. They'd told him Guam, but it was normal practice to say one place and wind up in another. Jim wrote her almost 500 letters during their time apart. I have them just the way my mother organized and stored them, bundled in his black military valise with his name and Army dog tag number stenciled on the side. I've read every one of them. They were conscientiously nondescript, each seeming just like the one before and the one after. They were obviously written with sensitivity toward the censors who would cut out anything revelatory. He wrote of tedious, dull days in featureless locations with lots of mud, rain, and insects. Occasionally two or three words were cut out by a censor's scissors, a reminder that these seemingly innocuous dispatches were being reviewed somewhere, by someone unknown.

Even so, Jim wrote fluid prose, describing each day as if it were one of a kind, as though all it needed to be perfect was to have Norma there with him. In one letter he switched to using the fountain pen she'd sent him and thanked her for it, telling her that the base secretary spared some ink for him until he could procure his own. From that time forward, that pen point curled and looped across hundreds of letters written from places he wasn't permitted to identify and which vexed me as I read them, being unable to drop a pin on any map to notate his whereabouts.

Though Norma saved his letters, hers to him are nowhere to be found. Jim would have treasured them, so they either perished in the elements of his swampy camps or had to be discarded for some arcane reason of military security. Or, since she was never sentimental about physical objects, except for her jewelry, and given her propensity for secrecy, she may have destroyed them. It feels unbalanced to me to have his sentiments so lovingly preserved, but not hers.

Jim and Norma had plans for their post-war lives. Neither had family resources to give them a kick-start, but they had ambition and resolve. Norma kept a strict record of every penny she spent, applying what she'd learned from her weekly Nuuanu accounting to Clarence Young. In her marriage, as in her youth, her role was to make sure that they made every penny work for them, and never ran out. Jim was equally disciplined. From the beginning, he deducted what he needed from his military paycheck and sent her a money order for the balance, along with a list of what he'd spent, to be put toward their postwar future.

Jim's discharge from the military came suddenly and unceremoniously. One of his buddies came into his tent during his tour of South Pacific islands and told him that the commanding officer wanted to see him. There were some jibes about misbehavior, about the KP duty to come, but what he got was news of reassignment to Westover Field in Massachusetts. He was put on a flight to Honolulu and stayed there just long enough to break the news to Norma and to re-jigger their plans. Never mind his hope to stay in the islands and make a life. He was soon on board a U.S. naval transport with his 11th Bombardment Group, all of them bursting with thoughts, memories, and emotions, many shared in raucous camaraderie, and many held inside in reflective grief. These were the gifts of their hard-won status as veterans of war. They arrived in the northeast in the middle of a snowstorm in May of 1945. The war seemed far away and unreal, just as far away and unreal as Norma and the islands. Their bittersweet wedding had been just six months earlier.

Jim spent his last few months of military duty fueling planes in wintry weather. He wrote that he had to scramble on the wing tops, very cold and slippery, and "I was longing for Hawai'i." Three months after he arrived back on the mainland, the Americans dropped atomic bombs on Hiroshima and Nagasaki. The Japanese surrendered on September 2, 1945, and the war was declared ended. Jim was notified that he had been discharged. He was to report to Chicago to complete the paperwork to end his service. He stared out the train window across the flat monotony of Pennsylvania, Ohio, and Indiana, comparing it to the tropical and oceanic environments he'd loved in the South Pacific, while contemplating the breadth of experiences he'd had there. From the station in Chicago, he sent a telegram to his mother that he'd be arriving the next day by bus, then he hoisted his duffel into the hold of the lumbering vehicle and found a seat near the rear. He spent much of the last ninety miles of his journey to his hometown remembering how they had so naively, impulsively, set out to enlist, and recalling "so vividly," he later wrote, "the four of us leaning on the ship rail singing 'Blue Hawaii.'"

Going home to his family, knowing they would celebrate him, he wondered how anyone could understand the shattering ordeal he and his buddies had survived. He was mourning the loss of his friend, missing his wife, and processing a store of inexpressible emotion. He needed Norma to bring the reality of the Hawaiian Islands back to him, and to buttress him against the continuing shock of the abrupt end of his military life.

Norma's journey to meet Jim in his hometown was more direct and less freighted than his, but she knew that daunting adjustments lay ahead, and she used the travel time to prepare for them. As a military wife, she'd been cleared to board one of the first Matson passenger liners that had been reconverted to civilian use after wartime appropriation by the U.S. military. After five days at sea from Honolulu to San Francisco, she disembarked amidst thousands of military personnel returning to civilian life, then met the military escort that accompanied her across the Bay to the Oakland train station. Traveling east, alone, she sat by a window and fell into days of trance, mesmerized by the craggy, snowcapped Sierra Nevada mountains, the rugged wastelands of Nevada, the grassy prairies of Nebraska and the windswept bluffs of Iowa, and on to Wisconsin's gently rolling, glaciated fields. She was traveling with the heavy baggage of war and felt the weight of it. She welcomed the time it took to cross those thousands of miles to think about all that had been gained and lost in the years of war. The placid, tidy countryside she passed through seemed surreal with a sense of safety and order that had been paid for with the sacrifice of her islands. Before entering the new places and people of her life with Jim, she needed to dispel her anger and still her sorrow.

As Norma's train crossed the border into Wisconsin, Jim was preparing his mother and her rented home to take in his wife. Getting ready for Norma energized him. His mother and sisters seemed eager to welcome her, though they did not help him prepare their space or plan a meal to celebrate her. On the long-awaited day of her arrival, Jim borrowed his brother-in-law's car and drove the sixty miles to Milwaukee to pick her up and bring her to their new home. He was besotted to have her there, but Norma was travel-weary and anxious, perhaps not aware that she was pregnant and at the mercy of hormones. She may have been short-tempered or hypersensitive, and Jim may have been over-eager to please, and Norma's new in-laws may have been stiff and diffident with their Germanic coldness. Whatever the combination of forces, something happened that was seismic, causing a door like heavy immovable steel to drop around her heart. Through the years of tirades against my father's family that formed the backdrop to my childhood, she never said what they'd done to wound her so deeply that she got back onto the train and made the interminable journey back to her islands, alone.

THE REGION THAT MY MOTHER HAD ENTERED SO OPTI-mistically and then left so traumatically is called by many names. Most of them – the Heartland, the Midwest, Mid-America, and Flyover Country – fail to stimulate the imagination, nor to conjure attributes that are attractive or distinctive. What they suggest is a sense of, literally, middling. They suggest a kind of dullness that is positioned as soothing, a kind of stability and steadiness that is positioned as superiority, as if a magic formula had been concocted to eliminate anything jarring or untoward. Except, of course, for the extreme winters, which Midwesterners speak of with an inverse braggadocio that is off-putting to anyone else wanting to move there.

My mother was intrepid and would have risen gamely to those challenges. But I often wonder how she thought she could fit into a place that was so utterly devoid of racial diversity. The largest racial group in Wisconsin in 1950 was African American, and they were fewer than one-eighth of one percent of the state population. They clustered in the manufacturing areas between Milwaukee and Chicago, a world apart from my father's hometown.

Like so many aspirational newlywed couples, my parents believed in the American myth of meritocracy, a commonly held belief that drove people to work too hard for too little, usually for too long, believing they would be commensurately rewarded. My parents resolved to overcome barriers with hard work and intelligence. They could "better" themselves, using this model for success, and transcend the barriers posed by my father's unwelcoming family and the region's inherent racial bias.

Having lived in Hawai'i's high-functioning, multi-racial culture for many years, my father may have forgotten how small-town Midwesterners felt about what they called Orientals. He'd not been around to see attitudes toward Asians harden after the Japanese invasion and internments. He believed that his family and the people of his hometown would open their arms to Norma, and he conveyed that to her in the many letters he wrote to her throughout his tour of duty. Based on things Elizabeth had written to Jim during the war, it seemed that they had intended to. They all went forward on this momentum of good feeling, until Norma arrived in their realm. Fissures in the foundation appeared when she stepped over Elizabeth's threshold, or stopped into a local store, bank, or post office. Being so visibly Asian, she triggered racial bias that people probably didn't even realize they had and couldn't help letting leak through the porous "Midwest Nice." I believe her response to her perceived rejection was commensurate with the high expectations that had lured her to the Midwest. Until she finally felt accepted, which seemed to occur sometime in her fifties, she'd carried herself with public dignity. Privately, she'd raged and became the bitter, harsh woman who'd raised me.

DESPITE MY MOTHER'S FLIGHT FROM WISCONSIN BACK to Hawaii, my parents' marriage was solid. Her issue was always with the "in-laws" and not with my father. He joined her in Honolulu within a few months and they celebrated that she was pregnant. Raising their family in Hawai'i would be even better than in Wisconsin, they admitted, with Honolulu transitioning back to a strong civilian economy. Norma took charge of their Hawaiian future with protective sympathy toward my father's sadness over wartime losses and the conflict with his mother. He'd lost confidence in his ability to create the future they'd mapped out, and she tried to bolster him.

She also tried to counsel her sisters, who were planning to accompany their haole GIs back to their hometowns, or to wherever else the military chose to send them. She cautioned them not to be naive about racial biases they'd encounter on the mainland, and that it was delusional to think that love would conquer all. I can imagine the sisters pushing back on what Norma counseled, clinging to the promise of new life with their young men, discounting the risks Norma had posited based on her own harsh experience. By the late 1940s, Norma's sisters had married their GIs and gone with them to the mainland.

Norma missed the company of her sisters, but her worry about them was eclipsed by the birth of my brother in 1946 and me in 1947, followed by my sister eighteen months later. She was happy to be on Oʻahu, with its mild weather and proximity to Grandma Rosa. The "boom" of postwar babies, together with postwar rationing, created shortages of diapers and the laundry soap to wash them. But otherwise, things were going as planned. Jim had a civilian job with the Navy that came with affordable military housing. But their happiness came crashing down when Jim developed allergies to Hawaiian plants and molds. Forced to leave Hawaiʻi with three children under four years old, the only feasible option was to return to Wisconsin. Luckily, they'd had saved enough to buy a small house of their own, because Norma would have camped out on the street before imposing on Elizabeth again. If she had to go back, it would be on her own terms.

O'ahu and Wisconsin, 1948 to 1952: Our young family in Honolulu, in front of the ocean liner that took us to the mainland, and after we'd settled in the Midwest

TALK STORY: Norma — 1949

> Norma put one foot in front of the other, trudging up the steep, narrow gangplank to the first deck of the U.S.S. Matsonia. These were the first hard steps of her new life. She was leaving the Hawaiian Islands, probably forever. Even with Jim and their keiki and their nest egg, she felt dread. Her son George, hardly three years old, gripped her skirt and whined that he couldn't see anything. She looked down at him, such a little being in the throngs, and asked Jim to carry him. Jim, already holding Nina, lifted his son with his other arm, nearly losing balance in the jostling, sweaty crush of passengers. Everyone was pushing toward the rails to catch final glimpses of

loved ones on shore. Norma knew those last looks could not fill all the lonely months ahead, but she craned for a view of her mother Rosalie just the same. Nina reached to catch the confetti and streamers swirling and drifting in the air, like the snowflakes her dad had told her she would see in the place they were going. She was only two years old, too young to understand, but it helped Jim to talk about what lay ahead, as if by preparing her he was preparing himself. Norma worried that the cloying flower lei piled over hundreds of passengers around them would trigger his allergies. As the boat edged out of the harbor, the lei would be ritually tossed into the ocean, a poignant farewell that Norma would welcome to relieve his watering eyes and raspy cough. Nina fussed, prickled by the *maile* leaves woven into Jim's lei, and grabbed at the satin ribbons holding the strand into a loop. Norma took her from Jim and moved her wrist back and forth, making a wave. "Say bye-bye" she said, hardly audible as the strains of "Aloha Oe" burst through the loudspeakers, the record scratchy and the sounds distorted by amplification. The crowds on shore, ten or twelve deep, waved as the blast from the ship trumpeted and the crew nimbly pulled up the gangplanks. The huge boat's enormous engines began their droning hum and the blast from the horns signaled that they were moving. Norma felt the barely perceptible motion and saw the distance between her and her mother slowly widening. A roar of farewell went up from the people on shore and the ones on deck. "Wave 'bye bye, Tutu," she said to Nina, pointing into the crowd of faces. Nina looked, but there were too many waving tutus down there to find her own.

With her last glimpse of Rosalie, already unreachable though she was still in sight, Norma felt a surge of remorse. They should be bringing Rosalie along. Who else would help her with these babies? She looked around at the other wahine going to the mainland with their new husbands. They were easy to spot, all a bit over-dressed, over-anxious, in their early twenties. She wished they could all get together in a year or so, to compare the differences between what they'd expected and how it had turned out to be.

Chapter 20

Ambition and Ambiguity

In the years just after World War II, most of the passengers on the Hawai'i to mainland-bound ocean liners were people like my parents: discharged military personnel taking their hapa spouses "back home." We would arrive already tagged with labels like "war babies," as well as epithets like "Nip" or "slant." Though the Chinese Exclusion Act had been repealed in 1943, legal limits on the number of Chinese people allowed to enter the United States remained in force. Being a citizen of a U.S. territory, also called an American protectorate, exempted my mother from those quotas and from the delays in processing endured by more than sixty thousand "War Brides" of GIs who'd been stationed at over fifty-five theaters of war on four continents. The influx of those military spouses was such an immigration and logistical challenge that Congress passed legislation called "The War Brides Act" in December, 1945 to expedite their admission to the U.S.

That Americans across the country were preparing to take in these wives may have created a wake of acceptance for the untold number of Hawaiian brides arriving on the mainland after the war. Most of the European war brides were white, while most of the Hawaiian brides were multiracial. The ambiguity of the Hawaiians' right to be in the U.S. in uncontrolled numbers, while it was still legal to limit the number of Chinese admitted, and while white brides were being stalled due to administrative backlog, may have played into the resistance against taking in brides like Norma. Hawai'i was not yet a state, and the consistency of rights accorded to citizens of U.S. territories has always been problematic. American immigration courts have struggled with legal language to apply to them. The Supreme Court ruled in the early 1900s that, in reference to the Hawaiian and Virgin islands, citizens of U.S. territories who wished to enter the United States were "foreign in a domestic sense. . .inhabited by alien races." Accordingly, Hawaiians were granted some, but not all, of the rights of American citizenship.[26] This area of immigration law left the door open to question whether people of U.S. territories were *bona fide* citizens.

Complicating this inherent ambiguity was the wide and often unbridgeable gap between Hawai'i culture and the culture of most of the mainland. This was, and remains, true of other U.S. protectorates that have distinct cultures, like American Samoa and Puerto Rico, whose citizens often feel isolated and alienated in American locales where they'd expected to feel like they belonged. Their alienation has led to street gangs and turf wars in areas where failure to assimilate has driven them to band together for companionship, protection, and safety. The musical *West Side Story*, based on the 1957 book by Arthur Laurents and set to music by Leonard Bernstein and Stephen Sondheim, brought this to American awareness with the fictional depiction of the Jets and Sharks, two warring New York City gangs with different ethnic backgrounds. Anyone raised in Hawai'i would have witnessed foreign nationals struggling to blend into the melting pot, bewildered that the model belied the ease of entry. Norma mirrored this struggle, in her own way and in her own circumstances, in trying to get a foothold on the mainland. She had to be on guard, assertive and watchful, to know when to step in and when to step back. And she would have to pass the need for that vigilance on to us, her children, without pointing out why we had to know it.

As she settled into her second trans-oceanic crossing, going back to the Midwest after her initial and disastrous first experience in that alien region, Norma felt the idealism of her first visit replaced by resolution. The war years were behind them, she was arriving with her husband and would be introducing their toddler children to Elizabeth. She expected it would go easier because her children were on the lighter side of brown. We hadn't inherited monolids, the typical shape of Asian eyes, so we could possibly pass as white, or the next closest thing – white mixed with some other stuff. We could say we were Polynesian, if anyone asked. "Polynesia. Isn't that in Tahiti? Oh, Hawaiian! The place with Pearl Harbor." Everyone knew about Pearl Harbor, and maybe that would be a good way to explain our origins, to help gain acceptance. She'd have to test what worked, to find a term that acknowledged difference but leaned toward white, to help avoid the label "Oriental" and sideswipe the truth that she was Chinese, a race that people still confused with Japanese, who we'd just defeated in war. To be Hawaiian was safe and innocuous, even if a bit brown-skinned. It would never be said that Hawaiians intended to take over American neighborhoods, as was claimed of other "colored" people. Hawaiians would not bring crime. Hawaiians tended to stay where they belonged, out there in the ocean somewhere. The ones who appeared in lily-white Midwestern communities came with a nice local boy who'd been in the war. Why else would they go there? Why else would they stay?

I've often wondered how many Hawaiian women moved to the mainland with World War II GIs, and how many stuck it out. People returning to the mainland from Hawai'i, or who've left the islands to live somewhere less beautiful, are repeatedly asked: "How could you leave a place like that to come to a place like this?" My own experience is that Hawai'i splits one's inclinations with its palpable simultaneous tug to go away and to stay put. For my mother, the mainland was a chance to avoid getting stuck in a lifetime of lateral drift.

What was unusual was not that she managed to get off the "damned rock," but that she resisted the pull to return to it. In the 1950s, after Hawaiian brides had been on the mainland awhile, scattered across small and large cities, prairies, military bases, in wintry climes, how many buckled and hightailed it back to Hawai'i? My mother's sisters, after stints on the mainland with their military husbands, or the husbands after those initial ones, eventually returned to Oʻahu, where they lived until they died. My mother stayed the course. Despite her rage, headaches, and depression, she feared that the Hawaiian caste system would be harsher to us, her hapa haole children, than any challenges we'd face on the mainland, where identification with our father would facilitate us passing for white.

Getting to know my cousins during the few times we got together on Oʻahu, I wished I could have asked the ones who'd gone to the mainland – of which there were several – why they'd returned. Part of the calculus must have been having to live with parents in cramped quarters, and having relatively limited investment and professional opportunities than on the mainland. But the door marked "personal" had never been cracked open enough to hear their stories. I'm left observing that going to the mainland was a rite of passage usually generated by a goal to get a college degree, to accept a job, to get to know extended family. I've noticed that Hawaiian tour and hospitality staff often make small talk about the time they lived on the mainland. They describe where they'd gone and what had taken them there. I'd ask strangers the questions I couldn't ask my cousins: the reasons they'd returned to Hawai'i. Their responses usually pointed toward difficulty: it was hard to find a job, to be so far from family, to fit in. If they had to be broke and poor, they'd rather do it "home," among their people.

Thinking about the untold numbers who'd gone to the mainland with a plan and had wanted to stay but didn't, reinforced my respect for my mother's tenacity. She'd endured all the things she'd hated – her in-laws, the rural culture, and formidable weather – but she'd stayed, even after the development of over-the-counter allergy treatments would have made it possible for my father to move back to Hawai'i. She'd achieved a foothold in the mainland world of haole, which was no small thing. We, her children, had bridged the trans-cultural divide. The price we'd paid was our meaningful affiliation with our ancestral home and the loss of deep knowledge of our roots as Polynesians and Asians.

Apart from random incidents my sibs and I have shared as adults, we'd grown up feeling like we fit in. On the surface of our everyday lives, my mother's social engineering had paid off. But digging only a few thin layers deeper, which I have not had the courage to do until recently, I see that our integration was never seamless and never without delusion.

I chose to not notice many subtle signals that I wasn't haole, because to see them would have been to acknowledge that I didn't belong there. The veiled contra-indications that we were integrated were easy to miss, or to ignore, because there was no one nearby who was like us. I had no perspective on how unusual we were. I had an ethnic name that triggered questions about where I was "from," though I now see that the question about my name was an inquiry into my race. My response that I am Hawaiian generated the usual tiresome questions about how and why I got from Hawaiʻi to Wisconsin, which led back to World War II and to my mother being a war bride, and on and on. Beyond merely annoying, such questions were often the prelude to pigeon-holing me, so I learned to shape my responses to shut down the conversation.

My mother, on the other hand, learned to take intrusive curiosity in stride, and even to turn it to her advantage. She used charm to put people at ease, and once she'd disarmed them, she seemed to thrive on the attention. Today, living in a global world with broad exposure to geography and history, I want to believe that this same line of questions, which I continue to receive, are asked to tease out a story line that can help dissolve, rather than enforce, racial stereotypes. As children, in that time and place, it was enough to say we were "part Hawaiian." Only recently have the questions begun probing for "what part?" or "how much?" In the simpler time and place of my childhood, I never asked those questions. I was what I was. I was hapa, but that was a word not used outside our house. Had I been in Hawaiʻi, the simple declaration that I was "part Hawaiian" would have been the beginning of the questions, not the answer.

I was a young adult before I finally calculated that I was, precisely, one-eighth Hawaiian. It is a thin claim, but enough to qualify a place on the Native Hawaiian Roll, a certified list of people of Hawaiian ancestry who descended from the aboriginal people who lived in the Hawaiian Islands prior to 1778. I am not proud of my failure to take up the banner of such a distinct racial identity and raise it over and around myself. I am the manifestation of the approach that my mother believed was in our best interest. One day, while visiting her in their retirement home in Florida, I asked her why she'd never told us things about her childhood in Hawai'i, about her unmentioned siblings and ancestors. She flared with the kind of rapid-fire hostility I knew too well. "You were never interested," she said, an accusation more than an explanation. I told her I didn't know enough to know what to ask.

Norma's assimilation into Southeast Wisconsin, to the point where she preferred it to other places and considered it as good a place as any, took over forty years. Over time people stopped beginning every conversation with curiosity about where she was from. Her story was known among the town folk, so if anyone wanted to know her background, they could ask each other.

After I stopped using my Hawaiian name Moana, most strangers seemed not to see my hapa features. Those who did used a question about my race as a conversation starter and gave themselves permission to probe my background without offering anything about their own. This was annoying and I was told, good-humoredly by a man at my office, that I certainly "suffered no fools." Questions about my origins and how haole I looked suggested that I am not haole (a word I still use since the English language does not have a comfortably corresponding term, Caucasian being too academic and white being too "on the nose"). No one asked haole people where they were from, or how they got to be haole, or the components of their haoleness. They had some sort of *a priori* acceptability, devoid of the minefield of maps, cultural quirks, or biases that formed the core of prejudicial curiosity about everyone else.

After leaving my small town and immersing in a succession of college campuses, I noticed that fewer people were interested in my origin story. This was the desired outcome, to blend into the haole mainstream. It also reflected that I was moving into populations that were more diverse, accepting, well-traveled, and erudite. Being Asian/Polynesian was unremarkable in the cities that I moved to – San Francisco, Los Angeles, Portland, and New York. I was in my mid-twenties when Affirmative Action policies were enacted, with the goal of offering broader opportunities in education and employment to underrepresented elements of society. Doors to law schools, banks, communications companies, and other realms with low representation not only of other races, but of women, were suddenly cracked open. People like me were invited, encouraged, to step inside.

I was tempted to use Affirmative Action to ratchet up my chances, but I didn't want the weight of taking it away from someone else when I could "pass" without it. I could blend in, even if it meant shoveling my ancestry, culture, and genes under the rug. I'd seen that the buffet of abundance that we now call white privilege was a better bet than the token Affirmative Action successes I was witness to in its earliest days. I'd not yet gone deeply enough into my mother's story to understand the cost paid for our relative ease, as multi-racial citizens, in tapping into those advantages, but I recognized a fundamental truth in it. My family story was a variant of this eons-old imperative of seeking more security, safety, and prosperity by moving from one place to another. The details vary among us, but the impetus is universal. My family story, however individuated to our situation, is not unique. Nor were my mother's aspirations for her children, for me.

My year on the windward side of Oʻahu went by swiftly, though each day seemed to tarry in the distorted sense of tropical time. I existed in an effortless balance between languid solitude and sprees of exploration. I felt shamelessly exploitative, but curiously listless. I'd planned to finally settle into a writing routine and draft the short fiction pieces I'd carried in my head in for years. But then I'd succumbed to the undertow of the deep currents of our female forebears. Waipuilani had stirred up the waters, churning up the muck and sunken debris that lay at the bottom of my seemingly clear pond. The transparency created from that clouded swill came not, as one would expect, from the eventual clearing of the water, but from the quagmire itself. I'd gained insight into the overlap of Chinese and Hawaiian in our family. Fully understanding its impact might take me the rest of my days.

As respite from those deliberative hours, I ventured around the island, which is only 130 miles in circumference. The distance from my rented home to Honolulu was twenty-five miles. It was the distance between introverted solitude and the embrace of friends who kept me well-invited, well-fed, and well-indulged. They joined me in viewing the island's abundant treasures: the Hawai'i International Film Festival's splendid offering from faraway places like Iran, Okinawa, Korea, the Marshall Islands; the Honolulu Academy of Art's James Michener Collection of Japanese Edo era woodblock prints; in hearing Daw Aung San Suu Kyi, shortly after her release from years of house arrest in Myanmar, and His Holiness the Dalai Lama, who sat amidst dozens of hula dancing children swirling around him like blossoms falling from a swaying tree. I took a bus to the sprawling estate Doris Duke, the heiress my mother had mentioned so often with childlike infatuation, which had been converted to the Shangri La Museum of Islamic Art, Culture & Design that houses her priceless trove. Honolulu was as cosmopolitan as my mother had always said. Its gracious, seamless intermingling of arts and peoples are readily embraceable if one just reaches out.

As are its views: the stunning expanse of the Pacific ocean a daily gift, renewable moment by moment, from wherever I was coming to wherever I was headed, just a glance over my shoulder or a glimpse beyond. I hiked up Lanikai's Kaiwa Ridge with my daughter on my birthday, through gaudily painted ruins of World War II military bunkers called The Pillboxes, and fell to my knees before the ocean's full spectrum of blues splayed back from the horizon. I remembered a color chart I'd once seen listing ninety-nine poetic names for blue. There was one called Blue Yonder, the perfect name for that one below, or this one, or all of them visibly mutating in that moment. I rode a horse into the sacred Kualoa Valley where ancient chiefs had sent their newborns for immersion in Hawaiian history, rituals, and the arts of war. And like so many Oahuans that year, when the North Shore waves surpassed twenty feet, triggering the Eddie Aikau Big Wave Invitational, I dropped everything to get to Waimea Bay where the world champion surfers, who'd also dropped everything to fly to Oʻahu for "The Eddie," embraced and defied and redefined what we call extreme. Friday twilights were for the Barefoot Beach Cafe in Kapiolani Park, eating on the grass, listening to local bands, watching the late-day surfers paddle to the pier, biding time until the fireworks went off, or for happy hour with Eddie Kamae, the ukulele virtuoso, and his Sons of Hawaiʻi musicians, at the Elks Lodge.

Back on my own side of the island, I stood on the sea wall on the night of the full moon, month after month, watching it toss thousands of points of light across impenetrably black water. I'd count on my fingers how many Hawaiian moons I'd bathed in since arriving, and how many I had left before I had to go back to my prior life. Full as I kept my days, I also kept my life in the islands unfettered so that I arrived at each new day with an existential gratitude for once again achieving this elemental, extraordinary thing: opening my eyes and arising to a new morning.

But, eventually, Hawaiʻi began to affect me adversely. My ties to the islands seemed more tenuous the longer I stayed, rather than more binding, as one would expect. My feeling of not belonging was ironic, and probably akin to how my mother felt when she went to the Midwest. Except there was this major difference: she had no ties to that place except for my father and an expectation for a future there, whereas I had an ancestral connection to the islands and a present family with which I'd never established meaningful attachment. It was hard not to replay my mother's predictions, but I stilled her voice by reminding myself that it was my kuleana to bring Waipuilani's story into the light of present day.

Thinking back to the first time I saw our family chart and noticed Makatu's name floating in the space beside Waipuilani, I'd asked about him. He could not have been insignificant, a penciled-in coda in our great-grandmother's final chapter, as his unfixed notation on the chart suggested. The bits I was told about him were dismissive, verging on derogatory. Intuitively, I could not accept this, especially as I began to imagine their talk story. They'd been innocents, children, close to the land, indigenous. They'd been swept up by tumult, like a tsunami wave of debris they had to dodge through to keep above water, to keep from injury and collision, to survive. They had found their way back to each other and married. Her gravestone has his surname carved upon it. She had gone full circle.

Were I writing Waipuilani's life as a play, Act Two would have been the time with Sun Akana Wong. Makatu, older and more worldly, would re-enter the stage, as the star of Act Three, in which we see the resolution, the denouement of her drama. I'd been focusing on her marriage to a Chinese man as the whole production, but I came to see him as a link in the chain of events of her life. I celebrated this conclusion to Waipuilani's story. It seemed as if, having done her duty, she had found her way back to her roots, her culture, her love.

Still, I do not take from her returning to her culture a model for myself, nor did I ever sense that she was beckoning me to take my place in the fold as a Hawaiian. It had been imperative to spend a long stretch of time in Hawai'i to learn that, though I am Hawaiian, I wasn't of Hawai'i. At least, not of my mother's Hawai'i, the one she'd warned me away from. I'd manifested a different Hawaiian experience than my mother's. The Hawai'i I'd come to know was of the unseen and mystical, the arts and culture, the generous and open-hearted aloha of my chosen friends, all consumed with frequent, intentional baths in its gob-smacking gorgeousness. My appreciation may never have ripened into this depth of field in my mother's milieu, though it was the one I'd hoped to enter. I'd tried knocking on the door, tried entering the rooms she'd inhabited and left behind. But I was not allowed in. Perhaps that is for the best. In landing in this acknowledgement, I validate my mother's choices. Thwarted as small-town Wisconsin had always seemed, and much as I'd grown up pining to be somewhere – anywhere – else, I am grateful that she'd gutted it out in that place that she'd called "like Siberia."

As often happens with people who've migrated, the longer my mother remained in Wisconsin the more she attached to it as her home. Remaining close with her Hawaiian family became increasingly difficult. Though flights to Honolulu became less expensive and more accessible, the trip was still time consuming and costly. My parents saved to go every few years, but eventually my mother seemed as happy to leave Hawai'i as she had been to arrive. By that time, I'd had a close and decades-long friendship with a Hawaiian family whose ancestor, I learned much later, had built the Pioneer Mill that I believe was the cause of Waipuilani leaving her ancestral home. At their invitation I often visited Hawai'i, and through them I experienced the essence of aloha extended to me as Hawaiian kin. My mother was happy that I'd found my own way to Hawai'i through the embrace of these friends, and that because of them my children came to know themselves as Hawaiian.

From that a channel opened for them to know and appreciate my mother, their Granny, as an embodied Hawaiian.

Having lived thirty-five years in the high mountain desert of the American West, where my children were born and raised to adulthood, we felt deep attunement to Native American history, places, and rituals. We were hikers, campers, back-packers, skiers. We loved the back country, both high alpine and the red rock beauty of southern Utah. We became aware that most of the places where we recreated, including the national parks, had been stolen from indigenous people, often through violence. We knew this, and it colored our experience on the land, enhancing our appreciation for what had been given up by indigenous people so that we could refresh and renew.

After my children spent time in Hawai'i and had taken in many of its highlights and histories, they returned to our Utah home having already connected the dots between the American appropriation of Hawaiian land and the American theft of Native American land. It was apparent to them, by the time of their adolescence, that if indigenous people stood in the way of what the United States wanted, they would be mowed over.

Although the U.S. military and settlers hadn't killed off Hawaiians in the way they'd massacred Native Americans, they had brought the diseases that had resulted in more than one hundred thousand Kānaka Maoli deaths, and had reduced the native Hawaiian population to just twenty four thousand by the time they were measured in the 1920 U.S. Census. Few mainland American students are taught Hawaiian history beyond three milestones: the 1778 "discovery" by Captain Cook, the 1941 Japanese attack on Pearl Harbor, and Hawai'i's admission to statehood in

1959. James Michener's seminal tome *Hawai'i*, had my parents allowed me to read it when I first came upon it in high school, could have enabled a small-town girl in rural Wisconsin to understand how her Hawaiian ancestors had all wound up in the melting pot. Absent other talk story and lore, it might have triggered the interest my mother had accused me of lacking.

Putting it all together, slogging through half-formed recriminations, reaching past easy conclusions, filling the voids with imagined truth, I began to understand what lay beneath my quest to understand my relationship with Hawai'i. I was no longer seeking to identify as a Hawaiian, nor to feel more authentic when I made claim to being Hawaiian. Until I came upon Waipuilani, I'd sought to belong to a far-off place and to feel as if I were being welcomed home. After directly experiencing Hawai'i and searching for affinity with it, I felt aesthetic and cultural appreciation. But I did not feel my soul celebrating, nor relaxing into, a feeling of being where I belonged. What I yearned for was to be unburdened of the feeling that I'd been denied something.

Waipuilani's invitation, as I came to understand it, was to delve far enough into our family and our place in the Hawaiian Islands to open the channels toward forgiveness. As I stepped into that opening, all the paths began to converge into one that led to acceptance of their withholding, and to seeing that there had been wisdom in that course. My soul wanted to rest in that place I'd gotten to. I'd taken a long walk with Waipuilani, joined along the way by Grandma Rosa, and then by my mother. When I imagined us sitting down to rest together, we would talk about our personal and shared experience of trying to fit in, as Hawaiians, as

Chinese, as Asian Americans, as hapa haole. Waipuilani and my mother would tell of how they'd felt like immigrants in their own land, and their shame at feeling run off places where they belonged. They'd talk about standing out and taking risks, not as a choice as in my world, where one can embrace challenges as personal growth, but as necessity.

I'd ask them about love, and they'd tell me that they'd had love. Yes, I knew there must have been love, I'd say, adding that I'd not felt much heart, nor witnessed it. I am not blaming, I'd hasten to add, but I'd yearned for the kind of snuggly, petting, cozy feeling that I was a precious thing. In the turmoil of survival, things go, my mother would say, like charm and heart. We'd fall silent, imagining what it would have been like to have had it, and feeling the loss of it.

Chapter 21

Home Together, Forever

Thinking about my father who, like my mother, had been abandoned by his father, I began pondering the correlation between abandonment and the walling off of an open, tender heart. My mother, despite her capacity for raging against her in-laws, had always protected my father as a wounded man who'd been abandoned. She reminded us children of this when she thought we were being insensitive to him. The father I knew had a submissive, remorseful, whipped dog quality, a demeanor that had always made my heart ache for him. He kept a distance between himself and us, his children. He walked past us if we were gathered in the kitchen, whistling his tuneless tune, on his way to sit by himself in the dim TV room. I always wondered why he wouldn't join us, and I'd wish that he'd sit down for some talk story or to join in whatever board game we had going.

Until a few years after he died, I had no idea how much life he'd lived. I'd come across his twenty-page memoir of his tour of the South Pacific, written after prodding by my mother when she no doubt knew he was near his end. Put on paper in his quavering handwriting and deteriorating spelling, he vividly recapped the day he'd enlisted in the military in 1939 and the ensuing fifty-eight months of his duty. From these pages I learned that he'd been in the Hebrides, New Caledonia, Guadalcanal, Guam, Saipan, and many other remote areas of the South Pacific I had to look up on a map – places he'd not been able to write about in his daily, censored dispatches to my mother.

Reading of his squadron's tour with the 11th Bombardment Group, I discovered that not only had my mother withheld things I'd have loved to have known, but my father had as well. With laborious penmanship, he'd laid down the story of his years in World War II with anecdotes and lessons learned that flowed with a still-fresh sense of wonder, gentle humor, vivid impressions, and an essayist's sense of irony. Of Éfaté, in the Solomon Islands, he gave a glimpse of how much they'd been strangers in a strange land: "When the moon was full the natives would pound on their drums and shout and howell [sic]. The first time we heard it we slept with our rifles by our side." Of the attack on Pearl Harbor, he could find no one to blame: "That day has been cussed and discussed, trying to put the blame on somebody. But in the end, it was nobody, and it was everybody. It was the system."

But most poignantly, and perhaps with prescience, he wrote, "Of all the islands that I traveled to or passed by, Enewetak (in the Marshall Islands) made me cry. There was only one palm tree still standing on the island." I had to look up Enewetak, and learned it was an atoll of less than six square miles. He may not have understood that the atolls, comprised of coral, rarely supported plant life, but he was kind-hearted and wanted to see life thriving, even out in the vast Pacific during wartime. Four years after my father sailed past Enewetak, the United States began a years-long campaign of atomic and biological weapons testing in, on and above the Marshall Islands, detonating sixty-seven nuclear bombs, leaving in the area a tiny island that is today the most radioactive place on earth. No doubt that lone tree that my father had contemplated with such tenderness had been obliterated.

Despite his shy reticence within our family walls, my father was unfailingly kind and generous in his community. He was that man one always counted on to volunteer, whether building and maintaining the American Legion Hall, mowing lawns for the elderly, delivering holiday turkeys for the St. Vincent de Paul Society, ushering at Mass. His recreation was a small-town, modest diversion: going to the riverside "tap" to drink beer and play a round of pool with whoever was there, generally younger guys with whom he was funny and light. We were surprised, at his retirement party, to learn how amusing, playful, and popular he was at work, particularly among the generations behind him. My brothers and I have talked about our loss in not having experienced that part that he shared with others.

The other group to which my father always showed his most gregarious self was his wartime 11th Bombardment Group. I read years later, when the information was no longer classified, that the group had been moved to Guam in October of 1944 for the attacks in the Volcano and Bonin Islands. That would have been the transfer to Guam that precipitated my parents' marriage, and about which he could never speak. Reading this small inclusion in the group's web page history helped me to understand the solidarity my father felt with these men. Until the mid-2000s, when there were too few of them left to continue gathering, the 11th Bomb Group, as they were called, held reunions every few years at cities throughout the United States. My parents attended every one of them. I resented that they made those trips during years when they rarely visited their grandchildren, so I flew to join them at a reunion held at the Tucson Convention Center, an easy flight from my home in Utah. I was curious to see what these old geezers offered that was more attractive than visiting us.

Arriving in the echoing, bland convention hall, I saw a cluster of aged men at scattered, linen-draped tables. Several were at the continental breakfast buffet serving themselves from the standard fare of bakery and fruit, or holding their cups beneath the spouts of coffee urns. I spotted my father talking with his war buddies, basking in the vestige of wartime brotherhood that they'd created and had never, to such a degree, had since. The old vets wore their felt hats with emblems and badges. Their war-era tattoos were faded and blurred. They embraced me as if I were a daughter. They'd seen pictures of me since I was a baby and knew all the details of my life and whereabouts. My father had told them about me and my sibs, and spoke of his pride in us, though he had never expressed those feelings directly to me.

My father retired as quickly as he could after turning sixty. He'd put in forty years at the John Deere plant in our town, and he'd hated most of them. He and my mother had planned their retirement to Florida, just as they'd planned their move from Honolulu to the Midwest forty years earlier. I was surprised they'd not gone back to Hawai'i, as one would expect. Nor did they consider a state closer to where my sister and I lived, such as California or Arizona. By then the pull of their friends, who were also moving to Florida as so many Midwesterners do, was stronger than the pull back to Hawai'i or to having proximity to us, their grown children and grandchildren. They were among the earliest residents of the now infamous development near Orlando called The Villages. They spent summers in Wisconsin in a home my brother had scouted out for them, close to where he lived, in the next town over from the one where we'd all grown up. Every June, after they'd settled into Wisconsin for the season, my mother put together a picnic for my father's sisters and their husbands. They gathered at a local park and my mother laid out a thoroughly regional spread of ham, potato salad, and homemade white bread, pickles, and apple pie. By then, she was grateful that all my father's siblings were still alive and able to come, and that she could facilitate their last times together.

IN 1995, FROM MY PARENTS' RETIREMENT ADDRESS IN Florida, came invitations to their 50th wedding anniversary celebration on Oʻahu. It would be the first time any of us would be in Hawaiʻi with them, though by that time we had all been there on our own. They would pay for our airfare. Most of us, with our families, arrived early and scattered across the various islands to vacation separately. Then we all converged in Honolulu for the banquet and speeches, memories, and reflections. My mother looked delicate in a soft coral-colored dress, her still-dark hair crowned with one of the braided *haku lei* that are worn on the head, like a tiara, that she had gifted all of us daughters, daughters-in-law, and granddaughters.

Honolulu, 1995: My mother at her 50th anniversary celebration, with me on her left and my daughters Malia and Aja on her right

My father had always seemed most at ease in aloha shirts, as he did that day on the dais. Five decades fell away as he spoke of his Norma as a young bride. He told everyone of the ways she'd made a life in the Midwest, and of the small gestures that were unheralded by all but him: how she'd get up and go fishing alone with her bamboo rod and red bobber, how she'd put in a strawberry patch and made shortcake from scratch, how she'd rush outside to gather laundry from the clothesline when a thunderstorm rolled through. She'd bake pies and send my brothers out to deliver them to the neighbors. Above all, she'd always treated the less fortunate with generosity and dignity, giving them the best, not the dregs that no one else wanted. After the speeches he danced with her, swirling her about with dips and pirouettes, with the smooth moves they'd perfected at those social mixers in the torchlit Honolulu pavilions of the 1940s war years. We ended that day at twilight on Honolulu's Kaimana Beach at Kapiolani Park. The children played in the water until dark. My mother sat on the grass watching them, proud to have finally taken her entire family home.

Circa 2000: Jim and Norma as happy retirees in Florida

They spent their last twenty years enjoying the diversions of The Villages, hosting visiting grandchildren, and rolling through the extensive grounds in their golf cart. They took cruises and traveled, including trips to Hawai'i every few years, often stopping en route to visit my sister in San Diego or me in the western places I lived – San Francisco, Park City, Portland. They were healthy, agile, and independent until their early eighties, when suddenly they weren't.

As their health declined, I offered to escort them to Hawai'i. I would guide them through the airports on those beeping carts, use my airline points to secure them the comforts of seats in business class, and completely dedicate myself to ensuring a relaxing, secure visit. Once on Oʻahu, I'd stay with my father, by then advancing into Alzheimer's disease, so my mother could enjoy time with her sisters. It would be their farewell to Hawaiʻi, of course, and perhaps to Aunties Jan and Winnie. But my mother firmly declined to go, despite my urging. She was in treatment for the cancer that had been diagnosed on her eightieth birthday and didn't have strength for a final trip to Hawaiʻi, despite the support I offered. She had never indulged in emotional gestures if they didn't serve some practical purpose. Her more compelling need was to conserve strength in order to stay well enough, long enough, to outlive my father. She was determined to take care of him to the end.

But the cancer would claim her a year before the Alzheimer's took him. In the months before she died, she'd been seeing her mother in dreams. Grandma Rosa was coaching her to cross over and the two of them were actively, consciously visioning her ending. My mother seemed to be preparing for death in the ways women prepare for birth, as an inevitability that would also be both an end and a deliverance. From her bed in Wisconsin beneath a large poster of a Hawaiian waterfall, seemingly comatose, she heard her sister Jan's poignant farewell in fluent Hawaiian. She died later that evening. A year later, after fighting infections and dementia, my father followed.

They'd wanted to be inurned at the National Memorial Cemetery of the Pacific in the volcanic crater above Honolulu, and had arranged and prepaid for a place there. The Hawaiians call this place *Pūowaina*, which means "Hill of Sacrifice." It is a place of deep spiritual significance to Hawaiian people, and is the resting place of over sixty thousand veterans of war and their families. I took my parents' urns there and arranged a gathering with my mother's remaining ohana – her two sisters, a hānai (adopted) sister, and several nephews and nieces, and a few step- or once/twice-removed relatives. The military had set up a canopy for us to gather beneath and had sent an honor guard to play taps. He presented me with the iconic, triangular-folded flag given to veterans of American wars. I said a few words, as did a few others, and then we all took a somber walk to the wall where they would be inurned. Their plaque had already been inscribed "Home together, forever" and was ready to be affixed after my cousin's sons, who'd borne their urns to the vault, placed them inside. And then, with finality, I realized that my mother had made it back home.

Visiting Jim and Norma at the National Cemetery is often the first stop many of us make after arriving in Honolulu, and the last stop before heading back to the mainland. Leaving a lei, laying a hand on their plaque, feeling the trade winds sweep across the crater's hallowed ground, absorbing the respectful silence, affirms our connection with them and with Hawai'i.

A few years after their inurnment, I spent several months house sitting for friends at the end Tantalus Drive, a winding, ascending road that ends at the highest residential reaches of Honolulu. It is an area of primeval, cloying vegetation and cushioning quiet. Coming or going there entailed passing the entrance to the Pūowaina cemetery and feeling its emanation of so many thousands of resting souls.

Nervous about jogging in the root-clogged paths surrounding the house where I was staying, and fearful of encountering wild boar, I began going down to the cemetery to run on its perfectly paved, looping roads. I'd route my run past the wall where my parents' remains rested. It was at the edge of the crater, on a ridge where the land fell away into a steep ravine. On some days I'd pass by them three or four times, always pausing to lay my hand on their names, tracing the raised letters on the plaque like a blind person feeling Braille. Someone once told me to keep talking to your deceased parents, so I did. Though I am an inveterate oversharer, I had never been with them. But there, I suddenly felt free to spill whatever was on my mind. Because running generates thoughts, and running through a cemetery escalates the number and dimensions of those musings, much bubbled up to say. But mostly what I told them, in words that arose unbidden from some deep well of sadness, was "I'm sorry. I'm sorry, I'm sorry." Just that. I could never have said why because I myself didn't know. But I knew the list would be long and that I'd cave under the sorrowful weight of it if I ever tried to explain.

    I let the sorrow lie in the fragrant air of memorial bouquets and lei until it floated away, and then I'd turn away to run another loop. Sometimes, slowing to mount the steps to the rows of memorial walls, each densely inscribed with the names of thousands who'd died in the Pacific theater, I'd recount the milestones of my parents' lives, trying to conjure their physical presence that was so irrevocably gone. They'd been Jim and Norma. They'd met in Hawai'i during World War II. They'd stayed together for over sixty years. They'd died within fifteen months of each other. Their lives were slipping from memory like sand through fingers. I was trying to stop time from taking the last vestiges of them.

    Jogging on, circling the massive crater, I'd take in the panorama: Diamond Head, Pearl Harbor, the Honolulu skyline, and the ocean on all sides. I'd pass families tending graves with tools they'd brought to brush moss from headstones, snip overhanging grass, carry water from the spigot to refresh blossoms in vases. I'd slow down at an area of many dozens of markers set off by itself with an aura of abandonment. The caretakers had trimmed around each one, but there was no sign of personal care amongst its rows of flat plaques, each with the same heartbreaking inscription – *Unknown Soldier, Korean War*. I'd push on, weeping, unaccountably overwhelmed. "Such waste, such waste. All those good men." I'd stumble away, toward a maintenance path across a field that would take me back near my parents one more time. Nearing my last day of this time on Oʻahu, I'd tell them that I'd miss being close to them.

Approaching them those last times, this truth arose and encircled me: we all long to feel endeared in the places we call home. My mother had needed that, as a scrappy Chinese woman conscripted to serve her brothers, as a war bride transplanted to the Midwest where she'd had to earn her place. I felt the plaintive urge to let Lillina rest. She could never have helped me feel Hawaiʻi was my home. She had lost the sense of that herself, and so she could not impart it. For her, growing up in years of transition and war, Hawaiʻi had become as fluid as the lava pouring from the craters, as the heaving ocean eroding the shore. It was a place of displacement, yet it continued its hold, claiming and reclaiming and forever holding its own to itself in its bowl of souls. Hawaiʻi would take my mother back and would always be home for her, as it would always be for me, if I could fully open to being fully received.

ACKNOWLEDGEMENTS

I thank my brothers and sister for sharing their memories of our childhood, often offering a different perspective than my own. I am grateful to Jeremiah Cahill and Theresa Tate for their editorial suggestions and guidance, to Leikula Rebecca Merryman Carr and James Dittmann for help with the photos, and for the many workshop writers who read, critiqued, and encouraged sections of the draft narrative. Above all, I extend boundless gratitude to Judith Flanders for awakening me to my heritage and for steadfastly bearing witness to this project. Every page bears the impress of her heart and wisdom.

ABOUT THE AUTHOR

Nina Macheel writes short fiction, essays, articles, and opinion pieces for the causes she feels strongly about. Her work was most recently published in *The Midwest Review* and *Out of Print*, an online literary journal published in India. This is her first book.

ninamacheel.com

NOTES & REFERENCES

1 John Yau, "What Hollywood Does to Asian Actors," *Hypoallergic.com*, https://hyperallergic.com/ Brooklyn, NY, June 20, 2020.

2 Lydia Maria Child, lyricist. "The New-England Boy's Song about Thanksgiving Day," 1844.

3 Noenoe K. Silva, *The Power of the Steel-Tipped Pen*, Duke University Press, 2017, p. 9, quoting Kekuewa Kikiloi, "Rebirth of an Archipelago: Sustaining a Hawaiian Cultural Identity for People and Homeland" from *Hulili: Multidisciplinary Research on Hawaiian Well-Being*, published by Kamehameha Schools, Volume 6, 2010, p. 74.

4 John Dominis Holt, *Waimea Summer*, Topgallant Publishing Co., Honolulu, 1976, p. 172.

5 Martha Henriques, "Can the legacy of trauma be passed down the generations?" BBC Future, March 26, 2019. https://www.bbc.com/future/article/20190326-what-is-epigenetics

6 Jonathan Kamakawiwoʻole Osorio, *Dismembering Lahui: A History of the Hawaiian Nation to 1887*, University of Hawaiʻi Press, 2002.

7 James A. Michener, *Hawaiʻi*, Random House, 1959.

8 *South Pacific*, a musical by composer Richard Rodgers and lyricist-dramatist Oscar Hammerstein that premiered on Broadway in 1949, was released as a film in 1958, and was based James A. Michener's *Tales of the South Pacific*, a collection of short stories published in 1947.

9 Oscar Hammerstein II, "Carefully Taught," from *South Pacific*, 1958.

10 Oscar Hammerstein II, "Some Enchanted Evening," *South Pacific*, 1958.

11 King Kamehameha I (1736-1819) united the Hawaiian Islands into one kingdom in 1810, after years of inter-island conflict between warring clans. Unification of the islands was strategically key to preventing competing western interests from tearing apart the Islands to serve their disparate interests. https://www.

gohawaii.com/culture/history/king-kamehameha and https://www.crownofhawaii.com/kam1sov

12 Dr. Larry Kimura, professor at Ka Haka 'Ula O Ke'elikōlani College of Hawaiian Language, quoted by Jan Wizinowich, *Hawaiian Naming Traditions, A Cultural Legacy*, Ke Ola Magazine, September-October, 2020.

13 Jean Iwata Cachola, "Kamehameha III: Kauikeaouli," Kamehameha Schools Press, Honolulu 1995, https://himonarchy.weebly.com/the-great-mahele.html The Great Māhele of March 1848 is considered the second most important episode of Hawaiian history, behind the overthrow of the Hawaiian sovereignty in 1893, and is an example of a grand intention that went terribly wrong. The name comes from the Hawaiian word *māhele* (to divide or portion). King Kamehameha II sought to protect Hawaiian lands from foreign ownership and to provide Hawaiians with secure title to land. Guided by foreign advisors who may have understood that Hawaiians, who had no concept of private land ownership, would fail to optimize their chance to own land, the King through The Great Māhele reallocated of one-third of Hawaiian land to the monarch, one-third to the chiefs and managers of the ahupua'a, and one-third to the people. Per the Kuleana Act of 1850, historical land tenants could get permanent title by documenting their claims to specific parcels within two years. In accordance with traditional Hawaiian belief that the land is for all, few Hawaiians made claim to their plots or fulfilled obligations like payment of taxes on the land. Unclaimed land reverted to the government, which sold or auctioned it to US mainlanders or to Hawaiian enterprises to use for their own profit. In the end, only 1% of the Kuleana lands was retained in the hands of the Hawaiians for whom the division was intended.

14 Deborah Saito and Susan Campbell, "Pioneer Mill Company History," Hawaiian Sugar Planters Association Plantation Archives, University of Hawai'i at Manoa Library Hawaiian Collection. http://www2.hawaii.edu/~speccoll/p_pioneer.html

15 Carol Wilcox, *Sugar Water: Hawai'i's Plantation Ditches*, University of Hawai'i Press, Honolulu, 1997.

16 John E. Seward, "A Kingdom Lost: The U.S. Annexation of Hawai'i," Defense Technical Information Center, Army War College, Carlisle Barracks, PA, 2001.

17 Milton Diamond, PhD, *Sexual Behavior in Pre Contact Hawai'i: A Sexological Ethnography*, Chapter 16: pp. 37-58. The Pacific Center of Sex & Society, University of Hawai'i, 2004.

18 Kip Fulbeck, *Part Asian, 100% Hapa*, Chronicle Books, San Francisco, 2006.

19 Sarah Miller Davenport, "Racists in Congress Fought Statehood for Hawai'i, But Lost that Battle Sixty Years Ago", *The Conversation*, March 18, 2019. https://theconversation.com/racists-in-congress-fought-statehood-for-hawaii-but-lost-that-battle-60-years-ago-113499

20 Collin Makamson, "Coming To America: The War Brides Act of 1945," from National World War II Museum Media & Education Center, December 28, 2020. https://www.nationalww2museum.org/war/articles/war-brides-act-1945

21 Amy Tan, *The Joy Luck Club*, G. P. Putnam's Sons, 1989.

22 C.L. Haliniak, *A Native Hawaiian Focus on the Hawai'i Public School System*, SY2015. (Ho'ona'auao (Education) Fact Sheet, Vol. 2017, No.1). Honolulu, HI: Office of Hawaiian Affairs, Research Division, Special Projects.

23 DeSote Brown, *Hawai'i Recalls: Selling Romance to America*, The Limited Editions Books, 1982.

24 Christina Giordano, "Pearl Harbor Remembered," *Ocala Star-Banner*, December 14, 2006.

25 Maggie McNeill, "Honolulu Harlots," *The Honest Courtesan*, July 5, 2011, https://www.thewhoresofyore.com/sex-history/honolulu-harlots-by-maggie-mcneil

26 The National Immigration Policy Forum, *Foreign in a Domestic Sense*, U.S. Territories and Insular Areas, April 12, 2021. https://immigrationforum.org/article/foreign-in-a-domestic-sense-u-s-territories-and-insular-areas/

Made in the USA
Monee, IL
17 August 2023

41156020R00184